THE
CASTAWAY'S
WAR

THE

CASTAWAY'S
WAR

ONE MAN'S BATTLE AGAINST IMPERIAL JAPAN

Stephen Harding

DA CAPO PRESS
A MEMBER OF THE PERSEUS BOOKS GROUP

DESIGNED BY LINDA MARK
Set in 11 point Stempel Garamond LT Std by The Perseus Books Group

Cataloging-in-Publication data for this book is available from the
Library of Congress.
ISBN: 978-0-306-82340-4 (hardcover)
ISBN: 978-0-306-82341-1 (e-book)

Published by Da Capo Press
A Member of the Perseus Books Group
www.dacapopress.com

Da Capo Press books are available at special discounts for bulk purchases in the
U.S. by corporations, institutions, and other organizations. For more information,
please contact the Special Markets Department at the Perseus Books Group,
2300 Chestnut Street, Suite 200, Philadelphia, PA 19103, or call (800) 810-4145,
ext. 5000, or e-mail special.markets@perseusbooks.com.

10 9 8 7 6 5 4 3 2 1

As always,
for Mari, with love

Eternal Father, strong to save,
Whose arm hath bound the restless wave,
Who bidst the mighty ocean deep
Its own appointed limits keep;
O, hear us when we cry to Thee
For those in peril on the sea!

—THE NAVY HYMN

CONTENTS

MAPS

PRELUDE

JUST BEFORE MIDNIGHT ON JULY 4, 1943, LIEUTENANT HUGH BARR MILLER Jr. stood on the windswept flying bridge of the *Fletcher*-class destroyer USS *Strong* as the warship steamed southwestward through Kula Gulf, the deep but relatively narrow waterway separating the islands of Kolombangara and New Georgia in the Japanese-occupied Solomon Islands. Bracing himself against the vessel's motion as it sliced through moderate swells, the thirty-three-year-old officer peered through his binoculars at the barely discernible shape of the destroyer *Nicholas*, fifteen hundred yards directly ahead. And though he could not see them because of the darkness and passing rain squalls, Miller knew that following in *Strong*'s wake were the light cruisers *Honolulu*, *Helena*, and *St. Louis*, with the destroyers *O'Bannon* and *Chevalier* bringing up the rear of the two-mile column.

The seven warships, part of Rear Admiral Walden L. "Pug" Ainsworth's Task Group 36.1, had come to shower death and destruction upon Japanese positions on both sides of Kula Gulf. The mayhem was intended to prevent the enemy from interfering with the amphibious landing of American forces at Rice Anchorage, on the northwest coast of New Georgia, an operation to be conducted by troop transports, mine vessels, and destroyers that were also—though only temporarily—part of TG 36.1. Ainsworth's light

1

cruisers and their escorting destroyers were to first shell an auxiliary airfield, gun emplacements, and other targets on the southern tip of Kolombangara, then switch their fire to the area immediately surrounding the enemy-held harbor at Bairoko, on New Georgia. The bombardment was scheduled to begin during the first minutes of July 5 and last for approximately a half hour, with the landings slated to commence shortly afterward and be completed by dawn.[1]

As the lead vessels in Ainsworth's bombardment group, *Nicholas* and *Strong* were tasked with conducting an intensive radar and sonar search along the course that the column of warships would follow. That roughly U-shaped route would first parallel the east coast of Kolombangara and then turn directly across the gulf and—upon completion of the mission—take the ships of the task group out of the gulf to the north. The two lead destroyers were to engage any enemy aircraft, surface vessels, or submarines they detected anywhere along the task group's track and would join in the general bombardment only after the light cruisers shifted their fire to the targets on New Georgia.

While the task of pummeling the enemy positions ashore would be left to *Strong*'s big guns—five 5-inch/.38-caliber weapons in two single mounts forward and three aft—the close-in defense of the destroyer was up to the ship's 40mm and 20mm rapid-fire cannon. Miller, a lawyer in civilian life, was in charge of the 20mm weapons and the score of sailors who manned them. Intended primarily for air defense, the guns could also prove murderously effective against small boats and surfaced submarines. Though *Strong*'s 5-inch mounts could be radar directed, the lighter weapons had to be manually aimed and fired, and it was up to Miller to assign potential targets for his gunners based on the general bearing and range information he received from the radar operator or gunnery officer. By stationing himself on the open flying bridge—the second-highest manned position on the ship—Miller had an all-around view of the surrounding sea and could better determine which of his guns should engage a given target, passing the information to his gun captains via sound-powered telephone.[2]

Though Miller didn't yet realize it, however, the greatest threat to *Strong* was far beyond the range of his 20mm guns.

JUST OVER TWENTY MILES TO THE NORTH OF WHERE THE SHIPS OF Ainsworth's bombardment group were preparing to open fire on their initial targets, another senior naval officer was pondering his own next move. Captain Kunizo Kanaoka, commander of the Imperial Japanese Navy's (IJN) Destroyer Division 22, had just been told that the sole radar-equipped vessel in his four-ship flotilla had detected several presumably hostile surface combatants moving south along the west side of Kula Gulf. This was decidedly unwelcome news, for only minutes before Kanaoka had ordered a course change that would take his four destroyers—*Nagatsuki, Niizuki, Satsuki,* and *Yunagi*—into the increasingly crowded gulf. The Japanese warships were packed with troops that Kanaoka was to have landed at Vila Plantation—the very place on Kolombangara that was about to become the first target of the American bombardment. Though the Japanese officer was unaware of his enemy's intentions, he immediately understood that the U.S. Navy's mere presence in Kula Gulf would make it extremely difficult, if not impossible, for his ships to land their embarked troops.

Yet Kanaoka was loath to immediately abort his mission. The Japanese were well aware that the capture of New Georgia was a key component in the Allies' campaign to neutralize the sprawling air and naval base at Rabaul, on New Britain, a vital prerequisite to the capture of the entire Solomon Islands chain. The troops packed aboard the four Japanese destroyers that night were ultimately intended to bolster New Georgia's defenses, thereby helping to slow or even halt the Allied advance through the Southwest Pacific, and Kanaoka's failure to put the men ashore on Kolombangara as planned could have dire consequences.

Though he realized there was little chance of slipping past the Americans undetected and landing the troops, Kanaoka decided to hold his course a bit longer, until he had a better idea of the enemy's intentions.

He didn't have to wait long.

AT TWENTY-SIX MINUTES AFTER MIDNIGHT—FOUR MINUTES AHEAD of the planned zero hour—*Honolulu* commenced firing. *Helena* and

St. Louis immediately joined in, with *O'Bannon* and *Chevalier* adding their voices to the chorus as their guns came to bear. After dispatching more than three thousand 5- and 6-inch high-explosive rounds in less than nine minutes, the column turned east across the gulf, and all of the ships—now including *Nicholas* and *Strong*—opened fire on the eastern shore of Bairoko Harbor. Exactly fourteen minutes after *Honolulu*'s senior gunnery officer prematurely kicked off the bombardment, the American warships ceased firing and the two lead destroyers turned hard to port to start the first leg of the withdrawal, TG 36.1's mission apparently having been successfully concluded without incident.

WHEN AINSWORTH'S SHIPS COMMENCED THEIR BOMBARDMENT OF southern Kolombangara, the deep rumble of their gunfire and the distant flashes of the shells exploding on their targets in and around Vila Plantation immediately convinced Kanaoka that it would be pointless to continue his troop-delivery mission. The radar-equipped American warships would have a distinct advantage over the Japanese destroyers in the darkness and rain, and the loss of the soldiers and naval infantry embarked aboard Kanaoka's vessels would be catastrophic. He therefore ordered the ships of his small flotilla to reverse course and head back toward their base at Buin, on the southern tip of Bougainville Island.

But Kanaoka had no intention of simply turning tail and slinking off without at least taking a parting shot at the enemy. In addition to their gun turrets, his destroyers carried deck-mounted launching tubes for the Type 93 torpedo, a technically advanced and extremely lethal long-range weapon far superior to anything then in the U.S. Navy's arsenal. When the Japanese ships had come about and steadied up on their withdrawal course, Kanaoka ordered *Nagatsuki*, *Niizuki*, and *Yunagi* to each unleash a fan of torpedoes. Within minutes fourteen of the sleek weapons were in the water, churning toward the American warships at speeds in excess of forty miles an hour.

ELEVEN MILES FROM WHERE THE JAPANESE TORPEDOES HAD JUST leaped from their tubes, *Strong* was turning onto the course that would take it—and the other ships of TG 36.1—out of the confines of Kula Gulf and into the relatively open waters of New Georgia Sound. Hugh Miller was still in his position on the destroyer's flying bridge, now joined by Lieutenant James Curran, the ship's gunnery officer. Both men, as well as the port-side lookout standing some fifteen feet aft of them, were attempting to pierce the darkness and light rain, their binoculars trained ahead and to the left of the destroyer's track. *Nicholas*, still in the lead, was occasionally visible fifteen hundred yards dead ahead.

As *Strong* steadied up on its new northerly track, some two miles off Rice Anchorage, first Curran and then Miller spotted a thin, phosphorescent torpedo wake streaking toward the destroyer's port side. Even as he reflexively shouted a warning into his telephone handset, Miller intuitively knew there was no time to prevent the tragedy that was about to engulf his ship. What he had no way of knowing at that moment, however, was that the looming disaster would launch him into an unexpected and harrowing adventure that would pit him against an implacable enemy; test his mind, body, and spirit in ways he had never imagined; and, ultimately, make him famous as the fighting castaway of Arundel Island.

1

ROLL TIDE

A S WITH MANY OF THE YOUNG MEN OF HIS GENERATION WHO EVENTUALLY went in harm's way aboard ships of the U.S. Navy, Hugh Barr Miller Jr. spent most of his early life far from the sea.[1]

Born on January 19, 1910, in Tuscaloosa, Alabama, he was the second son of Hugh Barr Miller and Bertha (Lewis) Miller, both of whom came from families long considered part of the "southern aristocracy." Hugh's paternal grandfather, Robert N. Miller, was a well-known lawyer, district attorney, and onetime president of the Mississippi Bar Association. He also owned a plantation in Center Point, some eight miles outside Hazlehurst in Mississippi's Copiah County. Robert's son, the first Hugh Barr Miller, was born on January 7, 1879, in Hazlehurst. The young man grew up with all the benefits his well-to-do parents could provide, though his formal education was leavened by plenty of time spent in the outdoors, riding, camping, and prowling the plantation's extensive grounds with fishing rod and shotgun.

The first Hugh Miller—known to the family as H. B.—graduated from the University of Mississippi's School of Law in 1903 and initially joined his father's practice in Hazlehurst. He eventually hung out his own shingle and also entered state politics, representing Copiah County for several terms in the Mississippi Legislature.

Within weeks of his graduation from law school, H. B. also got married, a union of two fine old aristocratic southern families. His bride was the former Bertha Boykin Lewis, born in Tuscaloosa in 1878. The new Mrs. Miller was one of seven daughters of Colonel Burwell Lewis, a Confederate veteran of the Civil War, a postwar member of the U.S. House of Representatives, and from 1880 to 1885 the president of the University of Alabama as well as a professor of constitutional and international law. Bertha spent her early years in the president's mansion at the school, a building the Lewis family considered something of an ancestral seat.

Bertha's maternal grandfather, Dr. Landon C. Garland, had been president of the university before and during the Civil War. Following her father's death in 1885, Bertha went to live with her grandparents in Nashville, Tennessee, where Dr. Garland was now chancellor of Vanderbilt University. Upon reaching eighteen, she returned to Tuscaloosa and enrolled in the university, graduating with an AB degree in art—an accomplishment that years later she would follow with a master's degree in the same subject from Columbia University. How and when she met H. B. is unclear, but the young people obviously hit it off and became engaged in 1902. After the wedding the following year, they settled in Hazlehurst, where H. B. went back to his father's law firm and Bertha set about creating a home. Their first son, Robert Burwell Miller, was born in 1905, followed by Hugh Jr.—as he was always referred to by his immediate family—five years later.

ROBERT AND HUGH JR. BOTH GREW UP ON THE CENTER POINT plantation, and, not surprisingly, their father ensured that the boys' formal schooling was supplemented by the same sorts of outdoor activities that he had enjoyed as a young man. H. B. introduced Robert and Hugh Jr. to firearms at a relatively early age, schooling them in

gun safety with unloaded weapons until he was sure they could handle the shotguns and hunting rifles responsibly. He then went on to
teach them the secrets of successful wing shooting—being able to lead
a fast-flying duck or quail accurately enough to bring it down before
it sped out of range—and how to take a deer with a single well-placed
shot from a high-powered rifle.

As keen as H. B. was to introduce his sons to the "manly pursuits"
of nature, his very busy professional life meant that most of the boys'
outdoors education was undertaken by a trusted and respected family
retainer, an elderly black farmhand named James Michael. Uncle Jim,
as he was known, was a tall and courtly man with a crown of white
hair. While he had helped introduce Robert to hunting and fishing, it
was Hugh Jr. who received the full benefit of his deep knowledge of,
and experience in, the great outdoors. The classroom in which Uncle Jim schooled H. B.'s second son was the acres of dense, swampy
woodland that made up much of the Center Point plantation.

Young Hugh's informal education began at eight years old, when
his parents gave their permission for Uncle Jim to take the boy into
the great outdoors.[2] The curriculum was nothing if not comprehensive, for Hugh learned to distinguish the various sounds of the forest,
how to track, how to move silently, and how to make himself completely at home in the outdoors.

Uncle Jim's lessons were taught during frequent woodland forays,
many of which started right after school on Friday. Despite the occasional misadventure, the time Hugh spent in the woods with Uncle
Jim taught the boy, as he later remembered, "everything there was to
know about the woods, and how to get along in them."[3] They were
lessons that years later would literally save his life.

A CHILDHOOD SPENT RIDING, CAMPING, HUNTING, AND DOING THE
strenuous and "character-building" chores his parents assigned to him
ensured that Hugh Miller grew into a sturdy and self-reliant teen-
ager. By the time he reached fourteen, he was sinewy and athletic, and
during his four high school years he played on each of the institution's
organized sports teams. Hugh's first love was football. At first glance,

it seems an odd choice, for he never topped five foot seven and until well into middle age rarely weighed more than 140 pounds. But he excelled as a placekicker—he set several school records that stood well into the 1950s—and could hold his own as a running back.

Football became a key aspect of Hugh's college years. When in September 1928 he entered the University of Alabama, he immediately tried out for the "Crimson Tide," the school's highly regarded team. He was initially assigned to the seventh string, but through determination and because of his capabilities as both a running back and a placekicker he made the varsity squad before the end of his freshman year. It was at that point that Hugh came under the tutelage of Wallace Wade, Alabama's head football coach and a man who was to have a profound and lifelong influence on Hugh.

Himself a college football star, at Alabama Wade turned what had been a relatively mediocre team into a football powerhouse. That metamorphosis was revealed to the nation as a whole on January 1, 1926, when Alabama went to the Rose Bowl for the first time and beat the vaunted and overwhelmingly favored University of Washington Huskies 20–19. The upset victory in Pasadena—gained in large part through two scoring runs and a spectacular and game-saving last-minute tackle by halfback Johnny Mack Brown—gave Alabama its first national title and helped bring southern teams into the mainstream of American college football.[4]

The Crimson Tide's transformation into a football force to be reckoned with was almost entirely the result of Wade's rigorous and uncompromising coaching style. He was a perfectionist, and he demanded that his players take the game as seriously as he did. Wade enforced an almost military discipline that required his players to give their maximum effort at all times. Hugh Miller later recalled the famed coach as "a terrific task master, a hard driver who had only the sharpest sarcasm for complainers, whiners [and] loafers."[5]

But the real secret to Wade's coaching success was his ability to motivate his players. Even as he was driving them hard, asking the most from each and every man on the team, he was imbuing them with an indomitable spirit built on both a belief in their own abilities and the conviction that they could accomplish anything they set out to do. He was firmly convinced that a man who *would not* be defeated *could not* be defeated, and he passed that conviction on to the young men he coached. It was a mantra that held special meaning for Hugh, whose single-minded determination to excel as a running back despite his stature quickly caught Wade's attention. The older man took a special interest in Hugh, sharpening his already considerable skills as a placekicker and turning him into a ruthlessly efficient tackler—though, as Hugh later jokingly recalled, Wade "damn near killed me in the process."[6]

The training and motivation paid off, for in 1930 the Tide was invited to return to the Rose Bowl. The game, played on January 1, 1931, against the Washington State Cougars, was Wade's last for Alabama—he had already accepted an offer to become head coach at Duke University in North Carolina and would leave at the end of the 1930 season. The looming departure of their coach did nothing to dampen the determination of the Tide players, however, for soon after they took to the rain-dampened field before some seventy thousand spectators in Pasadena they began what would ultimately become an unstoppable assault on the clearly overwhelmed Cougars. With Hugh participating in several plays as a guard, Alabama dominated Washington 24–0.[7]

The Rose Bowl game was not just Wade's last hurrah for the University of Alabama but also Hugh's final game. As dedicated as the young man was to football, he also had other interests. On the one hand, he was a full-time student, and to achieve the grades both he and his family expected him to meant that he had to make a choice—his studies or the game he loved. Given his family's history, social standing, and tradition of public service, it was perhaps inevitable that he would choose the books over the gridiron.

But there was also another distraction in Hugh's life. Soon after starting at Alabama, he'd met Anne Elizabeth Gayden, the well-to-do daughter of an eminent Mississippi physician, Dr. Hugh Dixon Gayden, who had died in France while serving in the American Expeditionary Forces during World War I. Anne had been raised by her mother, Anne McComb Gayden, in Leland, Mississippi, and despite the tragic loss of her husband the widow had ensured that her daughter grew up as a proper southern belle.

That was exactly the sort of woman Hugh's upbringing had taught him to seek as a prospective mate, and what apparently began as a casual acquaintance following a chance meeting in class soon blossomed into something much more. The two were married in a lavish Tuscaloosa ceremony on November 29, 1930, after which they set up housekeeping in a small off-campus apartment. With the help of twenty-year-old Hugh's parents, the couple was able to pay eighteen-year-old Anne's train fare from Alabama to Pasadena for the Rose Bowl game, and she cheered from the stands as the Crimson Tide rolled to victory.[8]

Having ended his college football career on a high note, Hugh devoted himself to both his studies and his young bride. Hugh received his AB degree in May 1931 and graduated from the University of Alabama's College of Law two years later. He and a now-pregnant Anne moved to Greenville, Mississippi—near where the young woman had grown up and where her mother still lived—where Hugh had been offered a position as an associate attorney with the prestigious law firm Percy & Farish.[9] The young couple had hardly settled into their new surroundings when their son, Hugh Barr Miller III, was born on August 20, 1933.

During Hugh's first year at Percy & Farish, the former football star displayed the same determination he'd shown on the field, putting his full effort and attention into even the most mundane assignments. His attitude and work ethic helped him move up the office pecking order, and by 1935 he'd amply demonstrated his skills as a litigator.

In the decade following his graduation from law school, Hugh's legal career seems to have moved from success to success, but the same period unfortunately saw a marked decline in the state of his marriage. He and Anne drifted steadily apart, and in August 1940 they officially separated. Hugh moved to Gainesville, Florida, and found a position with one of the city's law firms. At some point after his arrival in the city, he met and began a relationship with Frances Lee Nipper, a young woman eight years his junior.

Born in Alabama on November 13, 1918, Frances was the oldest of six children of Cicero and Emma (Southerland) Nipper and moved with her family to Gainesville soon after her birth. By all accounts a responsible, caring, and attractive young woman, Frances obviously captivated Hugh, who asked her to marry him when that became possible. On August 28, 1941, Anne filed for divorce in Greenville, seeking both alimony and permanent custody of their now eight-year-old son. Hugh did not contest the action and agreed in full to Anne's requests, and the final decree of divorce was granted by the Washington County, Mississippi, Chancery Court on October 7, 1941.[10] Just over a month later, on November 27, Hugh and Frances were married in Key West—where Hugh had started a new job barely a month before.

Hugh Barr Miller, former attorney, was now Ensign H. B. Miller, U.S. Naval Reserve.

BY THE TIME HUGH AND ANNE DECIDED TO GO THEIR SEPARATE ways in the summer of 1940, war had been raging in Europe for almost a year. Like many of his fellow citizens, Hugh was convinced, as he later recalled, that the United States was already "unofficially in the war and would get into it officially at any time."[11] President Franklin Roosevelt's September 1940 signing into law of the Selective Service and Training Act made it clear that Hugh—like millions of the country's other able-bodied men—could look forward to being drafted into military service sooner rather than later. While Hugh was a patriotic and proud American who wanted to do his part in what was obviously soon to be a national war effort, he didn't particularly relish the idea of ending up as an infantryman. He therefore began exploring other possibilities, and his research led him to the Navy.

As America geared up for war, all of the military services were in desperate need of officers. This need was particularly pressing for the Navy, given that its existing officer corps was already being stretched thin and the traditional source for new commissioned officers—the Naval Academy in Annapolis, Maryland—graduated fewer than one thousand new ensigns a year.[12] Moreover, the Navy's college-based Reserve Officers Training Corps (ROTC)—authorized by Congress in 1925—had developed slowly and by December 1939 was active on only nine campuses. To a greater extent than the Army, the Navy required officers with advanced skills—individuals with college degrees and professional expertise in engineering, in particular, but also in medicine, science, and law. One way to procure qualified persons was to provide for the direct commissioning of university graduates into the Naval Reserve, and after the September 1939 outbreak of war in Europe what had previously been a fairly low-key program was so inundated with applications from young college men around the country that boxes overflowing with the completed forms were stacked in the halls of the Navy's Bureau of Personnel (BuPers) by the thousands.[13]

Hugh's first step in obtaining a direct commission into the Naval Reserve was to apply through the commandant of the Seventh Naval District in Gainesville. In his cover letter, dated June 23, 1941, he called attention to both his sports background and his legal training as foundations for his leadership abilities.[14] Attached to Hugh's application were letters of recommendation, the most impressive—and prescient—of which came from Wallace Wade, who closed his very positive character reference by saying that Hugh was a young man with "plenty of fortitude" who could "take care of himself in any circumstances." The commandant of the Seventh Naval District was apparently appropriately impressed by Hugh's qualifications, for he forwarded the application to Washington with his recommendation that it be approved.

The packet of forms was obviously not one of those that ended up stacked in an endless corridor at BuPers, for Hugh's application was received, reviewed, and approved in less than ninety days. Hugh was notified of his acceptance in mid-September, and on the twenty-ninth he was commissioned in a brief ceremony in Miami, his wife at his side. The man born far from the sea was now officially an officer in the U.S. Naval Reserve.[15]

In his initial application for a commission, Hugh had said he didn't care where he was stationed, but it must have come as a pleasant surprise that his initial duty station was in Florida. After taking a few weeks to settle his business affairs, Hugh reported to Key West in mid-October to take up his new position as an aide to Captain Russell S. Crenshaw, assistant commandant of the Seventh Naval District. The long-serving and very well-respected officer proved to be an ideal mentor for Hugh. Crenshaw took the younger officer under his wing, introducing him to the Navy way of doing things and providing a master class in the subtleties of command. In return, Hugh brought his professional expertise to bear, advising Crenshaw on legal questions concerning the Navy's expansion of its facilities in and around Key West.

The workload for both Hugh and his superior increased dramatically following Japan's December 7, 1941, attack on Pearl Harbor and other military facilities on Oahu. On February 1, 1942, the headquarters of the commandant of the Seventh Naval District was moved from the Charleston, South Carolina, Navy Yard to Key West, and Crenshaw was elevated from assistant to acting district commandant. Days later, Crenshaw was tapped to also command the Gulf Sea Frontier, the Key West–based organization created to patrol the waters off Florida, the Gulf Coast states, the Bahamas, and Cuba.

The threat of enemy activity within the Gulf Sea Frontier's area of responsibility was very real. German submarines had been active off the East Coast of the United States even before Pearl Harbor and had damaged several American merchant vessels and in October 1941 sank the destroyer USS *Reuben James* as it was escorting a Britain-bound convoy. America's December 8 declaration of war against the Axis resulted in the arrival off Florida of several German and Italian submarines, and on February 19, 1942, the tanker *Pan Massachusetts* had the dubious distinction of being the first U.S.-flagged vessel to be sunk by enemy action in the Gulf Sea Frontier when it was torpedoed by *U-128* off Cape Canaveral. Four days later, the sub sank the tanker *Cities Service Empire* thirty miles east of Cocoa Beach, almost at the same time *U-504* was sinking another tanker, the *Republic*, some eighty miles to the southeast.[16]

While Hugh later recalled his time in Key West as interesting and personally rewarding, America's entry into the war and the string of enemy submarine attacks that followed within sight of the Florida coast convinced him that he wanted to take a more active role in the conflict. He put in his first request for sea duty within days of Pearl Harbor, seeking assignment to a destroyer because he'd spent one or two days at sea aboard the World War I–era training vessels homeported in Key West. That request—and the several that followed it—was denied because Hugh had never had any sort of training that would qualify him for a sea billet and, as one senior officer commented, there wasn't much need for lawyers on destroyers. Hugh's quest to "get into the fight" seemed to be going nowhere fast when, sometime in the early spring of 1942, a chance meeting with a senior officer set in motion a chain of events that would ultimately help "the lawyer" go to sea.

Boston-born Lieutenant Commander Joseph H. Wellings, known to friends and family as Gus, had enjoyed an interesting and varied career since graduating from the Naval Academy in 1925. He'd spent time afloat on the battleships *Utah*, *Florida*, and *California* and the destroyers *King* and *Tillman*; was a Navy ROTC instructor at Harvard for two years; and had served as aide and flag lieutenant to Vice Admiral William D. Leahy. From July 1940 to June 1941, he had been an assistant naval attaché at the U.S. Embassy in London, tasked with studying the Royal Navy's fleet operations and tactics. Following his return to the United States, Wellings was temporarily assigned to the Office of the Chief of Naval Operations to help develop doctrine for antisubmarine operations. It was in this role that he visited Key West—home to, among other commands, the Navy's Fleet Sonar School—in the spring of 1942.[17]

During the several days that Wellings spent in Key West, he called on Crenshaw, commander of the Gulf Sea Frontier, and was at some point introduced to Hugh. In the course of conversation, Wellings mentioned to the younger officer that the antisubmarine doctrine assignment was only temporary; in June Wellings was scheduled to take command of a *Fletcher*-class destroyer then under construction at Maine's Bath Iron Works (BIW). Seeing a chance to get himself to sea despite his lack of formal naval training, Hugh told Wellings of his predicament and asked if there was any way he might join the crew of the new vessel. He promised he would do whatever it might take to turn himself into a qualified shipboard officer and was apparently quite convincing, for Wellings agreed to ask BuPers to transfer Hugh to the crew then forming in Maine. As Hugh himself later recalled, he and Wellings "had a terrible time" convincing BuPers to authorize the transfer, though the two officers—with an additional endorsement by

Crenshaw—finally succeeded through "sheer persistency."[18] In late April Hugh received orders assigning him to Bath Iron Works as part of the precommissioning crew of DD-467, the soon-to-be-launched USS *Strong*.

Hugh's orders directed him to report to his new duty station no later than May 1, but authorized him several days of "leave en route." After wrapping up a few loose ends in Key West, he and Frances drove first to Gainesville for a brief reunion with her mother and sisters and then headed to Hazlehurst to see Hugh's family. After that, he and Frances made the fourteen-hundred-mile railway journey from southwestern Mississippi to the coast of central Maine; they had decided that she would accompany him and stay in Bath until the ship was ready for sea. At that point, the young Mrs. Miller would head south, to stay either with her mother or with Hugh's.

For Hugh, at least, some of the sadness of the imminent parting eased on May 1. Having signed in at the temporary building that served as the administration office for Navy personnel assigned to the Bath shipyard, he walked the several hundred yards to the slipways that fed into the tidal waters of the swift-flowing Kennebec River. There, impossibly elegant of line despite being high and dry, sat the vessel that would carry him to war and—though he didn't yet know it—launch him on the most challenging and dangerous adventure of his young life.

2

TAKING SHIP

THE VESSEL THAT WOULD EVENTUALLY CARRY HUGH MILLER TO THE SOUTH Pacific bore the Bath Iron Works hull number 193, and its construction had been officially authorized some twenty-two months before the young officer's first sight of it.

On July 1, 1940, William S. "Pete" Newell, president of BIW—as the Maine firm was universally referred to in shipbuilding circles—had traveled to Washington, D.C., to sign a contract his company had worked diligently to obtain. The agreement covered the construction of six 2,100-ton *Fletcher*-class destroyers and had a value of nearly $41 million.[1] BIW was more than qualified to produce the new vessels; the company had been building ships on the Kennebec River since the 1880s and had launched a World War I battleship, Coast Guard cutters, and a variety of yachts, passenger steamers, freighters, and other commercial vessels. More important, beginning in 1909 the company had built several varieties of destroyer for the Navy, and even as Newell entrained for Washington in that

eventful summer of 1940 BIW was already constructing examples of
the 1,630-ton *Gleaves* class.

BIW was one of the smallest of only six private shipbuilding companies to have survived the Great Depression, and it stood to lose orders
to the larger concerns as the Navy geared up for war.[2] As early as 1937
Newell had begun the expansion process, and in the early summer of
1940—before the signing of the *Fletcher*-class contract—the U.S. government stepped in to help. A telegram from Secretary of the Navy
Frank Knox informed Newell that Congress had authorized the re-
imbursement of private companies for funds spent to enlarge facilities
vital to the national defense. Knox directed Newell to "take immediate
steps to expand your facilities with the view to greatly enlarged shipbuilding program." And, to underscore the urgency of that program,
Knox pointed out that "speed is of the essence."[3]

Newell's foresight in acquiring lands adjacent to the existing shipyard and beginning the construction of new facilities—including
additional slipways, matériel storage yards, and a steel fabrication
plant[4]—was quickly vindicated. The expansion gave BIW the ability
to have eight vessels under construction at the same time and allowed
the firm to begin work on the *Fletcher*-class destroyers well before
most of the other private and Navy-owned yards that ultimately received contracts.[5] The keels of the first two ships, BIW hull numbers
190 and 191—the future USS *Nicholas* and USS *O'Bannon*—were laid
on adjoining slipways on March 3, 1941. The second pair, *Chevalier*
and *Strong*, was started—also on adjacent slipways—on April 30 and
the final ships of the initial order, *Taylor* and *De Haven*, in August and
September, respectively. The six destroyers were the first of an eventual 31 BIW-built *Fletcher*s, the largest number constructed by any of
the eleven private and government-owned shipyards that ultimately
produced the 175 ships of the class.

While BIW was ahead of the game in terms of being able to start
construction of its *Fletcher*s nearly seven months before the lead ship
of the class was laid down at New Jersey's Federal Shipbuilding,[6]
production of the new vessels was not without some fairly significant
challenges. The ships were, after all, the largest and most complex destroyers thus far ordered for the U.S. Navy.

THE CERTAINTY THAT BIW's CONTRACT FOR ITS FIRST SIX *FLETCHER*S would be followed by orders for additional examples—all of which would have to be produced as quickly as was humanly possible— prompted the company to abandon its traditional "custom-built" approach to ship construction and adopt the sort of assembly-line process already in use in automobile and aircraft production. Each team of workers performed a certain set of tasks, then moved to the next vessel to do the same job. This process quickened the pace of ship construction and ensured that the vast numbers of inexperienced workers drawn into BIW as replacements for seasoned employees called up for military service would have to master only a few special- ized skills rather than a myriad of general tasks.

In the months preceding the Japanese attack on Pearl Harbor, a three-shift, six-day work schedule kept the shipyard humming. Just as important, an improved supply-chain system ensured that the var- ious standardized systems, subassemblies, and government-furnished items required for each hull—everything from boilers and turbines to 5-inch guns and torpedo tubes—arrived on time and in the proper condition for installation. BIW encountered difficulties as it geared up, of course, but overcame many of the early issues while working on *Nicholas* and *O'Bannon*, and when *Chevalier* and *Strong* took their places side by side on the slipways the construction process was run- ning relatively smoothly. By the time Hugh Miller first saw his new ship it had been under construction for 366 days, had experienced no significant delays, and was just 16 days from taking to the water for the first time.

THOUGH HUGH WAS ONE OF THE INITIAL MEMBERS OF *STRONG*'S prospective crew to arrive at BIW, he was not the first.

That honor belonged to thirty-year-old Lieutenant Marvin I. Rosenberg, who had been tapped to be the destroyer's engineering officer. The 1934 graduate of the U.S. Naval Academy had been at the shipyard since shortly after the ship's keel was laid and soon thereafter was joined by his assistant engineering officer, twenty- four-year-old Lieutenant (Junior Grade)[7] Delavan B. Downer, and several enlisted men. The group's purpose was twofold. First, they had closely monitored each step of *Strong*'s construction on behalf of the Navy's supervisor of shipbuilding at Bath, Commander J. M. Kiernan. And, second, Rosenberg and the others had used their time at Bath to familiarize themselves with every aspect of the new destroyer's oil-fired boilers, its two General Electric steam turbines, and all of the associated systems that would ultimately take the ship where it was needed.

But overseeing *Strong*'s gestation was not Rosenberg's only responsibility. Owing to commitments in Washington, Gus Wellings was not scheduled to arrive at BIW until June 1, so his engineering officer had been tapped to command the destroyer's precommissioning detail. Though Hugh Miller and the other officers and enlisted men who arrived at BIW while the ship was under construction were officially assigned to temporary duty in Kiernan's office—and though they were attached to the Boston-based First Naval District for administrative purposes—their day-to-day welfare and activities were Rosenberg's concern.[8] The hectic pace of the work at the shipyard undoubtedly made his personnel-management task easier, for the officers and men of his detail rarely had time to do anything but work or sleep. They were all intensely focused on the ship's first milestone—its launching. That momentous event had been set for May 17, and any delay would cause serious ripple effects through the shipyard's production schedule.

For Hugh, the sixteen days following his arrival in Bath were a blur. Wellings had tapped him to be *Strong*'s machine-gun officer—apparently deciding that years of wing-shooting experience made the former lawyer a reasonable candidate for the job of overseeing the crews who would man the ship's four .50-caliber Brownings. Having had no previous experience with automatic weapons of any kind, Hugh had immersed himself in technical and operator manuals even before leaving Florida, only to find upon arriving at the shipyard that the .50s had been deemed inadequate for modern air defense and were being replaced on all *Fletcher*s by 20mm guns. License-built versions of the Swiss-developed Oerlikon autocannon, these weapons were significantly larger and more complex than the Brownings they were to replace. Though the cannon would not be installed until after *Strong*'s launching, Hugh threw himself into learning about both the guns and the Mark 14 gyro-stabilized, lead-computing gunsight with which they'd ultimately be fitted. He also spent time on the ship while it was still on the ways, familiarizing himself with the four locations where the guns would be placed—two in individual semicircular "tubs" just forward, below, and to either side of *Strong*'s bridge structure, and the other two on either side of the vessel's main deck amidships—and with the location and capacity of the 20mm ammunition lockers.

Thanks to the round-the-clock effort of BIW's workers—and to the work of Rosenberg and the men of his precommissioning detail—hull number 193 was ready to slide down the ways exactly on schedule.

OWING TO WARTIME SECURITY REGULATIONS, THE DATE AND TIME of *Strong*'s launching had not been publicly announced ahead of time. Yet by the midafternoon of May 17, some four hundred civilian onlookers had gathered just outside the shipyard's gates, primarily along the north side of the Carlton Bridge spanning the Kennebec River. While launchings at BIW almost always drew crowds—Bath was, and remains, a maritime town—the throng on that particular day was somewhat larger than usual, perhaps because the event marked the first Sunday launching in the shipyard's history.[9]

Strong had been constructed at the upper end of the outermost of the two new inclined slipways built on land BIW had acquired adjacent to the original shipyard, with the future *Chevalier* barely forty feet away on the port side. *Strong*'s hull rested atop a series of supporting wooden blocks, and about sixty days before the scheduled launch date shipyard workers had begun laying two lines of heavy timbers parallel to the ship's keel all the way down the slipway and into the river. On top of those timbers, known as groundways, workers then laid a thick coating of grease before adding another parallel line of timbers, the sliding ways. To keep the latter from moving prematurely, the workers installed diagonal bracing timbers referred to as dog shores. The next step in the preparation for launch was the construction of a wooden cradle that fitted the shape of *Strong*'s hull; on the morning of May 15, teams of workmen wielding massive sledgehammers began driving huge wooden wedges between the sliding ways and the cradle, slowly transferring the weight of the ship from the shores to the sliding ways. The supporting blocks beneath the hull were then removed, and *Strong* was ready for its baptismal slide into the Kennebec.

The destroyer had been named in honor of Rear Admiral James Hooker Strong, who served with distinction during the Civil War and ended his career in 1876 as commander in chief of the South Atlantic Squadron. In searching for an appropriate sponsor for the new vessel, the Navy's Bureau of Navigation was able to locate the admiral's great-grandniece Mrs. Susan Hobart Olson of Milwaukee. At 3:45 on a dreary, rain-soaked May 17, she and her husband joined Marvin Rosenberg; BIW's general manager, George Connard; and a few other dignitaries atop a small wooden platform built at the base of the destroyer's stem. After remarks by the Navy and company representatives, Mrs. Olson stepped before the microphone, quickly read the short christening statement, and then gamely swung a bottle of champagne against the destroyer's stem.

The shattering of the bottle was the signal for workmen to knock out the dog shores, and almost immediately *Strong* began its 90-second journey down the slipway. As the vessel picked up speed, the colorful flags flying from a line stretched from the bow to a temporary mast atop the bridge and all the way to the stern flapped in the wind, as onlookers both in the shipyard and outside the gates cheered. The destroyer slid stern first into the calm Kennebec—the launch had been planned for slack tide—and waiting tugs quickly shepherded it the few hundred feet to BIW's fitting-out wharf. The ship was quickly tied up inboard of *Chevalier*, itself launched just over a month earlier. Even as the people who had witnessed the afternoon's ceremony began to disperse, workers started preparing *Strong* for the next step in its evolution.

Most of the destroyer's vital internal systems—including boilers, turbines, fuel tanks, and miles of wiring and ducting—had been installed during the 382 days it had sat on the ways, and the basic superstructure was complete by the time it took to the water. But it was during *Strong*'s 82-day fitting-out period that the vessel evolved into a combat-ready warship. Much of the work involved the addition of such structural components as the main mast, searchlight platforms on either side of the forward funnel, davits for the ship's two motor whale boats, and so on. But arguably the most important transformation that occurred was the addition of weaponry.

The main armament of the initial *Fletcher*-class destroyers consisted of five 5-inch/.38-caliber dual-purpose guns that could be used against both surface targets and aircraft. Each of the weapons was completely enclosed within a gun house, also referred to as a turret, and all five were lifted aboard *Strong* by a crane on the fitting-out wharf and installed as complete units. The two forward guns were placed directly ahead of the bridge area, with Mount 51 on the main deck and Mount 52 stepped above and directly behind it on the 01 level. Mounts 53 and 54 were secured atop the aft deckhouse, also on the 01 level, with the former pointing forward and the latter aft. The final gun, Mount 55, was placed on the main deck, stepped just below and aft of Mount 54. The addition of the Mark 37 gun director atop a pedestal on the flying bridge completed *Strong*'s main battery.

Next to go aboard was the destroyer's secondary armament. First came the torpedo tubes, with one five-tube launcher fixed immediately aft of each funnel on the 01 level. On the ship's fantail workers installed depth-charge rails and then added three K-gun projectors amidships on either side. And finally, much to Hugh Miller's relief, the four 20mm cannon he was to command were winched aboard and installed in the forward and amidships gun tubs.

THOUGH MARVIN ROSENBERG HAD BEEN OFFICIALLY IN CHARGE of *Strong*'s precommissioning detail, the destroyer's prospective captain had not been idle.

Gus Wellings had visited BIW whenever his duties in Washington had allowed, taking the opportunity to gauge the progress of the vessel's construction and talk with the men who were building what would ultimately become his ship. But he had gone even further: once he was released from his duties in the Office of the Chief of Naval

Operations, Wellings had traveled to Boston, where he spent three days inspecting *Nicholas*, a product of BIW and the first *Fletcher* to be launched. Its captain, Lieutenant Commander William Brown, allowed Wellings to examine every inch of the vessel and talk to the crewmen about their impressions of the new ship.

Upon officially reporting aboard at BIW in mid-June, Wellings requested Kiernan's permission to sail aboard *O'Bannon* when it left Bath for Boston and the official turnover to the Navy. When the destroyer departed for the one-day voyage, Wellings was on the bridge with the captain, Commander Edwin Wilkinson, a longtime friend. Both during the trip and after *O'Bannon*'s arrival in Boston, Wellings relentlessly prowled the entire ship, undertaking a personal inspection and asking questions of both the Navy personnel onboard and the BIW workers who were in charge of the vessel until its official handover. Once back in Bath, Wellings also spent considerable time aboard *Chevalier*, which had been launched in mid-April and was soon to depart for Boston for its own additional work.

During the last few days of June Wellings wrote a comprehensive report detailing his observations about the *Fletcher*-class ships in general and *Strong* in particular. The document was addressed to Captain Edward L. "Ned" Cochrane, at that time the assistant director of the Design Division in the Navy's Bureau of Ships.[10] BuShips, as it was known within the service, was responsible for the development, construction, and modification of all Navy vessels. Cochrane was a vigorous promoter of destroyers and other "small" combatants. *Strong*'s prospective captain apparently felt that his honest assessments of the first few *Fletcher*s would be both of value to and appreciated by Cochrane and other senior officers in BuShips.

Dated July 1, 1942, Wellings's evaluation was characteristically thorough. Though he found several things to like about the design and layout of the first *Fletcher*-class destroyers—he pronounced the engineering spaces to be "apparently excellent," for example, and the arrangement of the bridge "very good"—he noted far more things that were "deficient." These included everything from poor ventilation in the officers' and crews' quarters to a chart house that was "barely large enough" to fuel oil tanks that were too small to permit the destroyers to achieve their projected cruising radius. *Strong*'s prospective captain was particularly displeased with his ship's armament, which he termed "not much better, if any," than the considerably smaller destroyers already in service.

While Wellings signed the letter to Cochrane "With kindest personal regards," his irritation and frustration were palpable. He was a conscientious and capable officer who realized all too well the challenges he and his men would soon face, and he knew that the *Fletchers* would have a vital role to play in the coming battles in both the Atlantic and the Pacific. Although he understood the need to build the ships as quickly as possible, he clearly saw no benefit or logic in rushing them to launching only to have them sidelined for months while they underwent modifications that could have been done on the ways.

CATALOGING THE SHORTCOMINGS OF THE *FLETCHERS*' DESIGN WAS not Wellings's only task during his time at BIW, of course; the man who would soon be responsible for *Strong* and all who sailed in it had myriad other administrative and matériel issues to deal with while the ship was alongside BIW's fitting-out wharf. He was able to delegate some of the work to Rosenberg, Hugh Miller—who had been promoted to lieutenant (jg) on June 13—and the few senior petty officers assigned to the precommissioning crew, but Wellings must have sighed with relief on June 26 when his new executive officer reported for duty.

Lieutenant Frederick W. Purdy was cut from the same cloth as his new captain. A 1933 Naval Academy graduate, Purdy had held significant assignments both ashore and afloat. He was serving aboard the battleship *California* when it was damaged during the Japanese attack on Pearl Harbor and helped supervise repairs to the vessel until his return to the United States in April 1942. At that point he'd briefly joined the staff of the 12th Naval District in California, but had gladly given up that job when Wellings—a longtime acquaintance—had specifically requested him to be *Strong*'s second in command. As executive officer, or XO, Purdy would be both the destroyer's navigator and its chief administrator, handling personnel issues and many other bureaucratic chores on Wellings's behalf. The two men respected and trusted each other, and *Strong*'s commanding officer considered himself extremely fortunate to have secured Purdy's service before he could be snapped up by some other captain.

Among the most important issues Purdy tackled was coordinating the assembly of *Strong*'s crew. By the time he arrived in Bath, the ship's precommissioning complement totaled 4 officers and about 15 enlisted men, with another 10 or so individuals scheduled to come aboard before the ship's departure for the Boston Navy Yard. However, the destroyer's planned complement on the day of its commissioning in Massachusetts—tentatively scheduled for the first week in August— was to be 15 officers and 264 men.

Wellings's officers would include two highly capable lieutenants, six lieutenants (jg) with between one and three years' time in service, and six recently commissioned ensigns. All of the chief petty officers and about a third of the enlisted sailors earmarked for *Strong* were experienced men who would be coming from other ships or such shore stations as Norfolk, Portsmouth, New York, and Boston itself. The remainder of the ship's complement, however, was to consist of men who were relatively new to the Navy, with a surprisingly large number having entered the service only sixty to ninety days before being assigned to the ship.[11] It was Purdy's job to review the prospective crew members' personnel files and coordinate with BuPers and the Boston Navy Yard's receiving station to ensure that all of the new arrivals would be available well in advance of the day when the destroyer would officially commission.

That the vast majority of *Strong*'s crew would not report aboard until after the destroyer's arrival in Boston resulted from the simple fact that they would not be required. The destroyer would remain the property of BIW until its official acceptance by the Navy just prior to commissioning, and it would make the one-day voyage from Maine to Massachusetts with an operating crew made up of shipyard employees. Wellings and the other members of the precommissioning detail would not take part in the navigation or operation of the vessel—except for the evaluation of its weapons—though they would be very interested observers.

The need to meet the destroyer's contract delivery date led the Navy and BIW to streamline the process by which *Strong*'s propulsion systems and general seaworthiness were evaluated. Rather than subjecting each destroyer to weeks of traditional builders' trials and customer acceptance trials, both parties agreed that other than a low-power engine test conducted during the "dock trails and inspection" alongside the BIW wharf on August 3, all other system checks would be done while the vessel was under way to Boston.[12] BIW completed the ship's fitting-out on Wednesday, August 5, and by dawn the following day it was ready to put to sea.

The morning of departure dawned cool and overcast, the sun struggling to pierce the low-hanging clouds. As workers let go the lines holding *Strong* to the fitting-out wharf, tugs moved in to turn it away from the Carlton Bridge and point the bow toward the Atlantic, 12 miles downriver. On the ship's bridge BIW employees manned the helm and engine-order telegraphs, with the company's assistant port captain (and veteran Kennebec River pilot) George C. Stacey in command. Workers also staffed the engine room and other key areas of the vessel, and George Connard stood on the starboard bridge wing, chatting with Gus Wellings, Marv Rosenberg, and Kiernan. From vantage points throughout the ship, Hugh Miller and the other members of the precommissioning detail looked on as their civilian counterparts got the destroyer under way for the first time, the BIW house flag flying from the signal yard.

Strong slowly moved downriver in the central channel, the forested hillsides on either bank gliding past in the brightening sun. At several points on its journey to the sea the destroyer had to thread its way between small islands and the river's bank, though the tide was high and the navigation presented no real challenge for Stacey. As the ship passed through the thousand-foot-wide channel between Long Island and the Civil War–era Fort Popham—just a mile from the river's mouth—the veteran BIW captain ordered the revolutions on the twin shafts progressively higher. By the time *Strong* passed Seguin Island, some 3 miles offshore, it was clocking nearly 35 knots—roughly 40 miles per hour.

The destroyer could easily have covered the 128-mile straight-line distance to Boston in about four hours, but the trip was more than a delivery run. It was the only sea trial it would have before being turned over to the Navy, and Stacey, Kiernan, and Wellings all had a vested interest in seeing that it met the minimum acceptance criteria. Over the next eight hours the ship was put through its paces, with frequent high-speed dashes interspersed with hard turns and even a "crash stop." Other than the fact that its turning radius was unimpressive—the *Fletchers'* single rudders ensured that even a heavy cruiser could turn with greater agility—the engineering plant and propulsion systems all passed muster. As seaworthy as *Strong* proved itself to be, however, there were other tests that were equally important.

Before leaving Bath the destroyer had taken on depth charges and ammunition for the main guns and the four 20mm cannon. While this was partly out of common sense—there were German U-boats operating off the East Coast, and it might actually need to defend itself—it was also so the weapons could be tested. Once clear of the coast, gunner's mates who were part of the precommissioning detail systematically fired rounds from each 5-inch mount, varying the distance and direction of fire so that each turret's range of motion could be verified at the same time its gun was being tested. When they moved on to the 20mm weapons, Hugh Miller, "pulling rank," gave himself the chance to fire the weapons for which he would soon be responsible. As a finale, each of the six K-gun projectors tossed a 300-pound Mark 6 depth charge far to the side of the ship's track, as 600-pound Mark 7 charges rolled off both of the fantail-mounted racks. The resulting explosions produced an impressive series of subsurface convulsions, each of which was quickly followed by the eruption of a dome-shaped geyser of roiling seawater.

With the abbreviated "acceptance trial" successfully completed, *Strong* headed for Boston and was alongside one of the Navy Yard's piers just after 3:00 p.m. Stacey then rang up "finished with engines," and he and the other BIW employees gathered on the ship's quarterdeck for the brief handover ceremony. Once Kiernan signed the acceptance forms that transferred ownership of the destroyer to the Navy, the dignitaries shook hands, the shipbuilder's house flag came down from the signal yard, and the BIW contingent rushed off to find

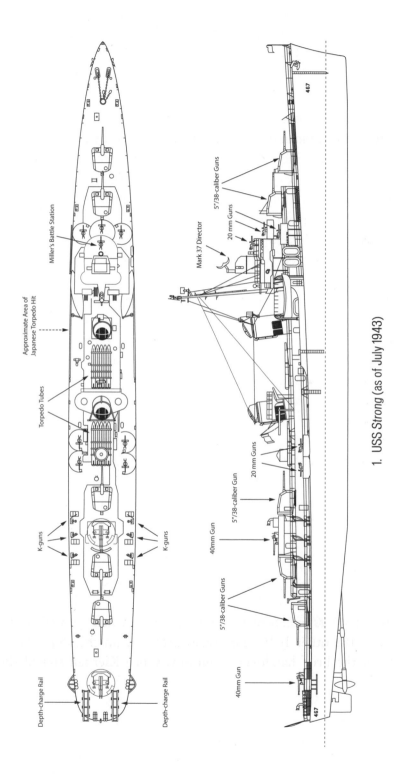

Miller's Battle Station

Approximate Area of
Japanese Torpedo Hit

Torpedo Tubes

K-guns

K-guns

Depth-charge Rail

Depth-charge Rail

Mark 37 Director

5"/38-caliber Guns

20 mm Guns

5"/38-caliber Gun

40mm Gun

20 mm Guns

5"/38-caliber Guns

40mm Gun

467

467

1. USS *Strong* (as of July 1943)

the cabs that would take them to Boston's North Station in time to catch the 4:30 train back to Bath.[13]

ALMOST AS SOON AS KIERNAN OFFICIALLY ACCEPTED *STRONG* ON the Navy's behalf, the enlisted men who would constitute the bulk of the crew began streaming aboard, sea bags over their shoulders. For the rest of the afternoon and well into the evening, scores of young sailors—most of whom had never before walked a warship's decks—sought out their berthing areas with help from the members of the precommissioning detachment, stowed their gear, and generally began settling in aboard the vessel that was to be their home for the foreseeable future. The arrival process was, not surprisingly, somewhat less hectic for new officers joining the ship. As each man stepped aboard, a runner guided him first to his shared stateroom to drop his luggage and then to the wardroom, one level below and immediately aft of Mount 52. There the officer was greeted by the captain and XO and, after handing over his orders, was officially welcomed aboard.

While Wellings obviously had much to discuss with his officers on that evening of August 6, the most pressing issue was the following day's commissioning ceremony. Scheduled for the afternoon, the event would be brief, in keeping with wartime priorities but nonetheless important, for it would officially make *Strong* a "United States Ship" and mark Wellings's official assumption of command. The fact that a representative of Rear Admiral William T. Tarrant, commandant of the First Naval District, would be participating in the ceremony was also likely a topic of discussion, and Wellings made certain his officers fully understood the need for the event to go off flawlessly.

Just after 4:00 p.m. on August 7, the men who at that point constituted *Strong*'s entire crew were gathered on the destroyer's fantail. Wellings and Purdy stood side by side in front of Hugh and the other 12 officers, who were drawn up in two lines at the base of Mount 55. The 258 enlisted men were arrayed several rows deep along both sides of the ship from the second funnel aft and all, officers and sailors alike wearing service dress-blue uniforms. The "transferring officer"— the captain representing Admiral Tarrant—stood just forward of the depth-charge rails, flanked by Kiernan and a Navy chaplain. Facing Wellings, the captain called all present to attention, then read the directive officially placing the ship in commission. The First Naval District band struck up the national anthem from the pier, and a 9-man Marine color guard hoisted the national ensign on *Strong*'s stern flagstaff. At almost the same instant, other Marines hoisted the blue forty-eight-starred Union Jack on the ship's bow jackstaff, and a team of 3 sailors ran the four-foot red, white, and blue commissioning pennant to the top of the mainmast. Wellings then walked forward, turned to his officers, and read the orders assigning him to command. That done, he faced Purdy and ordered the executive officer to set the first watch. The ceremony had lasted barely twenty minutes, and at its conclusion the enlisted men dispersed as Wellings, his officers, and the dignitaries retired to the wardroom for coffee and cake.

Although the commissioning meant that *Strong* was now officially in the Navy, it was not yet structurally ready for war. Indeed, the primary reason for the voyage to Boston was to have key equipment installed and to undergo a variety of modifications and updates that had not been possible at BIW because of tight production schedules or the lack of necessary government-furnished equipment.

Among the most important additions to be made were the installation of the Mark 4 fire-control radar atop the Mark 37 gun director and the destroyer's SC-1 and SG radars. The former, referred to as Sugar Charley (from the phonetic pronunciation of the letters), was an air-search system. Once its four-foot-by-fifteen-foot "mattress" antenna was operational at the apex of *Strong*'s mainmast, operators would be able to detect aircraft at a range of eighty nautical miles and up to an altitude of ten thousand feet. While the other system, known as Sugar George, could also detect aircraft, its main purpose was searching for surface targets at ranges out to fifteen miles. Because the SG's display could present images of nearby landmasses, it was also used for navigation. Both radars would help *Strong* "see" the world around it, as would the keel-mounted QCL-5 sonar that had been installed by BIW.[14]

Though many of the design deficiencies Wellings had pointed out in his July letter to BuShips' Ned Cochrane could be remedied only in later versions of the *Fletcher* class, there were several things that could be done in Boston. Most of these concerned the installation or re-positioning of relatively small pieces of equipment—radios, antennas, ammunition lockers, and the like—but *Strong*'s time in the Massachusetts Navy Yard would also include a major modification that would address one of Wellings's key complaints, the ship's armament.

The original design for the *Fletcher*-class destroyers had included a four-barreled 1.1-inch/.75-caliber antiaircraft gun mounted in a large tub atop the aft deckhouse separating Mounts 53 and 54.[15] Designed in the late 1920s as a replacement for the .50-caliber machine guns then in antiaircraft use, by 1942 the 1.1-inch quad mount was totally inadequate for engaging fast-moving and low-flying aircraft. Even as production began on the first *Fletcher*-class ships, the Navy had therefore decided to replace the 1.1-inch mount with a license-built dual-barrel version of the vastly more capable Swedish-developed 40mm Bofors autocannon, but production schedules and the scarcity of the new weapon led to *Strong* and several other early examples of the class being constructed with the tub associated with the 1.1-inch/.75. The first three BIW-built *Fletcher*s—*Nicholas*, *O'Bannon*, and *Chevalier*—actually deployed to the Pacific with the outmoded weapon, but *Strong*'s was never installed.

Wellings's ship and the USS *Saufley*, launched on July 17 by New Jersey's Kearny Shipbuilding, were the first two *Fletcher*s to be modified to what was intended to be the class's new antiaircraft armament configuration. This consisted of a dual 40mm in place of the 1.1-inch/.75, a second dual 40mm and its Mark 51 director in a new centerline tub built on the ship's fantail between the depth-charge rails, and the four single 20mm mounts that were to be Hugh's responsibility. In *Strong*'s case it was up to workers at the Boston Navy Yard to undertake the necessary modifications, which began on August 8. The list of necessary work items ran to four single-spaced typed pages just for the armament upgrade and included the complete removal of the tub associated with the 1.1-inch/.75 and the substantial structure that supported it.[16] As daunting as that list may have been, the yard workers managed to complete all the necessary modifications by August 26—a total of just eighteen workdays.

GUS WELLINGS AND HIS CREW HAD CERTAINLY NOT BEEN IDLE while their ship was undergoing modification. Indeed, almost as soon as the August 7 commissioning ceremony had ended, *Strong*'s captain and executive officer had begun the process that would ultimately turn a diverse group of men into a disciplined, effective, and motivated ship's company.

The first step in that metamorphosis had been Wellings's assignment of his various officers to particular tasks, commensurate with both their skills and the needs of the ship. In addition to those already outlined for the captain, executive officer Purdy, and engineering officer Rosenberg, by August 26 those included, in order of rank:

Lt. (jg) James A. Curran, USN, Gunnery Officer

Lt. (jg) Hugh B. Miller, USNR, 20mm and Stores (supply) Officer

Lt. (jg) Robert J. Foley, USNR, 1st Lieutenant and Damage Control Officer

Lt. (jg) Donald A. Regan, USNR, Assistant Gunnery and Commissary Officer

Lt. (jg) Delavan B. Downer, USNR, Assistant Engineering Officer

Lt. (jg) Henry P. Laughlin, MC, Medical Officer

Ens. James W. Ellis Jr., USN, Assistant Damage Control Officer

Ens. Alton B. Grimes, USN, Radar and Sound Officer

Ens. Orivall M. Hackett, USNR, Torpedo Officer

Ens. Benjamin F. Jetton, USNR, Communications Officer

Ens. Albert E. Oberg, USN, Signal Officer and Assistant Navigator

Ens. Ralph E. Trost, USNR, Assistant Engineering Officer

Ens. Virgil M. Wheeler Jr., USNR, Assistant Gunnery Officer

As the 20mm officer Hugh Miller was responsible for four weapons and twenty-six people. Each mount had a crew of four or five—the gun captain (who was also the talker), the gunner, the trunnion operator (who raised or lowered the column on which the weapon was mounted as directed by the gunner), and one or two loaders, who kept the gun supplied with ammunition in 60-round circular magazines. While Hugh's team included several qualified gunner's mates and at least two highly experienced chief petty officers, the majority of his men were new to the service. Not surprisingly, the Crimson Tide alumnus therefore set about molding his men into an effective unit in characteristic fashion: "I trained my gun crews as you would train a football team, having them compete against each other, and built up a perfectly wonderful and very skillful organization of a bunch of kids with terrific spirit."[17]

Hugh chose the flying bridge, directly above the pilot house and the site of the Mark 37 director, as his personal battle station. In combat it would be the most exposed spot on the ship, but it offered a clear view of every gun and would allow Hugh to see targets long before his gunners could. He would be able to concentrate the weapons' fire if appropriate or split it if necessary. Dispensing with a talker, he wore his own phones so that he could instantly receive target information from the radar operators and communicate the data directly to each gun captain. Realizing that the Sugar Charley wouldn't necessarily detect all incoming threats, Hugh also devised his own low-tech spotting system—he chose two young enlisted men with excellent eyesight to work with him as lookouts. Both stood with their backs to him atop the flying bridge, one off each shoulder, and all three practiced turning as a unit to ensure that Hugh had "eyes in the back of his head" no matter which way he was looking.[18]

Commanding the 20mm guns was not Hugh's only responsibility, of course. Until Strong could obtain the services of a trained supply officer, his collateral duty as stores officer required him to manage the acquisition and disbursement of most every item consumed aboard the ship while it lay alongside the pier. He was also tasked with preordering all the items Strong would need when it left Boston, everything from food and cigarettes to ammunition and fresh water. And as if two jobs didn't keep the 20mm officer busy enough, Gus Wellings gave him a third. Because of his professional background and age—he was the third-oldest person on the ship behind the captain and Fred Purdy—Hugh was appointed Strong's unofficial legal officer. In addition to handling such normal issues as the men's writing of wills and the designation of beneficiaries for their government-provided life insurance, Hugh also advised and counseled them on such "civilian" legal issues as divorce, child custody, and the sale of cars and other property they certainly wouldn't be needing once the ship deployed.

THE TIME WHEN *STRONG* WOULD BE READY TO JOIN THE WAR CAME a step closer on the morning of September 1, when the ship cast off from the Boston pier and headed slowly toward Massachusetts Bay. The completion of its yard stint had resulted in its assignment to Commander, Destroyer Force Atlantic, for a seven-week shakedown period, and the first destination was Newport, Rhode Island. The 116-mile voyage marked the first time that most of the destroyer's crew had been out into open water aboard the vessel that would ultimately carry them overseas. The trip took *Strong* south along the coast toward Plymouth, through the 480-foot-wide Cape Cod Canal—transiting the inland waterway was intended to help the ship avoid German U-boats that might be lurking farther offshore—and into Buzzards Bay. Just after four thirty the destroyer turned north into Narragansett Bay, and a half hour later it was alongside the pier on Goat Island, since 1869 the home of the Naval Torpedo Station.[19]

By 1940 the Navy had adopted the Mark 15 torpedo as standard for destroyers, and *Strong*, like almost all wartime *Fletcher*s, was equipped with two quintuple launchers for the 21-inch-wide, 24-foot-long weapon.[20] Each set of five tubes was installed on the ship's centerline and could rotate to either side but could not elevate or depress. Two men—a mount trainer and a gyroscope setter—sat atop each launcher and physically input the course, speed, and depth information provided to them from either of the two bridge wing-mounted Mark 27 torpedo directors. The steam turbine–powered Mark 15 weighed nearly two tons and had a maximum range of about 9 miles, depending on sea conditions. *Strong* spent September 2 taking on its full complement of Mark 15s and the following day fired two—one from each launcher—on a range off Newport.

On the morning of September 4 the destroyer sailed for Maine, again via the Cape Cod Canal. As part of its shakedown period *Strong* spent the next three weeks operating out of Casco Bay, barely 17 miles southwest of where it was built. It was an eventful time, combining both training and real-world tasks. From the eleventh through the thirteenth, *Strong* joined the destroyers *Radford* and *Murray* in screening the recently commissioned battleship *Massachusetts* as that massive warship traveled from Maine to Boston to undergo some modifications and take on ammunition for its nine 16-inch main guns. On the twenty-second and twenty-third, *Strong* and the destroyers *Emmons* and *Rodman* screened *Massachusetts* as the battleship fired day and night target practices. Each of these occasions saw Gus Wellings and his crew operating in full wartime mode; the very real threat of attack by German U-boats ensured that the antisubmarine sweeps *Strong* undertook were done with all weapons loaded, manned, and ready for immediate use. By the time the destroyer returned to Boston on September 28 to begin a weeklong yard period, its shakedown was for all practical purposes concluded. Indeed, so satisfactory had *Strong*'s performance been while operating from Casco that official engineering trials by the Navy's Board of Inspection and Survey were canceled.

The successful completion of the destroyer's at-sea evaluation led the Navy to list it as ready for regular duty, and the seven days the ship spent at the Navy Yard were busy ones. Workers undertook some minor repairs and modifications on *Strong*, and Wellings and his crew welcomed aboard an additional forty-four enlisted men. The ship also took on fuel oil, ammunition, and pallet after pallet of fresh and canned food. Despite the frenzied activity, Wellings set up a rotational liberty system to ensure that each of his men got at least one full day off in Boston. While this was undoubtedly a much-appreciated gesture, it also likely convinced all aboard that it would probably be some time before they had another opportunity for shore leave.

Strong sailed from Boston on the morning of October 6 and after more gunnery practice arrived in Portland just after dark. The destroyer took up an antisubmarine patrol off the busy port and then at dawn shifted a few miles north to Casco Bay.[21] Though some members of *Strong*'s crew may have assumed the ship was destined to spend more time in the increasingly frigid waters off New England, it was in fact bound for warmer climes. Just hours after arriving in Casco Bay,

Wellings was directed to rendezvous with the tanker USS *Mataponi* off Portland and escort it the 650 miles to Hampton Roads, Virginia, where *Strong* was to await further orders. The two vessels found each other without difficulty and steamed south through the night, zigzagging to throw off the aim of any lurking U-boats.[22]

After seeing *Mataponi* safely into Hampton Roads on October 9, *Strong* was directed to join its fellow *Fletcher*-class destroyer *La Valette* in escorting the troopship *Antaeus* and cargo transport *Ariel* to San Juan, Puerto Rico. After dropping the two transports in San Juan on October 13, *Strong* spent the remainder of the month escorting a variety of vessels around the Caribbean. Operating both alone and in company with *La Valette*, its port calls included St. Thomas in the Virgin Islands; Port of Spain, Trinidad; and repeated visits to San Juan. This routine lasted until October 24, when *Strong* and *La Valette* left Puerto Rico as escorts for *Antaeus* and *Ariel*, which were returning to Hampton Roads. During the three-day passage Wellings repeatedly exercised his ship's 20mm and 40mm guns in the antiaircraft mode, sending up weather balloons as targets. While Hugh Miller later called the practice "great fun," he also declared the balloons to be "damned hard to hit."

Strong remained in Virginia until the early afternoon of October 29, when it departed in company with *La Valette* and *Saufley*. The three *Fletcher*s were escorting the oiler *Chicopee*, freighter *Polaris*, and minelayer *Terror* to New York's Brooklyn Navy Yard, which the mini convoy reached without incident early the following day. Soon after coming alongside the pier, Wellings notified the crew that *Strong* had been granted five days' "availability" in port. His men were understandably elated by the idea of taking some time off in New York City after shuttling up and down the East Coast and in the Caribbean, though they would likely have been less enthusiastic had they known that following its short time in Brooklyn *Strong* would embark on a much more ambitious and potentially far more dangerous voyage.

In late December 1941—just as Hugh and Frances Miller were celebrating their first month of married life in Florida—President

Franklin Roosevelt was hosting British prime minister Winston Churchill for what would become known as the First Washington Conference. Despite the huge shock of Pearl Harbor and the obvious requirement to ultimately engage and defeat Japan in the Pacific, the two leaders agreed that some major military operation had to be conducted against the Germans in 1942, in large part to take pressure off the hard-pressed Soviets.[23]

The location of that first joint effort was ultimately determined by Germany's successes in North Africa. By June 1942 Field Marshal Erwin Rommel's Afrika Korps had enjoyed significant success in Libya and was apparently moving to take the Suez Canal, and there was increasing evidence that Adolf Hitler was pressuring Vichy French leader Marshal Philippe Pétain to give Germany military access to France's African colonies and control of the French navy. The threat of a newly enlarged and significantly more capable Kriegsmarine sallying forth from additional Mediterranean and Atlantic ports ultimately convinced the combined Anglo-American chiefs of staff to settle— somewhat reluctantly—on an invasion of French North Africa as the "major military operation" of 1942. The decision was formally made in London in late July, and by early September the plans had been finalized for Operation TORCH.

On November 8, 1942, three British-American formations conducted the largest amphibious operation thus far in the war, landing both in Algeria and at three locations in French Morocco. Allied planners had attempted to persuade the Vichy French not to resist the landings, and the invading troops were instructed to hold their fire unless fired upon. This turned out to be an unfortunate decision, for the French defenders responded with small arms and artillery. The resulting firefights ultimately claimed some five hundred British and American lives, as well as about thirteen hundred French dead. However, on November 10 Admiral François Darlan, commander of all French forces in North Africa, was persuaded to order the cessation of hostilities against the incoming Allies. The fighting quickly ended, and the landing units shifted from combat operations to consolidation.

The American effort to sustain the buildup of forces in North Africa was to be undertaken by large convoys of cargo vessels and tankers sailing from the East Coast of the United States. The first such armada, designated UGS-2, consisted of forty merchant vessels and four Navy ships—three minelayers and a fleet oiler—and was assembled in New York and nearby ports during the first ten days of November. On the morning of the fourth, Gus Wellings was notified that his ship would be part of the escort force for the convoy. *Strong* would join the destroyers *Benson*, *Chevalier*, *Davison*, *La Valette*, and *Taylor* to form Task Force 37, with *Taylor*'s captain serving as commander of both the task force and the convoy. In preparation for the coming voyage *Strong* spent the fifth and sixth at sea off New London, Connecticut, conducting antisubmarine training in company with *La Valette* and the sub USS *Marlin*. Wellings noted that the two days provided "excellent training for lookouts, radar and sound operators."[24]

Upon returning to New York, *Strong* took on fuel, provisions, and ammunition. It also loaded sixteen additional Mark 6 depth charges, for a total of forty-five of the 300-pound weapons. On November 13 the destroyer slipped its moorings at Brooklyn's Thirty-Fifth Street Naval Supply Depot just after six in the morning and soon joined the other escorts in patrolling off the coast as the convoy ships formed up. That process took several hours, with the vessels eventually arrayed in eleven columns of varying length. The *S* in *UGS* denoted a slow convoy, meaning it traveled at the speed of the slowest ship. It was very quickly evident that this would be a glacial nine knots, though *Strong* and the other destroyers would average fifteen knots as they moved back and forth shepherding the merchantmen and investigating sound contacts.

Though Gus Wellings and Fred Purdy knew the convoy's ultimate destination, their crew did not. Most of the men believed they were bound for Iceland or England, and the weather the armada initially encountered seemed to back the assumption that the ships were headed for northerly climes. As Ensign Al Grimes, the twenty-four-year-old radar and sound officer, later recalled, "The wind blew and we rolled and pitched. . . . Giant swells looked like mountains as they rolled toward the ship, but we always seemed to pop up and ride over them. . . . This was the North Atlantic in winter."[25]

Much to everyone's relief, the weather and seas quickly began to moderate as the convoy changed course to the southeast—the crew's first indication that the ship might be bound for somewhere other than Iceland or Britain. But the men aboard *Strong* had little free time for speculation about their ultimate destination. The crew was frequently called to general quarters when the sonar or radar operators detected suspicious activity, and on several occasions the destroyer was sent off to investigate distant contacts or to round up straggling cargo vessels and return them to the relative safety of the convoy. The voyage also afforded time for the officers to hone the skills of the men in their teams; in Hugh Miller's case this meant live-fire training for his 20mm gun crews whenever possible, the targets either the hard-to-hit balloons or occasional clumps of floating debris.

As busy as things were aboard the destroyer, Gus Wellings knew that nonstop work doesn't make for a happy crew. His previous at-sea stints had convinced him that sailors need more to look forward to than just the usual shipboard routine of watches, instruction periods, drills, and sleep—they need ways in which to relax and have as much fun as circumstances allow. Early on in the UGS-2 voyage Wellings therefore appointed a "morale officer" for the ship. The man he tapped for the job was none other than Hugh Miller, who approached the task with his usual enthusiasm. In addition to showing occasional movies in the ship's large messing compartment, he used musical instruments the ship carried in its "recreation locker" to put together a string band. Hugh also organized frequent "Happy Duty Hours" for all hands off watch, during which the men could put on skits, tell jokes, or sing. He apparently outdid himself on Thanksgiving Day, November 26, for Gus Wellings noted in a letter to his wife that Hugh "was in grand form. His rendition of 'His Dolly With a Hole in Her Stocking' was marvelous. Needless to say, he got a big hand."[26]

Strong and the other destroyers of TF 37 investigated several suspicious sonar contacts during the course of the eastward voyage, but the convoy never came under attack, and on the morning of November 30—at a point some sixty miles off Morocco's southwest coast—TF 37 handed responsibility for the UGS-2 ships over to the Royal Navy. *Strong, Benson, Chevalier, La Valette*, and *Taylor* were then officially transferred to duty with TF 38, which consisted of the battleship *Arkansas* and the destroyers *Gleaves, Mayo, Niblack*, and *Plunkett*. The warships were tasked with shepherding the twenty merchant vessels and troopships of convoy GUF-2 back to Hampton Roads. The westward voyage was uneventful, and on December 10 *Strong* was detached from the convoy to escort the troopship USS *Monticello* to New York. Both ships arrived safely the following day, and by two in the afternoon the destroyer was alongside a Navy Yard pier.

While Gus Wellings and his crew were not yet aware of the fact, their return to New York marked the end of the only round-trip Atlantic voyage their ship would make. Though the destroyer would spend nearly two weeks in and around New York, Navy Department planners in Washington, D.C., were already charting a very different course for *Strong* and the men who sailed in it.

THE MONTH OF DECEMBER 1942 WAS FRIGIDLY COLD IN NEW YORK City, with temperatures hovering just above zero for the first few days following *Strong*'s return. Wartime priorities ensured that the cold was not allowed to disrupt the round-the-clock bustle of activity at the Navy Yard, however, as workers sought to repair, provision, and dispatch scores of vessels.

Strong was itself in need of work. The voyage to North Africa and back had been hard on the ship, and dozens of items needed to be replaced or repaired. The vessel's New York yard period also saw the addition of many entirely new items, ranging from updated radios to a mast-mounted "stovepipe" antenna for the IFF (identification, friend or foe) system that determined whether incoming aircraft were friendly or hostile. The most obvious structural change, however, was the installation of a fifth 20mm gun on a raised platform built out from the rounded front section of the ship's bridge, on the centerline just aft of and slightly above Mount 52. At least three of *Strong*'s 20mm weapons were also fitted with the Mark 14 lead-computing gunsight.

The material alterations made to the destroyer in New York were mirrored by personnel changes. Several dozen sailors left the ship for other duty and were replaced by new men, many of whom transferred from the World War I battleship turned gunnery training vessel USS *Wyoming*. There were also changes among the officers. Lieutenant (jg) Robert Foley left *Strong* for the soon-to-be commissioned battleship USS *Iowa,* and three new ensigns came aboard—John A. Fulham Jr. as the new damage control officer and William C. Hedrick and Jack B. Howard as assistant communications officers.

The ultimate goal of *Strong'*s time in New York was to prepare it for the next assignment, of course, and on the afternoon of Christmas Day the ship set out from Brooklyn's Thirty-Third Street Pier on the first leg of what would prove to be a very long voyage. After clearing the harbor, *Strong* joined forces with the destroyers *Rodman* and *Emmons*, and the three ships took up escort positions around the trooper *Monticello* for the overnight passage to Hampton Roads. Gus Wellings and his crew didn't linger long in Virginia, however, for at just after ten on the morning of the twenty-seventh *Strong* stood out to sea, again in company with *Emmons* and *Rodman*. A few miles off Virginia Beach the ships joined *Cony, Ellyson, Macomb,* and *Murphy*. The seven destroyers then rendezvoused with eight Navy cargo and troop transports—*Arcturus, William P. Biddle, Charles Carroll, Joseph T. Dickman, Hermitage, Thomas Jefferson, Monticello,* and *Oberon*—to form Task Force 39. Once the ships had gotten themselves organized into two columns, the mini armada shaped a course for the Panama Canal.

The two-thousand-mile voyage south took TF 39 to the east of the Bahamas, through the Windward Passage separating Cuba and Hispaniola, and to the east of Jamaica. Though there were several sonar and radar contacts, none proved to be hostile, and the days passed aboard *Strong* in the usual way. Indeed, the normal convoy routine was interrupted by only two unusual events. On December 29 the ship's medical officer, Henry Laughlin, performed a successful emergency appendectomy on a young crewman.[27] And shortly after the convoy reached Panama on the morning of January 2, *Strong* had just entered the swept channel leading to the northern entrance to the canal when aft of it the *Charles Carroll,* command vessel for the task force, hit a drifting mine. The explosion damaged the attack transport's rudder and propeller, but there were no serious injuries and it was able to limp into port for repairs.[28]

The instructions Gus Wellings had received before the Christmas Day departure from New York specified that upon the task force's arrival in Panama, *Strong* and *Cony* would "receive further orders." These were transmitted by TF 39's commander as *Charles Carroll* was tying up to the pier that would be its home while it was under repair. In addition to saying "Well done, duty completed" to the escorting destroyers, the task force commander notified *Strong* and *Cony* that they were being transferred to the control of the Commander, U.S. Pacific Fleet. Both destroyers were directed to transit the Panama Canal immediately upon arrival and await further orders. *Strong* entered the Gatun Locks at 12:25 and by a few minutes before 9:00 p.m. it was tied up alongside *Cony* at Pier 16 in Balboa.

In a later letter to his wife, Gus Wellings wrote that he'd "had no information that we were going west until we arrived in Panama and I was ordered through the canal." He, like Hugh and many other members of *Strong*'s crew, had apparently assumed that the destroyer would return to the East Coast for more Atlantic convoy duty and was understandably sad that he now wouldn't have the chance to see his family again for some time. "However," he wrote, "[the transfer] had to happen sometime and perhaps it was for the best. We have got to get on with this war and good destroyers are needed here in the Pacific."

Whatever his personal thoughts on this new development, in his *War Diary* entry for January 2 Wellings was characteristically professional, writing simply, "Thus ended *Strong*'s duty in [the] Atlantic, at least for the present."[29] In fact, the destroyer and many of those aboard it that warm, star-filled night in Panama would not survive their coming sojourn in the vast and dangerous Pacific.

3

WAR AMONG THE ISLANDS

WHILE STRONG'S TRANSFER TO THE PACIFIC FLEET WAS MOMENTOUS AND would ultimately result in tragedy for both the ship and its crew, the first few days following the destroyer's transit of the Panama Canal were decidedly anticlimactic. Rather than immediately charging out to join the pivotal battles raging eighty-three hundred miles to the west, *Strong* remained tied to its Balboa pier as the captain awaited further instructions and the crew prepared it for whatever was to come.

One of the first tasks was to repaint the ship. At the time of its launching *Strong* bore a simple color scheme referred to by the Navy as Measure 18—a sea-blue hull and haze-gray upper works—though during its stay in Boston the destroyer was redone in the navy blue hues widely used on vessels operating in the North Atlantic. In September 1942 all surface vessels operating in the Pacific—except hospital ships—had been ordered to adopt Measure 21, which was basically navy blue from the waterline on up and was supposed to provide the lowest visibility to enemy aircraft. So the destroyer's crew set about applying the new war paint on the morning of January 3.[1]

Painting was not the only preparation, of course. In the days following transit of the Canal *Strong* underwent a range of minor repairs and took on provisions, fresh water, and 20mm and 40mm ammunition to replace the rounds expended during practice on the voyage south. Always thinking in terms of the crew's morale, Gus Wellings and Fred Purdy ensured that as many men as possible had the chance to rotate ashore in between work details, though most barely had time to drink a cold beer or have a souvenir picture taken in front of a painted backdrop—generally either swaying palm trees, if the photo was to be mailed home to family, or a scantily clad senorita if the image was to remain in the sailor's possession.

On the evening of January 4 Wellings received the orders for which he'd been waiting. *Strong* was to continue escorting the transports of Task Force 39, though the group had been redesignated TF 19 upon its arrival in Panama. The need to redistribute the troops and equipment from the damaged *Charles Carroll* to the other vessels caused a twenty-four-hour delay in the original sailing schedule, though by the morning of January 6 the remaining six transports were ready to begin the first leg of their journey across the Pacific. *Strong* and *Cony* moved out through the swept channel of the harbor's protective minefield at about seven thirty and were soon joined by the destroyer *Warrington* and the aging but still formidable light cruiser *Concord*, which took up a lead position five miles ahead of the other vessels. The transports formed into two three-ship columns, while the three destroyers formed a semicircular screen around them.

Life aboard *Strong* quickly settled back into the familiar routines of convoy-escort duty—the crew operating on rotating watches, manning general quarters at dawn and dusk, and the ship making occasional forays away from the task force to investigate suspicious sonar or radar contacts. Hugh Miller and his 20mm crews were able to undertake a few live-fire exercises, shooting both at balloons released from *Strong*'s fantail and at a sleeve target towed by one of *Concord*'s catapult-launched observation aircraft. The destroyer's machine-gun officer noted with pride that "his boys" were getting better every day and that the pesky balloons weren't as hard to hit as they once had been.

In a letter written to his wife on January 7 Gus Wellings noted that in a few days, the majority of his crew would undergo a once-in-a-lifetime experience, the traditional "crossing-the-line" ceremony commemorating a sailor's first transit of the equator. The "shell-backs," those who have already made the crossing, initiate those who have not—the "pollywogs"—into the domain of His Royal Highness Neptunus Rex. The ceremony involves the appearance aboard ship of King Neptune and members of his court—portrayed by costumed shellbacks—and the ritual subjection of the pollywogs to various good-natured types of hazing. "Of course, we cannot have the usual peacetime elaborate ceremony," Wellings wrote. "However we will have an abbreviated ceremony in order to give the boys something to think about before, during and after crossing the line."

That "abbreviated ceremony" began on the morning of January 10. *Strong*'s *War Diary* for the day merely dryly noted that "at 0830 His Royal Highness Neptunus Rex and his royal party were received on board and initiated into the royal order of shellbacks all pollywogs (274). Ceremonies consistent with war operations were conducted." Wellings was more descriptive in a letter to his wife written that evening. Noting that King Neptune and his court had come aboard and "taken command of my ship," he added, "The Jolly Roger was broken at the top of the mast and after a very color-ful parade his Royal Highness held court and awarded sentences to all the pollywogs."

Wellings also described how "the royal barber ran his clippers over each [pollywog's] head . . . which meant practically all my crew . . . had all their hair cut off." Noting that he, Fred Purdy, Marv Rosenberg, and Del Downer were the only commissioned members of *Strong*'s crew to have crossed the line before, Wellings wryly observed that none of his other officers would require a haircut "for a long while." Indeed, a group photo taken on the destroyer's flying bridge the af-ternoon of the ceremony depicts *Strong*'s captain surrounded by his officers, most of them sheepishly sporting little hair and, in Hugh's case, none at all.

The crossing-the-line ceremony helped keep morale relatively high aboard *Strong* as it and the other ships of TF 19 plowed ever westward, though there was also increasingly intense speculation about the ship's next port of call. While the destroyer's officers and enlisted men were obviously well aware that they were bound for the South Pacific, that vast region offered a myriad of possibilities. Were they en route to the romantic isles of French Polynesia perhaps, or possibly New Zealand or Australia, or, less enticing, embattled New Guinea or some godforsaken port in the Indian Ocean? Opinions ran the gamut, and more than one enterprising sailor took wagers from his shipmates about where and when *Strong* would next drop anchor.

The destroyer's crew didn't have to wait long to find out. At 7:45 on the morning of January 18 *Strong* was ordered to detach from TF 19 and in company with *Cony* make for Bora Bora in the Society Islands. The initial American advance base established in the region following the 1941 declaration of war, the island was code-named BOBCAT and was a key fueling station on what U.S. war planners had dubbed the "Southern Lifeline" to Australia. The French colonial authorities on the picturesque isle were solidly on the Allied side, and since the Japanese had shown no inclination to attack BOBCAT it remained relatively unspoiled—except, of course, for the sprawling refueling base that dominated Teavanui Harbor.[2]

The two destroyers arrived off the island just after dawn on January 19 and were soon moored to buoys in the harbor, their crews gazing raptly at the first tropical island most of the men had ever seen. Al Grimes, *Strong*'s young radar and sonar officer, was mesmerized by "the bright blue of the water in the little harbor, the bright green of the water around the coral reefs, and the palm trees that came right down to the broad white beaches."[3] Unfortunately, the men aboard *Strong* and *Cony* would have no opportunity to explore the island or sample its rumored charms; the destroyers' visit was strictly business, and after completing the refueling both ships would be on their way back out the narrow Teavanui Pass and into the open sea.

Before that happened, however, *Strong* took aboard a passenger who would prove in the short run to be a popular, if temporary, shipmate and in the longer term would become a good friend of Hugh's.

The man was Lieutenant Colonel Edward Nicholson Fay, a forty-seven-year-old Army Quartermaster Corps (QMC) officer and World War I veteran. Fluent in French, he had been dispatched to the Pacific to help organize the Army's logistics operations in Polynesia.

The ship's officers soon took to Fay. As Gus Wellings noted in a letter to his wife written soon after the destroyer departed Bora Bora, the Army officer "has a large number of good stories and in addition is a grand shipmate." Fay's gregariousness, Wellings added, was more than matched by Hugh's: "Miller has been at his best in the wardroom and has had all of us roaring with his Alabama stories, particularly the political stories. Apparently Hugh has political aspirations after the war. He promised to give us all soft government jobs when he [is] elected to congress or Governor. Tonight he is having a Strong happy hour which I know will be good since Hugh loves to perform before strangers."[4] The lawyer turned Navy officer and the "grand shipmate" obviously hit it off, for Hugh would from that point on address the older man affectionately as "Colonel Eddie."

The days following *Strong*'s departure from Bora Bora passed in the by now usual way. After rejoining TF 19 the ship and *Cony* had settled back into their normal escort positions—at that point assisted by the destroyer *Mahan*, because *Concord* and *Warrington* had been detached for duty elsewhere—with the only out-of-the-ordinary occurrence being the convoy's transit of the international date line on the night of January 23. Four days later land again hove into view—this time the southern end of the island of New Caledonia—and early in the evening *Strong* and the other ships of TF 19 slowly wended their way into Nouméa's Dumbea Bay, home to the naval station code-named WHITE POPPY. The base was one of several Allied military installations on the island, which was far more exposed to possible attack by Japanese forces than was Bora Bora, and as *Strong* moored alongside the tanker *Pasig* crewmen aboard the destroyer noted numerous large-caliber antiaircraft guns dotted around the bay.

The convoy's arrival in New Caledonia marked changes both in *Strong*'s complement and in the destroyer's tasking.

On the morning of January 28 "Colonel Eddie" Fay thanked Wellings and his officers for "a fine trip and great companionship"

before leaving the ship for temporary duty in Nouméa before returning to Bora Bora. The QMC officer would spend the remainder
of the war organizing Army logistics operations on several islands,
during which time he would become good friends with a thirty-six-
year-old Navy lieutenant named James A. Michener, who would
later use his own wartime experiences as the basis for the Pulitzer
Prize–winning book *Tales of the South Pacific*.[5] Fay was soon followed ashore by Marv Rosenberg, the ship's engineering officer since
before its launching, who had received orders to report to the 12th
Naval District in San Francisco, pending further assignment. His assistant, Del Downer, stepped into the senior engineer slot, and Ralph
Trost became Downer's assistant. Though none of the young officers
knew it at the time, Rosenberg's orders to return to the United States
almost certainly saved his life.[6]

Just hours after Rosenberg left the ship, two of TF 19's six transports—*Biddle* and *Oberon*—were detached and held in port, and
the remaining ships were redesignated Task Force 66.19. *Strong* and
Cony, now the sole escorts for the four transports, sailed out in the
early evening and patrolled offshore until their charges assembled.
The reconfigured convoy soon got under way and headed southwest
toward Australia, but any hopes Wellings's crew might have had of
seeing "the Land Down Under" were dashed early on January 30. The
destroyers *Henley* and *Selfridge* appeared just after six in the morning
and relieved *Strong* and *Cony* of their convoy responsibilities.

The release from TF 66.19 marked the end of a marathon elev-
en-thousand-mile escort voyage that for Wellings and his crew had
begun in New York on Christmas Day. After receiving a sincere
"Well done" from the task force commander, *Strong*—with *Cony*
steaming alongside—turned to the northeast and shaped a course
back to Nouméa. By the afternoon of January 31 both destroyers
were safely back in Dumbea Bay, with *Strong* moored alongside
Shasta. The ammunition ship immediately began passing over the
first of nearly two thousand rounds of various types for the destroyer's 5-inch/.38-caliber mounts, even as small boats from the nearby
stores tender *Whitney* arrived with food and other provisions. It
was the first comprehensive replenishment *Strong* had received since

leaving the United States and the largest amount of main-gun ammunition the ship had yet taken aboard. Many members of Wellings's crew saw the latter fact—rightly, as it would soon turn out—as an indication that their days of shepherding slow convoys were ending and that they were about to get into the war in a very serious way.

BY THE TIME *STRONG* RETURNED TO NOUMÉA FOR ITS MUCH-needed replenishment, America had been at war in the Pacific for twelve months and twenty-four days.[7] The conflict had initially not gone well for the United States and its allies, of course. In the weeks and months following Pearl Harbor, Japanese forces had taken the U.S. outposts on Wake Island and Guam, captured the Philippines, rolled over the former European colonial holdings in Southeast Asia, and surged southward into New Guinea and the island chains north of Australia.

While those early setbacks were due in large part to Japan's military prowess—and, to some extent, the Allies' failure to heed intelligence warnings that the outbreak of a Pacific conflict was imminent—they also stemmed from the joint decision made by the United States and Britain in the spring of 1941 that Europe and the Atlantic Ocean were to be considered the "decisive theater" and that if Japan entered the war, the Allied strategy in the Far East would be defensive until Hitler and Mussolini had been defeated.[8]

American military planners had subsequently incorporated that decision into Rainbow 5, the latest iteration in a series of numbered war plans the United States had begun developing in June 1939. While Rainbow 5 acknowledged that America's far-western Pacific bases would likely fall to the Japanese, U.S. activities in the vast region were not intended to be mere holding actions—they were to be strategically defensive. In addition to preventing the Japanese from seizing additional territory, American forces would undertake various tactical offensives meant to secure the enemy-held islands that would ultimately serve as the springboard for the full-throated Allied offensive against Japan that was to follow the defeat of the Germans and Italians. The eventual necessity of fighting a wide-ranging conflict against Japan in the Pacific had been a staple of American war planning since the mid-1920s—under a color-code system the various strategies developed for possible use against the Japanese were referred to as the Orange Plans—and the campaign that unfolded in the months following Pearl Harbor generally followed the precepts set forth in those documents, at least insofar as they dovetailed with the requirements of Rainbow 5.[9]

Japan initially sought to neutralize the U.S. Navy in the Pacific through the Pearl Harbor attack, then went on to capture Wake Island and Guam in order to sever the United States' traditional maritime supply route to the Philippines, which also ultimately fell. Nor did the Japanese ignore Europe's long-standing logistical links to the Far East and Pacific. By defeating British and Commonwealth forces in Malaya, Japan was able to dominate much of the eastern Indian Ocean between British India and Australia, and by taking the Netherlands' colonial holdings Tokyo gained direct access to New Guinea.

The latter was a key objective of the Japanese advance into the Southwest Pacific. At the time, the western half of the island was part of the Netherlands East Indies. The eastern half was itself divided; the northern quarter was referred to as the Territory of New Guinea and was administered by Australia under a post–World War I League of Nations mandate. The southeastern quarter was known as the Territory of Papua and had been formally ruled by Australia since 1906. The island as a whole dominates the waters in several directions—the open Pacific to the north, the Arafura and Timor Seas to the southwest, the Coral Sea to the southeast, and the Solomon Sea to the east. Just as important in a strategic sense, at its closest point New Guinea is less than one hundred miles from the Australian mainland. Taking the entire island would allow the Japanese to launch aerial strikes against ports, airfields, military posts, communication hubs, and other vital targets throughout northern Australia. Moreover, possession of all or part of New Guinea would give Japan a base from which to establish a string of bastions throughout the British-administered Solomon Islands and eventually capture the New Hebrides, New Caledonia, and Fiji. If successful, the campaign would allow Tokyo to command the entire Southwest Pacific, isolate Australia and New Zealand, and

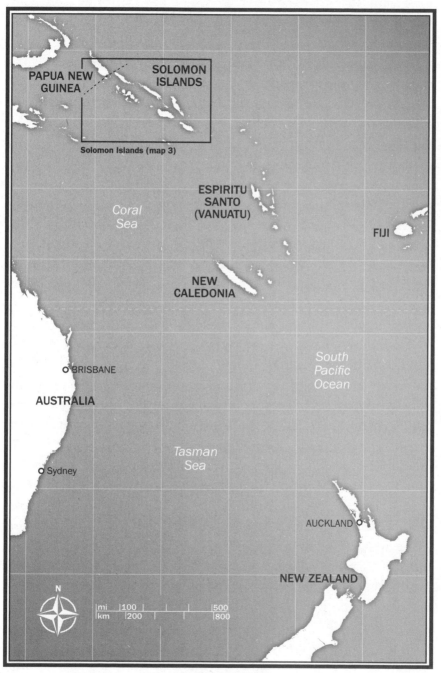

2. South Pacific

potentially permit Japan to land troops on the territories of each at a time when the majority of both nations' combat forces were fighting in the Middle East.

The assault on New Guinea began on January 21, 1942, when Japanese aircraft bombed several areas on the island's Australian-controlled northwestern and western coasts. Two days later Rabaul—the seat of government for the Territory of New Guinea on the Bismarck Archipelago island of New Britain—was taken by Japanese forces that immediately began turning it into a formidable air and naval base. The occupation of the rest of New Britain and adjoining New Ireland quickly followed, as did the capture of the Admiralty Islands and Bougainville—all politically joined to Australian-administered New Guinea but geographically part of the northern Solomon Islands. Taken together, these actions posed a very real threat to northern Australia—a threat that was underscored by Japan's carrier-launched air attack on Darwin, the capital of the nation's Northern Territory, on February 19.

The first step in America's response to Japan's initiation of hostilities and initial campaigns in the Pacific was, of necessity, logistical. From the American point of view, the logical response to Japan's severing of the maritime supply routes and the only way to guarantee that Australia and New Zealand did not become Japan's next conquests was to establish the alternate "Southern Lifeline" to the Pacific. This "sea line of communication," as it was formally known, stretched from the West Coast of the United States and Panama to Hawaii, through the islands of French Polynesia to Fiji, and thence on to New Zealand and Australia. The importance of Australia as a staging base for future Allied operations throughout the Pacific and Far East also added a wartime responsibility that the Orange Plans had not anticipated—the United States would have to commit to defending the island continent as well as the vital supply routes leading to it.

During the first months of 1942 ships of several Allied nations had begun rushing troops, equipment, and supplies along the southern route, the intention being to bolster the defenses of the various "way-point" islands and, ultimately, muster the forces necessary to both defend Australia and begin the buildup that would allow the commencement of the tactical offensives outlined in Rainbow 5. Indeed, so important was it to quickly reinforce Australia and the Southwest Pacific that between January and March, some seventy-nine thousand American troops were transported to the region, a number nearly four times greater than that shipped to the European theater over the same period.[10]

While the speed with which the United States began to pump personnel and equipment into the Pacific was something of a surprise to the Japanese, they were likely astonished by the rapidity of America's military riposte after what was supposed to have been a decisive defeat at Pearl Harbor. The aircraft carriers the attack had failed to destroy on that tragic Sunday on Oahu were soon at work, their embarked squadrons hitting Japanese installations in the Gilbert and Marshall Islands and on Wake in February 1942. In April sixteen U.S. Army Air Forces B-25 bombers commanded by Lieutenant Colonel James H. Doolittle launched from the carrier *Hornet* and stunned the Japanese by bombing targets on the Home Islands—the first time in centuries that Japan proper had been attacked and the first time *ever* that enemy aircraft had appeared over sacred Nippon.

These initial attacks did little, however, to slow the momentum of Japan's move into the Southwest Pacific. In early March 1942 Japanese troops had landed in the Lae-Salamaua area of New Guinea's west coast, and the following month the IJN and the Imperial Japanese Army (IJA) finalized plans for Operation MO, an offensive intended to seize Port Moresby on the island's southern coast, just four hundred miles across the Coral Sea from Australia's Northern Territory. MO also included the capture of Tulagi, an island some twenty miles north of Guadalcanal and the capital of Great Britain's Solomon Islands protectorate. The primary purpose of this second assault was to establish a seaplane base to support the Port Moresby operation while at the same time strengthening the defenses of Rabaul.

Elements of the IJN's Kure 3rd Special Naval Landing Force seized Tulagi on May 2 and 3, but the attempt to take Port Moresby was scuttled because Allied signals intelligence personnel had decrypted Japanese naval message traffic relating to the proposed invasion.

Task Force 17, a primarily American fleet under Rear Admiral Frank Fletcher, intercepted the Japanese in the Coral Sea northeast of Australia, and between May 4 and 8 the two sides fought the first naval action in history in which aircraft carriers engaged each other.[11] Though the IJN managed to so badly damage the carrier *Lexington* that it had to be scuttled, American aircraft mauled the Japanese fleet carrier *Shokaku* and essentially wiped out the squadrons embarked aboard *Zuikaku*. The Battle of the Coral Sea was thus a tactical victory for Japan but a strategic one for the Allies, in that the two IJN carriers were not able to participate in the decisive June 4–5 Battle of Midway, in which the U.S. Navy—again forewarned of enemy intentions through intercepted message traffic—sank four Japanese aircraft carriers and a heavy cruiser for the loss of the carrier *Yorktown* and destroyer *Hammann*. This engagement marked both Japan's first true naval defeat in almost a century and its first of World War II.[12] While Midway did not immediately shift the balance of power in favor of America and its allies, it was a solid and shocking blow to the IJN.

Even as they were absorbing that blow, however, the Japanese were seeking to counter it to some degree by emplacing an airfield at Lunga Point on the north coast of Guadalcanal. Such a field would allow IJN and IJA bombers and fighters to roam at will over the Solomons and, potentially, as far afield as the New Hebrides and New Caledonia. The threat posed by the field, and by Japan's possession of the entire island, was perceived to be so grave that it helped precipitate the first major Allied offensive of the Pacific war and the first of the tactical offensives foreseen in Rainbow 5—the amphibious invasion of Guadalcanal.

Operation WATCHTOWER, as the assault was code-named, kicked off on the morning of August 7, 1942. It was a two-pronged action, with the thirty-nine hundred men of the 1st Marine Division's Northern Landing Force going ashore first on Tulagi, the nearby islets of Gavutu and Tanambogo, and the south coast of adjacent Florida Island. The main assault group, also part of Major General Alexander Vandegrift's 1st Marine Division, began hitting the beach on Guadalcanal just after nine in the morning near the Japanese airfield at Lunga Point. The Northern Landing Force was able to secure all its objectives by August 9 with relatively few American casualties, and the Marines on Guadalcanal quickly took possession of the airfield—thereafter known as Henderson Field—after initially meeting only light resistance. That happy state of affairs quickly changed, however, as the beachhead and the ships offshore came under sustained attack by aircraft flying from Rabaul. Early on August 8 Japanese warships managed to slip into Savo Sound, off Guadalcanal's northwest coast, and by the close of the following day had managed to sink the Australian cruiser *Canberra* and the U.S. cruisers *Astoria*, *Quincy*, and *Vincennes*.

The Battle of Savo Sound was the first of several engagements that took place in the waters near Guadalcanal during the course of what ultimately became a six-month American effort to wrest control of the island from the Japanese.[13] Many of the maritime battles resulted from Tokyo's efforts to transport supplies and troops to Guadalcanal, initially in daylight aboard heavily escorted troopships. When that method proved ineffective owing to Allied air and surface attacks, the Japanese began packing the men and matériel aboard destroyers and light cruisers that traveled at high speed at night to avoid interception. Known collectively to the Allies as the Tokyo Express, these ships were based at Rabaul, Bougainville, and the Shortland Islands, and their normal route took them through New Georgia Sound. Some 400 miles long and 60 miles across at its widest point, that body of water runs southeastward from Bougainville through the approximate center of the Solomons and was quickly nicknamed "the Slot" by the Allies.

As the Japanese hold on Guadalcanal weakened and it became increasingly obvious that the island would ultimately fall to the Allies, the ships of the Tokyo Express were given a new task. In mid-January 1943 they began evacuating the first of some eleven thousand troops from Guadalcanal. Though this marked a definite turning point in the battle for the Solomon Islands, it certainly did not mean, as Hugh and many others aboard *Strong* feared, that the "real war" would be over before the destroyer and its crew got into it.

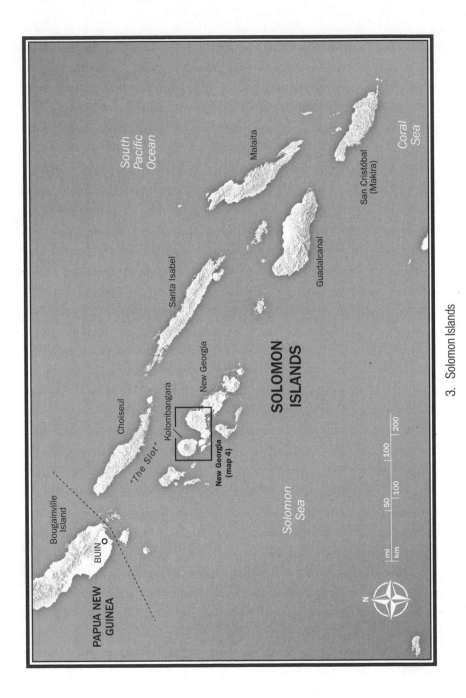

3. Solomon Islands

DAWN ON FEBRUARY 1, 1943, FOUND *STRONG* AND *CONY* ONCE AGAIN preparing to get under way. The crews of both destroyers had worked through the night to take aboard and stow the provisions and ammunition from *Whitney* and *Shasta*, and by 6:22 a.m. the ships were steaming slowly out to sea. Their mission was to escort *Biddle* and *Oberon* to what was already becoming the largest naval operating base in the South Pacific, the island of Espíritu Santo in the New Hebrides. Once the transports emerged past the reefs, the four ships steamed southwest and then, after passing the Isle of Pines, turned due north. The 440-mile trip was uneventful, and by 9:30 on the morning of February 3 *Strong* and its companions were safely moored in Segond Channel, just off Luganville, Espíritu Santo's main harbor.

Largely a Pacific backwater before the Japanese attack on Pearl Harbor, in June 1942 the heavily forested 75-mile-long island had been chosen as the site for an airfield intended to support projected Allied operations on Guadalcanal, 540 miles to the northwest. Code-named BUTTONS but known simply as Santo to virtually all the Allied service members who visited it during the war, the island ultimately hosted several airfields, and the sheltered Segond Channel became one of the most heavily used anchorages in the entire Pacific.

While Santo would become a familiar port of call for Gus Wellings and his crew over the following months, their first visit was a brief one. On the night of *Strong*'s arrival its captain received a secret dispatch from Commander, South Pacific Forces (ComSoPac),[14] directing him to prepare his ship and crew for their first foray into a decidedly active combat zone. On the morning of February 5 *Strong* was to lead the five-destroyer escort screen for a group of ships bound for Guadalcanal. Three of the vessels—*American Legion*, *George Clymer*, and *Hunter Liggett*—were attack transports carrying Army troops and their equipment, while the fourth ship, *Patuxent*, was an oiler bearing both fuel for the ships operating in the area and drums of aviation gasoline. The latter were bound for Henderson Field, as were scores of wooden crates stacked on *Strong*'s fantail during the night before the convoy's departure. The stout boxes contained a total of 440 auxiliary fuze boosters—Navy and Marine aircraft flying from the airstrip were conducting strikes against well-protected Japanese positions on the island, and the boosters enhanced the destructive effects of bombs dropped on enemy bunkers built of blast-absorbing coconut-tree logs.

Just after first light on the morning of the fifth *Strong* led the other escorting destroyers—*Breese*, *Conyingham*, *Humphreys*, and *Sheldrake*—out of Segond Channel to the east to await the appearance of the four slower transports. Once those ships emerged from the harbor, the convoy, dubbed Task Group 62.9, formed up and turned north, the five escorts encircling their charges in a protective screen with *Strong* in the lead. Several hours into the voyage the convoy swung to the northwest, shaping a course that would take the ships around the northeast coast of San Cristóbal Island, some 40 miles southeast of Guadalcanal at the southern end of Indispensable Strait. While there was little risk of air attack until the American vessels entered that body of water, Japanese submarines presented a very real threat along the convoy's entire route. The ships therefore undertook orchestrated zigzagging during daylight hours, and the escorts went to general quarters from sunset until thirty minutes after dark. Soon after lookouts aboard *Strong* sighted the southern end of San Cristóbal on the afternoon of February 6, two Allied escort aircraft appeared overhead and remained on patrol over the convoy until sunset.

At 4:25 the following morning Gus Wellings ordered the ships of TG 62.9 into single file, with *Strong* in the van and the other destroyers in trail behind the four cargo vessels. The column then moved slowly into Sealark Channel, the center of three narrow east-to-west passages leading from Indispensable Strait into Savo Sound through the reefs lying between Guadalcanal and Florida Island. *Strong*'s Sugar George radar was especially helpful in picking out waypoints ashore, as Fred Purdy carefully navigated the line of ships through the channel and into Savo Sound—already better known as Iron Bottom Sound because of the number of Japanese and Allied vessels that had disappeared beneath its surface. Once in open water the destroyers again took up a protective screen around the transports, and the entire convoy steered southwest toward the anchorages off Lunga Point, some 15 miles distant. Just before 6:00 in the morning the escorts took up patrol stations 2 miles offshore as *American Legion*,

George Clymer, Hunter Liggett, and *Patuxent* dropped anchor and their crews set about offloading men and cargo into landing craft for the short ride to the beach.

Three hours later *Strong* left the patrol line, moved in near *American Legion*, and went dead in the water. Gus Wellings and several of his officers looked on from the destroyer's bridge wings as two barges were brought alongside by a tug and watched with a certain amount of trepidation as the boxes of fuze boosters were winched over the side and stacked on the barges.

Strong had only just rejoined the other destroyers of TG 62.9 in patrolling offshore when, just after 11:00, an urgent radio message from the aircraft-warning center ashore announced that nine Japanese bombers were approaching Henderson Field. Wellings immediately ordered his crew to general quarters, directed the cargo ships to weigh anchor and make for open water, and then radioed the other escorts to re-form the protective screen. The hastily reconstituted TG 62.9 had just turned east toward Indispensable Strait when at 11:15 the warning center on Guadalcanal sounded the "all clear." The cargo vessels and oiler returned to their unloading anchorages off Lunga Point, and the escorting destroyers resumed their offshore patrolling. But the respite was short-lived, for just after 5:00 in the afternoon Wellings received a high-priority ComSoPac message ordering him to take the task group back to sea: reports from Allied patrol aircraft and coastwatchers on the enemy-occupied islands farther up the Solomons chain indicated that some twenty Japanese destroyers were conducting a Tokyo Express run down the Slot, and it appeared they might be heading directly for the Lunga Point area. Wellings got his charges rounded up and moving by 6:00, and *Strong* led the way east through Lengo Channel—the passage immediately to the south of Sealark—and back into Indispensable Strait.

Wellings kept TG 62.9 traveling east throughout the night and well into the day on February 8. In the midafternoon he received another ComSoPac message, this one directing him to turn the convoy around and return to Guadalcanal at best speed, the Tokyo Express threat having evaporated. Once again the destroyers and their charges turned west, and just after 11:00 on the morning of the ninth they passed through

Lengo Channel and proceeded to the anchorage off Lunga Point. The three cargo ships and the oiler resumed their twice-interrupted unloading, and the destroyers returned to their offshore patrol areas.

At 7:00 that evening the finally empty *American Legion*, *George Clymer*, and *Hunter Liggett* weighed anchor and departed for New Zealand, escorted by *Breese*, *Conyingham*, and *Sheldrake*. The oiler *Patuxent* had not yet finished unloading, so *Strong* and *Humphreys*—now aided by three Royal New Zealand Navy (RNZN) corvettes—remained on patrol between Lunga Point and Tassafaronga Point, some fifteen miles to the west on Guadalcanal's northern coast. In November 1942 that promontory had given its name to a battle in which a force of American heavy cruisers and destroyers had surprised eight Japanese destroyers attempting to put troops ashore; in the ensuing nighttime engagement the American ships sank one of the IJN vessels, but the waves of Type 93 torpedoes launched by the Japanese destroyers sent the cruiser *Northampton* to the bottom and severely damaged the cruisers *Minneapolis*, *New Orleans*, and *Pensacola*. The battle was yet another demonstration of the range and power of the Type 93, a highly sophisticated weapon vastly more capable and reliable than torpedoes then in use by the U.S. Navy—and one fated to play a role in *Strong*'s future.[15]

On February 10 *Patuxent* finished offloading its cargo of aviation fuel and, escorted by *Strong* and *Humphreys*, steamed the twenty miles north to Tulagi. Soon after the three ships reached the harbor and moored alongside each other, the oiler's captain passed Gus Wellings word that Major General Alexander M. Patch, commander of the Army's XIV Corps, had officially declared Guadalcanal secured.[16] While the announcement prompted Wellings to insert a terse "good news" in his *War Diary* entry, a ComSoPac order he received the following morning was even better: *Strong* and *Humphreys* were to depart that afternoon as escorts for *Patuxent*, which would be returning to Espíritu Santo. The best part of that message was that though *Strong* would make the entire journey back to the New Hebrides, roughly halfway to Santo the destroyer would detach from escort duty and rendezvous with elements of Task Force 67.

Commanded by Rear Admiral Walden L. "Pug" Ainsworth, the Santo-based TF 67 by that point comprised the light cruisers *Nashville* (as flagship), *Helena*, *Honolulu*, and *St. Louis*; the heavy cruiser *Louisville*; the RNZN light cruiser HMNZS *Achilles*; and a changing cast of U.S. destroyers that included *Chevalier*, *Fletcher*, *Jenkins*, *O'Bannon*, *Nicholas*, and *Taylor*. The task force had been reconstituted with light cruisers following the mauling of its original heavy cruisers at the Battle of Tassafaronga, and Ainsworth—the former commander of all Pacific Fleet destroyers—had arrived from Pearl Harbor in late December 1942 and took the helm of TF 67 during the first ten days of January. His brief from ComSoPac Admiral William F. "Bull" Halsey was straightforward—he was to "keep the sea closed to the southward [of] and in the vicinity of Guadalcanal in order to intercept the night forays of Japanese forces coming down The Slot."[17]

After working up in December and early January, TF 67 had helped cover the landing of reinforcements on Guadalcanal and then undertaken a highly effective night bombardment of the Japanese airfield at Munda, on the southwest coast of New Georgia Island. The action marked two milestones for the Navy—it was the first use of radar for both navigation and fire control against shore targets, and it was the first time the service coordinated the actions of aircraft, surface ships, and submarines in a night bombardment. While the raid was considered highly successful, TF 67 did not get off scot free—after returning to the waters south of Guadalcanal, the ships were attacked by Japanese aircraft. *Achilles* was hit by a bomb that killed thirteen men in one of its gun turrets, though the task-force gunners shot down two of the attackers and fighters from Henderson Field claimed at least three more.[18]

During January and early February elements of Ainsworth's command undertook a variety of missions, including bombardments of Japanese positions on Guadalcanal and Kolombangara Island, west of New Georgia across Kula Gulf; antisubmarine patrols; and conducting sweeps of the Coral Sea with Task Forces 11 and 16. When *Strong* rendezvoused with TF 67 shortly after seven on the morning of January 13, Ainsworth's ships were inbound to Espíritu Santo, and

Wellings was ordered to join *Chevalier*, *Jenkins*, and *Taylor* in screening the cruisers. The task force encountered no difficulties and entered Segond Channel early on February 14. By eight o'clock *Strong* was moored alongside its BIW-built sister *Chevalier*, and soon afterward Wellings called on Ainsworth to be officially welcomed to TF 67.

While *Strong*'s new assignment was certain to put it in the thick of the action in terms of the effort to wrest control of the Solomons from the Japanese, that action wasn't immediately forthcoming. From February 15 through 23 Ainsworth kept his ships at sea for intense training in tactics and gunnery, after which TF 67 returned to Santo so several of the vessels could undergo maintenance and modification. In *Strong*'s case this meant the repair of the power-train unit that controlled the movement of the fantail 40mm mount and, more important from Hugh's point of view, the installation of additional 20mm guns.

Given that the threat of air attack was deemed relatively high in the Solomons, most of the destroyers assigned to the region were being fitted with increased antiaircraft armament. Because 40mm cannon were still in short supply, *Strong* received three more 20mm mounts — one fixed to the flying bridge above the pilot house directly in front of the Mark 37 director and an additional one placed next to each of the existing weapons amidships on the main deck. Hugh was by all accounts delighted by this enlargement of his arsenal to eight guns, though it obviously meant he had to form new crews and introduce them to his Wallace Wade–inspired training regimen. Fortunately, the February 24 arrival of Ensign Keith Sherlie as the destroyer's new supply officer allowed Hugh to focus on that regimen by taking over a collateral duty he had handled since soon after his own assignment to the ship.

All the men aboard *Strong* had the opportunity to further hone their skills before going into combat with TF 67. In accordance with his ComSoPac orders, on March 3 Ainsworth took his ships to sea for patrol duty between the New Hebrides and the Solomons; for the next eleven days *Strong* and the other vessels of the task force crisscrossed the waters to the southeast of San Cristóbal with only one quick return to Santo for fuel. While the purpose of the voyage was to engage and defeat any hostile force that might be encountered, the complete absence of enemy activity meant that the days and nights at sea were also filled with still more training—gunnery practice, anti-submarine drills, coordination with friendly reconnaissance aircraft, radar navigation familiarization, and, perhaps most important, a constant emphasis on coordinated fleet maneuvering.

While the men aboard *Strong* certainly benefited from Ainsworth's exacting training regimen, Wellings had been working to prepare his men for combat since before the destroyer left the United States. The seasoned and experienced captain, ably assisted by his executive officer, had molded a disparate group of individuals—most of them new to both military service and the rigors of life at sea—into a capable and efficient wartime crew. During the many long hours of convoy-escort duty and routine patrolling, Wellings had been able to keep his sailors and junior officers focused and motivated, leading by his calm example and frequently reminding everyone in an honest and straightforward way that the skills they were honing would ultimately be put to the test against a resourceful, experienced, and implacable enemy.

And just after noon on March 14 Wellings received the assignment he had long expected and for which he'd been so diligently preparing his crew. *Strong* was ordered to detach from TF 18, as Ainsworth's force had been redesignated, and proceed to Tulagi in company with the destroyers *Nicholas*, *Radford*, and *Taylor*. The four warships—operating as Task Group 18.6 under the command of Destroyer Squadron (DesRon) 21's Captain Francis X. McInerney in *Nicholas*—would refuel and replenish and then proceed up the Slot and into Kula Gulf. Their mission was to bombard Japanese positions at Vila-Stanmore on the southern tip of Kolombangara Island.

After months of preparation, *Strong* was about to fire its guns in anger.

ONE OF ELEVEN MAIN ISLANDS IN THE NEW GEORGIA GROUP, Kolombangara is almost perfectly circular except for a small rounded projection of low ground on its southeastern end that in the 1920s became the location of the Vila-Stanmore coconut plantation operated by the British firm Lever Brothers. The site was divided by the Vila

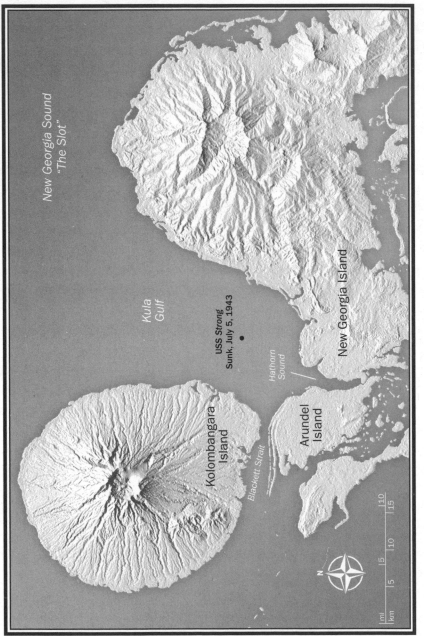

New Georgia Sound
"The Slot"

Kula
Gulf

USS Strong
Sunk, July 5, 1943

New Georgia Island

Hathorn
Sound

Kolombangara
Island

Arundel
Island

Blackett Strait

N

mi   5   10
km   5   10   15

4. New Georgia

River, with the plantation on the east bank and the settlement of Vila on the west. Ten miles west across Kula Gulf from New Georgia itself, 18-mile-wide Kolombangara is the summit of an extinct volcano and is dominated by the more than fifty-eight-hundred-foot Mount Veve. Following the Japanese occupation of New Georgia in October and November 1942, Vila-Stanmore was selected as the site for an airfield and various supporting installations. By the end of February 1943 there were approximately two thousand men—primarily of the IJN's Yokosuka 7th Special Naval Landing Force but also including IJA troops—concentrated in and near the former plantation.[19] The airfield was defended by artillery emplacements and large numbers of antiaircraft guns, as well as by fighters flying from Rabaul and from the auxiliary field at Munda.

Despite its considerable defenses the Vila-Stanmore complex had been repeatedly attacked by Allied aircraft in an attempt to disrupt the airfield's construction and operation and in February had also been subjected to naval bombardment by Ainsworth's task force. Allied intelligence reports indicated that Japanese ships operating from Buin, on the southeastern coast of Bougainville, and the adjacent Shortland Islands were continuing to reinforce the units at Vila-Stanmore with "Tokyo Express"–style nightly deliveries of men and matériel. There were also indications that the IJN had moved highly maneuverable motor torpedo boats into Kula Gulf, basing them in small harbors on Kolombangara's east coast and in coves and inlets along the north side of Blackett Strait, the narrow waterway that separates Kolombangara from Arundel Island to the south and connects Vella Gulf in the west to Kula Gulf in the east. The primary task assigned to McInerney's TG 18.6 was to bombard the Vila-Stanmore complex, though the destroyers were also authorized to engage Japanese torpedo boats and any other small enemy craft encountered during the foray into Kula Gulf.[20]

At the time they detached from TF 18 on March 14, McInerney's ships were roughly 130 miles southeast of San Cristóbal. The 340-mile passage to the east and then north of that island and into Tulagi was uneventful, and the destroyers were safely moored in the port by 11:00 on the morning of March 15. A problem soon cropped up, however. *Strong* was the last of the TG 18.6 ships to refuel, and when it moved alongside the tanker *Erskine Phelps* that vessel's captain informed Wellings that he did not have enough fuel oil left to top off the destroyer's tanks. Moreover, earlier delays in fueling *Taylor* meant that even if there had been enough fuel, there wouldn't be time to transfer it before TG 18.6's scheduled 6:00 p.m. departure from Tulagi. Some quick calculations by Fred Purdy and engineer officer Del Downer resulted in a determination that the 105,000 gallons left in *Strong*'s tanks was sufficient to get the destroyer through the night's operation and back to the rendezvous point with the rest of TF 18—providing there was no enemy damage to the ship's fuel tanks and that TG 18.6 refueled as scheduled on March 17.[21]

While his executive officer was dealing with the refueling issues, Wellings was aboard *Nicholas* attending a briefing being given by McInerney for the captains of his destroyers and the pilots of the four radar-equipped PBY-5A "Black Cat" flying boats of Patrol Squadron 12 (VP-12) that would accompany the destroyers—three of the aircraft would search the task group's route to and from the target for enemy ships, while the fourth would act as a spotter over Vila-Stanmore.[22] DesRon 21's commander emphasized that the ships of the task group would maintain complete radio silence from the time they left Tulagi until they rejoined the larger TF 18 the next day. They would follow the course and time schedule outlined in the operations order he passed out, with the destroyers making the entire journey in single-file, open-column formation. The entry into Kula Gulf and the retirement back into the Slot would be made at high speed, and all maneuvering during the bombardment would be follow-the-leader style. The line of vessels would initially approach Kolombangara head-on, but would turn to the south a few miles offshore in order to parallel the island's coast during the firing run. Each ship was assigned specific targets and would fire for ten minutes or until its assigned ammunition allotment was expended. McInerney ended his briefing by cautioning his captains not to be so fixated on the targets ashore that they neglected to watch for attacks from the seaward side, and he directed that they illuminate any inbound enemy surface craft with searchlights to warn the other destroyers without breaking radio silence.

Despite the old military axiom "No plan survives first contact with the enemy," Task Group 18.6's attack on Vila Stanmore went off without significant problems. *Nicholas* led *Radford*, *Strong*, and *Taylor* into Kula Gulf exactly on schedule at 1:15 a.m. on March 16, and the lead ship opened fire at 2:01. Two minutes and thirty seconds later *Strong*'s Mount 51 fired the first combat rounds of the destroyer's career, and by the time Wellings ordered "cease fire" ten minutes later the ship's 5-inch/.38s had sent a total of 368 high-explosive rounds hurtling toward the targets ashore. With the firing run completed, *Nicholas* led the column in a sharp turn to the northeast and increased speed to thirty-two knots. The destroyers emerged into the Slot at 3:00 a.m. and began the long haul back toward the rendezvous with TF 18, which occurred 124 miles southeast of San Cristóbal just after 10:45 on the night of the sixteenth.

Wellings's after-action report on the Vila-Stanmore bombardment showed overall satisfaction with his crew's performance. Noting that the operation was the first time his ship had fired its guns in anger—and that only he, his executive officer, and ten enlisted men had previously seen action—Wellings acknowledged his men for carrying out the complex and challenging mission in a professional way. He specifically lauded Purdy and Downer for their efforts, the former for his skillful navigating and the latter for ensuring that the ship's engines performed flawlessly despite having not undergone major overhaul since leaving the United States.

The three weeks following *Strong*'s combat debut were busy ones for the destroyer and the other ships of TF 18. On March 19 ComSoPac ordered Ainsworth to temporarily divide his command, with several vessels remaining on patrol south of San Cristóbal, while a slightly restructured Task Group 18.6—now including *Honolulu* in addition to the four destroyers—detached to go trolling for enemy ships trying to make nighttime runs between Buin and Vila-Stanmore. The two nights of searching the northern end of the Slot near the entrance to Kula Gulf turned up nothing, however, and by March 22 TG

18.6 had rejoined TF 18 and the entire force returned to Espíritu Santo for maintenance and replenishment.

While the time in port was also intended to provide the men of Ainsworth's command with a certain amount of downtime—Santo had separate clubs and recreation areas for enlisted sailors and officers—the ships of McInerney's DesRon 21 were nonetheless responsible for routine patrols of "Area George," the northeastern approaches to the harbor. The destroyers undertook the twenty-four-hour task in turn, with the crews of those vessels not under way being allowed liberty ashore as their work schedules permitted. After two days moored in Segond Channel, it was time for *Strong*'s shift on "Task George," and just after 6:00 a.m. on Thursday, March 25, Gus Wellings took his ship to sea for what everyone aboard assumed would be a routine patrol.

And the twenty-four hours the destroyer spent steaming back and forth were completely uneventful, at least in terms of its assigned mission. After relieving *Radford*, *Strong* had sailed various courses at differing speeds, probing the sea and sky around it with radar and sonar in search of enemies. It found none, and while its crew went to general quarters for forty-five minutes at dusk and again at dawn—the times of day favored by the Japanese for hit-and-run attacks—the only ships and aircraft Wellings and his men encountered were friendly. Indeed, the patrol would have been entirely unremarkable had it not been for an accident that befell Hugh Miller.

STRONG'S MACHINE-GUN OFFICER FAVORED THE DESTROYER'S FLYing bridge as his battle station because it offered excellent all-around visibility, but the position had obvious drawbacks: it was completely exposed to the elements and was also inherently unstable. The flying bridge's height above the ship's waterline ensured that even a slight roll or easy turn would be magnified several times, meaning that a motion that might be barely felt on the main deck could be severe at the base of the Mark 37 director. While the men inside that turret-like station were protected somewhat, anyone standing on the small deck around the director could easily be tossed about if not sufficiently well braced against the surrounding railing or wedged into one of the lookout positions. The other danger, of course, was that a sudden movement of the ship would catch a man ascending or descending one of the narrow ladders that connected the flying bridge to the bridge wings. That is apparently what happened to Hugh.

Sometime on March 27 the machine-gun officer was thrown from one of the ladders by a sudden movement of the ship. He managed to land on his feet, but in the process badly twisted his left knee—which he had previously injured several times playing football—and hurt one of his ankles. Henry Laughlin, the ship's medical officer, determined both injuries to be bad sprains. By the time *Strong* returned to Santo on March 28, however, the doctor had cause to reevaluate part of his initial diagnosis: Hugh's ankle had swollen considerably, and his pain level was well beyond what might be expected with a sprain. It was obvious that the injuries would make it extremely difficult for Hugh to carry out his duties. Moreover, Wellings had already been notified that TF 18 would sortie from Santo within forty-eight hours, and, rather than subject the hobbled officer to what could well turn out to be weeks at sea confined to his cabin, the destroyer's commander directed Laughlin to transfer Hugh ashore for treatment.

By the evening of March 28 Espíritu Santo's U.S. Naval Base Hospital No. 3—a sprawling complex of Quonset huts nestled among coconut palms not far from the harbor—had officially admitted Hugh. His knee and massively bruised foot were X-rayed, and the attending physician determined that the "bad ankle sprain" was actually a displaced fracture. A not-uncommon injury aboard ships, the condition is often caused by a fall or strong blow to the lower leg or ankle—exactly as happened when Hugh was thrown from the ladder—and results in one or more fractured bones being forced out of normal position. The procedure that puts the bones back where they should be without the need for surgery is known as a closed reduction, and this is from all indications what was required for Hugh. The follow-on care normally includes a splint or hard cast, and the patient usually spends several weeks on crutches as the fracture heals.

Surviving records do not indicate whether the ankle reduction was done at Santo's Base Hospital No. 3, but we do know that Hugh didn't

stay on the island long. After just six days he was transferred to the
casualty evacuation ship USS *Rixey* for transportation to U.S. Naval
Mobile Base Hospital No. 4 in Auckland, New Zealand. The reason
for this movement to what at the time was one of the largest rear-area
Navy medical centers in the Pacific Theater is unclear; it may have been
that the procedure on his ankle and any required therapy for his knee
could not be performed at Santo, or that both had been undertaken
but didn't produce the desired results, or that beds at the island facility
were more urgently needed for combat casualties, or that Hugh's need
for weeks of convalescence and physical therapy simply could not be
met at Base Hospital No. 3. Whatever the reason, when *Rixey* raised
anchor on the morning of April 3, *Strong*'s machine-gun officer was
one of twelve Navy personnel among the more than four hundred
casualties aboard. The ship took on additional patients during a call
at Port Vila on Efate, farther south in the New Hebrides, and by the
afternoon of April 8 *Rixey* was moored to Auckland's Queen's Wharf
and its casualties were departing for Mobile Hospital No. 4—stretcher
cases by ambulance and ambulatory patients aboard buses.[23]

MOB 4, as the hospital was referred to by staff and patients alike,
was constructed on a sixteen-acre former sports field at the foot of
Mount Hobson in the Auckland suburb of Remuera, and by the time
of Hugh Miller's arrival in the spring of 1943 the facility consisted of
more than seventy prefabricated buildings divided among the 1,160-
bed main hospital and a 1,000-bed convalescent-care center. While
MOB 4 treated mainly Navy and Marine Corps personnel evacuated
from the Pacific battle zones, it also admitted members of the U.S.
Army and the Australian, British, and New Zealand forces.

During his two months at MOB 4, Hugh was assigned to the con-
valescent center. He slept and ate in a section of the facility reserved
for officers and was under the care of an orthopedist. Though he arrived in New Zealand on crutches and with his injured ankle encased
in a full-foot cast, he made the transition to a lighter walking cast and
cane fairly quickly. Other than attending mandatory physical-therapy
sessions for both his knee and his ankle and occasional consultations
with his physician, Hugh's time was his own, and he took advantage
of the many leisure activities available to ambulatory patients. These

included bus tours of Auckland and day trips to North Island's many scenic areas, enjoying home-cooked meals with local families, and attending sporting events.

By the end of April Hugh was out of the cast and no longer using a cane. Though not perhaps ready to run a footrace, he was certainly fit to return to duty, and on the evening of June 6 he was discharged from the hospital and transferred to the evacuation transport USS *Pinkney*, then loading passengers at Auckland's Princess Wharf. The ship was bound first for Nouméa and then Espíritu Santo, where Hugh would rejoin *Strong*. When *Pinkney* sailed early on June 7, many of its passengers stood on deck and quietly watched as Auckland's lights faded into the rain and fog of a gloomy austral winter morning. For many of the men lining the ship's rails, it was undoubtedly a bittersweet sight; they were bound for sunnier but far less hospitable climes to the north, and most were unlikely to return to Aotearoa, as New Zealand is called by its indigenous people, the Maori.[24]

While we cannot know Hugh Miller's thoughts as he watched the coast of the North Island disappear over the horizon, we may assume that he was to some degree pondering what the future might hold for him. Whatever he envisioned, it almost certainly did not include the disaster that would engulf him and his shipmates less than four weeks later.

4

ON A COLLISION COURSE

H UGH MILLER'S RETURN JOURNEY TO ESPÍRITU SANTO FROM NEW ZEALAND ended up being a somewhat leisurely voyage. *Pinkney* made the passage to Nouméa relatively quickly, arriving on the evening of June 9, and over the following twenty-four hours offloaded several hundred passengers—Army and Navy personnel, Red Cross nurses, and Royal New Zealand Air Force aircrew—as well as some twelve tons of food, medical equipment, and other cargo.[1] But then, for reasons that are unclear, the transport remained in New Caledonia for a further five days—a delay that apparently gave Hugh the chance to go ashore to visit with Eddie Fay. Finally, on June 15 *Pinkney* raised anchor and departed Nouméa in company with the stores ship USS *Aldebaran* and the escorting Free French vessel *Cap des Palmes*.[2]

Though the chances of attack by Japanese submarines increased significantly the closer the convoy got to the New Hebrides, the two-day journey passed without incident. While still 150 miles short of Santo, *Aldebaran* left the group to call at Port Vila on Efaté, and *Pinkney* and

77

Cap des Palmes finally dropped anchor in Segond Channel on the afternoon of June 17. The evacuation transport's passengers began disembarking via tenders and whaleboats, and upon reaching the pier Hugh presented himself at the port captain's office to arrange transportation to whichever part of the crowded anchorage *Strong* was moored in. He must have been nonplussed when he was told that his ship wasn't actually in port and that until it returned he would be billeted in one of the several Quonset huts that constituted the transient personnel quarters.

Strong's machine-gun officer would certainly have been even more chagrined, however, had he known that while he was in New Zealand, the gun crews he'd worked so hard to train had their first opportunity to put that training to the test. Moreover, Hugh had missed the two most significant combat actions thus far in his destroyer's career.

THE MORNING AFTER HUGH'S MARCH 28 ADMISSION TO SANTO'S Base Hospital No. 3, his ship had sortied as part of the reconstituted Task Group 18.6. Now consisting of the cruisers *Honolulu* and *St. Louis* and the destroyers *Nicholas*, *Jenkins*, and *Radford* in addition to *Strong*, the armada had been ordered to patrol the area between San Cristóbal and the Solomons. There were no out-of-the-ordinary occurrences, and on the night of March 31 Ainsworth was ordered to take the task group to Tulagi for a new mission.[3]

That task was to hunt for the Japanese ships that were carrying troops and supplies to New Georgia and Kolombangara under cover of darkness. These were often the same vessels from Rabaul, Bougainville, and the Shortland Islands that had earlier been called the Tokyo Express, and now, as the Vila Express, they were attempting to bolster the defenses of what the Japanese correctly assumed were the next targets of Allied landing forces. TG 18.6 was directed to troll the northern end of the Slot for enemy vessels attempting to enter Kula Gulf, engage any that might be encountered, and then return to Tulagi each morning to prepare for the next night's patrol.

These interdiction sweeps began on the night of April 1, but no enemy vessels were encountered on the first four sorties. That situation changed, however, on April 5. A few minutes before 2:00 in the morning, as the ships of the task group were moving south through the Slot on the return passage to Tulagi, *Strong*'s Radarman 2nd Class Sigmond Butler picked up a contact some eleven miles away. After evaluating the radar image, he decided that he was looking at a surfaced submarine and passed the word to the bridge. Gus Wellings determined that *O'Bannon* was only three miles from the contact and notified its captain, Lieutenant Commander Don Mac-Donald, of the sub's position and course. *O'Bannon* immediately went to investigate the contact, by now some thirteen miles south of Santa Isabel Island and moving slowly northwestward. At 2:31 a.m. the destroyer's lookouts identified the contact as a Japanese submarine, and MacDonald ordered his 5-inch mounts to open fire under radar control. The destroyer's 40mm and 20mm guns joined in the action as *O'Bannon* closed with the target, and numerous hits were seen on the sub's conning tower and hull. For more than thirty-five minutes the destroyer threw everything it had at the frantically maneuvering enemy vessel, which was finally able to submerge at about 3:20. *O'Bannon* dropped several patterns of depth charges, and by the time MacDonald was directed to rejoin the task group he and his crew were firmly convinced that they'd sunk the sub. Unfortunately, they hadn't.[4]

The vessel on which *O'Bannon* had focused its considerable firepower was the 940-ton type K5 (*RO-33* Class) Japanese submarine *RO-34*, which had sailed from Rabaul at noon on April 2 with a threefold mission. First, Lieutenant Commander Rikichi Tomita was to take his ship to a patrol area east of the Russell Islands and engage Allied vessels operating off Tulagi and Guadalcanal; second, the sub was to provide reports on weather conditions at various points in the Slot; and third, *RO-34* was to act as a "lifeguard" for Japanese aircraft operating over the central Solomons. It is unclear which of these tasks the submarine was engaged in when discovered by "Siggy" Butler. What is clear from postwar investigation, however, is that *RO-34* somehow survived the mauling by *O'Bannon* and was able to leave the scene despite being damaged. The sub's good fortune wouldn't last long, however.[5]

At noon on April 7 TG 18.6—now bolstered by the addition of
Helena and *Taylor*—again sortied from Tulagi, this time to undertake a simultaneous night bombardment of the Vila-Stanmore area
on Kolombangara and the Japanese airfield at Munda Point on New
Georgia. The warships had barely cleared the harbor, however, when
Ainsworth was notified of an incoming Japanese air raid. TG 18.6
changed course to head for the relative safety of the seas north of
Florida Island, sweeping in a wide arc first to the northwest and then
directly north. Ainsworth's ships did not come under air attack, and
at 1:45 the bombardment mission was canceled and the task group was
ordered to withdraw to an area west of Vanikoro Island, 330 miles east
of San Cristóbal.[6]

By 9:51 p.m. the ships were about 145 miles to the southeast
of Tulagi and some 27 miles north of San Cristóbal. At that point
Strong's Radarman 2nd Class Dixon Garris reported a surface radar
contact a little more than 5 miles to the southeast of the destroyer's
track. The contact appeared to be dead in the water, and Garris and
Fred Purdy[7] quickly classified it as a surfaced submarine. Wellings
called his crew to general quarters and notified Ainsworth that *Strong*
would investigate the contact, then turned the destroyer due south.
As the range to the target closed, Wellings increased his ship's speed
to twenty-five knots and at 10:04 the surfaced and unmoving *RO-34*
appeared in the beam of *Strong*'s fire-control searchlight, some 700
yards off the destroyer's port bow. The words "Commence firing"
had barely left Wellings's lips when three of the ship's 5-inch mounts
and all of the 20mm and 40mm weapons that could be brought to bear
started pumping out rounds. Solid hits were observed on the hull and
conning tower of the sub, which had begun to move sluggishly forward and appeared to be trying to submerge. As *Strong* swept past
RO-34, it became obvious that the sub wasn't submerging; it was
sinking stern-first at a ten- to fifteen-degree angle. The smell of diesel
oil hung heavy on the night air as Wellings ordered his helmsman
to bring the destroyer about for a depth-charge run. At 10:25 the
destroyer dropped a pattern of eight charges, followed by another
minutes later. A sweep of the area after the second pattern revealed

oil and debris in the water, and at 10:53 Wellings notified Ainsworth that the submarine had been sunk.[8]

While the sinking of *RO-34* marked a high point in *Strong*'s war, the event did nothing to lessen the ship's operational tempo. From April 8 through April 10 the destroyer and Task Force 18 patrolled the area between the New Hebrides and the Solomons, and through the end of the month *Strong* operated from Santo, alternately engaged in antisubmarine patrols and training. May also proved to be busy, with TF 18 undertaking two significant operations. In the first, on the night of May 7–8, the task force provided cover for a mining operation undertaken between Ferguson Passage and the southern end of Kolombangara, in the process penetrating into the gulf that separates the latter from Vella Lavella Island to the west. In the second operation, *Strong* and the other ships of TF 18 undertook the simultaneous night bombardment of the Vila-Stanmore area and Japanese positions around Rice Anchorage, on the western coast of New Georgia. On May 20 and 21 *Strong* escorted a convoy to Guadalcanal and then remained off the island into the first week of June, screening the unloading berths near Henderson Field. *Strong* dropped anchor in Segond Channel on June 8, but four days later departed in company with *Nicholas*. The two destroyers escorted the oiler *Monongahela* to Guadalcanal and Tulagi, and it was in the dangerous waters between the two locations that *Strong* was able to directly engage the Japanese for the second time.

By June 16 *Monongahela* had completed its refueling of vessels berthed off Guadalcanal, and the oiler and its two escorting destroyers had shifted north across Iron Bottom Sound to drop anchor at Tulagi. At 1:15 p.m. *Nicholas* was refueling from *Monongahela* and *Strong* was moored about 400 yards away when all three vessels received warning of an impending air raid. The two destroyers immediately ushered *Monongahela* into Iron Bottom Sound, with all three vessels then taking up coordinated maneuvering at high speed. The radio circuits came alive with reports of Japanese aircraft attacking Henderson Field on Guadalcanal, and at 2:12 the men aboard *Strong* saw a formation of some fifteen Aichi D3A dive-bombers (referred to as "Vals" by the Allies) attack merchant ships off Lunga Point. At least one of the vessels was hit, and minutes later the Vals turned toward *Monongahela* and its escorts, flying low and fast. Another gaggle of enemy aircraft, a mixed group of Vals and escorting Mitsubishi A6M "Zero" fighters, approached the three American ships at higher altitude from the direction of Koli Point.[9]

The Japanese aircraft were apparently intent on clearing the area as quickly as possible, for none of them attempted to attack the three zigzagging warships. The enemy pilots' lack of interest in *Monongahela* and its protectors did not prevent the American vessels from putting up a wall of antiaircraft fire, however. *Strong* was the closest ship to the passing Japanese formations, and in the space of just seven minutes the destroyer's guns pumped out 194 5-inch, 750 40mm, and 980 20mm rounds. The hail of ordnance knocked down two of the low-flying Vals and a third that flew directly over the destroyer at higher altitude. Wellings ordered "cease fire" at 2:21 when the enemy aircraft passed out of range, and for the next half hour the men aboard *Strong* and its companions watched as American and Japanese fighters battled each other in swirling dogfights high above. The all clear was finally sounded at 2:58, and minutes later the three ships turned back toward Tulagi.

HUGH MILLER HAD SPENT TWO DAYS COOLING HIS HEELS IN SANTO by the time *Strong* finally dropped anchor in Segond Channel on June 19. While he must have been pleased to finally be reunited with his shipmates, the pugnacious machine-gun officer was also more than a little disappointed to have missed the sinking of *RO-34* and the downing of the Vals.

Hugh's dismay was assuaged somewhat, however, by a bit of other news he received during the course of his first meal back aboard *Strong*. Gus Wellings first introduced Hugh to three new officers who had joined the ship in his absence. The first was Lieutenant (jg) Albert M. Horne, who in late April had replaced Henry Laughlin as medical officer. The other two, Ensigns Jack J. Drath and Alfred R. Naphan, had come aboard the same day Hugh left the ship for Base

Hospital No. 3 and were still doing general tasks pending assignment to a particular duty. After motioning for quiet in the crowded
wardroom—there were now nineteen officers assigned to *Strong*—
Wellings announced that Hugh had been promoted to lieutenant as
of May 1. In response to the inevitable good-natured ribbing about
advancing in rank while "taking it easy" hundreds of miles from the
combat zone, Hugh, true to form, regaled his fellow officers with
tales of his "adventures" Down Under. As Wellings later wrote to his
wife, Hugh "has millions of stories about Auckland, NZ. He must
have had a grand time."[10]

While Hugh soon resumed his official duties aboard *Strong*, he just
as quickly regained his unofficial position as the ship's chief morale
booster. His first effort took place on June 23 at Wellings's request. The
event grew out of the efforts of Al Oberg and Keith Sherlie—respectively, the destroyer's assistant gunnery officer and supply officer—to
date nurses assigned to a hospital ship berthed in Espíritu Santo.[11] The
nurses were understandably popular, given that they were the only
Caucasian women within hundreds of miles. In order to boost the
morale in the officers' mess, Wellings suggested Oberg and Sherlie in-
vite the young ladies—and some of their friends—to a party hosted
by all of the destroyer's officers. Hugh was put in charge of arranging
the venue and went ashore early to secure a prime area of the officers'
club. The facility, a suitably "South Seas"–looking wooden building
with wide covered verandas and coconut-palm thatching, was nestled
among trees not far from Base Hospital No. 3. Hugh persuaded the
club manager to set aside tables usually reserved for captains and admirals and to provide several bottles of scotch and bourbon.

At 4:00 p.m. all the officers not on duty left *Strong* in a launch and
called at the hospital ship for the four nurses who had agreed to attend the soiree. A short trip across the harbor brought the boat to the
small pier at the officers' club, and the party was soon in full swing.
Hugh sang several songs, accompanied by a few of the others, and
after a couple of hours the entire party motored back to *Strong* for a
buffet supper. The nurses had a 10:00 p.m. curfew, and they were duly
escorted back to their ship by Oberg, Sherlie, Jack Fulham, and Don
Regan. In a letter to his wife Wellings noted that he had footed the

twelve-dollar cost of the party, saying it was money well spent "because the boys let their hair down. . . . We had more fun than we have had for weeks. . . . [I]t was our one and only party since the [ship's] commissioning . . . and the boys needed a little relaxation."[12]

While Wellings certainly could not have foreseen it at the time, the party on June 23 would be the last celebrated aboard his ship. It also marked the final time that anyone would hear Hugh Miller sing in public.

WHATEVER RELAXATION *STRONG*'S OFFICERS ENJOYED DURING AND immediately after the party likely dissipated quickly over the following days. On June 26 the destroyer sortied from Santo for twelve hours of gunnery and antisubmarine training, and the following day Wellings returned from a meeting aboard *Honolulu* with Ainsworth and the captains of TF 18's other vessels to announce a new mission: *Strong* was to be part of Operation TOENAILS, the invasion of New Georgia.

The sixth-largest island in the Solomons, New Georgia is some forty-five miles long on its northwest-to-southeast axis and about thirty miles across at its widest point. The Japanese had first explored the island in October 1942 and quickly determined that Munda Point would be an excellent location for an auxiliary airfield, and in November a significant landing force had occupied the area and begun construction. The Japanese had also established outposts on the island's southeastern and northwestern ends, as well as on Kolombangara, Arundel—less than a mile south of Vila-Stanmore across Blackett Strait— and Rendova, an island eight miles southeast of Munda across Blanche Channel. The intense Japanese activity on New Georgia and its neighbor islands quickly attracted the attention of Allied intelligence officers, and Munda and the other installations had been routinely subjected to heavy bombardment by aircraft and naval gunfire.

The first full-scale Allied offensive undertaken in the Solomons following the capture of Guadalcanal, TOENAILS was intended to wrest New Georgia, Rendova, and several smaller islands in Blanche Channel from the enemy as part of the larger Operation CARTWHEEL, the Allied isolation and eventual reduction of the massive Japanese base at Rabaul. The first part of the TOENAILS plan called for the Army's 43rd Infantry Division, the Marines' 9th Defense Battalion and 1st Raider Regiment, Navy Seabees (construction battalions), and various support units to go ashore on Rendova and at several points along southeastern New Georgia. These initial landings were to be quickly followed by operations intended to neutralize the Japanese airfield at Munda and two important positions fronting Kula Gulf on New Georgia's northwestern coast: the barge anchorage and logistics hub at Bairoko Harbor and a suspected battery of four 120mm guns at Enogai Inlet that, if actually present, could dominate the gulf almost all the way to the north end of Kolombangara.[13]

Wellings's announcement about *Strong*'s new mission would not have come as a surprise to his officers—the destroyer and the other vessels of TF 18 had been engaged for some time in the run-up to the invasion. Their bombardments of Vila-Stanmore and Munda and the nightly forays up the Slot had been intended to both degrade enemy defenses and prevent the Japanese from reinforcing the already significant garrisons on Kolombangara and New Georgia. The role undertaken by Ainsworth's ships during the landings—which were scheduled to begin on June 30—would initially be largely protective. Operating as Task Group 36.1, the three cruisers plus *Strong*, *Nicholas*, *O'Bannon*, and *Chevalier* would patrol to the south of New Georgia to prevent Japanese interference with the amphibious operations.[14]

TG 36.1 sortied from Espíritu Santo on the morning of June 28 and shaped a course for the patrol zone south of New Georgia. The following afternoon Ainsworth was notified that his command had been tapped for an additional task: Once the landings on Rendova and the south coast of New Georgia had taken place, TG 36.1 was to head up the Slot to Kula Gulf. There the warships would again bombard Vila-Stanmore and then shift their fire to Bairoko Harbor and Enogai Inlet on New Georgia's northwest coast as support for the mixed Army-Marine landing operations at nearby Rice Anchorage that were intended to block the flow of Japanese reinforcements from Kolombangara to Munda.

Soon after Ainsworth received his new tasking, he directed Wellings to take *Strong* to Koli Point on Guadalcanal to pick up the most recent charts and intelligence reports for Kula Gulf. The destroyer left the task group at 3:10 p.m. on the twenty-ninth and turned north, with Fred Purdy charting a 370-mile route that took *Strong* to the east of Rennell Island and then through the 40-mile-wide channel between the southern end of Guadalcanal and the northern tip of San Cristóbal and back into the familiar waters of Indispensable Strait and Sealark Channel. The ship arrived off Koli Point early on the morning of June 30—at roughly the same time as the first American troops were going ashore on Rendova and at Wickham Anchorage on the southeast coast of New Georgia—but didn't linger. As soon as a landing craft from shore delivered the charts, intelligence materials, and operations orders, Wellings got the destroyer under way and headed back to the rendezvous point on which he and Ainsworth had previously agreed. The return passage was uneventful, and *Strong* rejoined TG 36.1 at 6:30 on the morning of July 1 at a point 340 miles south of Kolombangara.

The operations order for which Ainsworth had been waiting—which along with the other planning materials was passed from *Strong* to *Honolulu* in a waterproof container attached to a high-line—directed TG 36.1 to complete one final westward leg of the current patrol line before making for Tulagi to refuel and, if necessary, rearm, in preparation for the sortie to Kula Gulf.[15] The task group finally came about on the morning of July 2 and took up a course nearly identical to that followed by *Strong* on its dash to Koli Point, and at 10:15 on July 3 *Honolulu* led the flotilla into Tulagi. As it turned out, however, it was a brief stay. On the night of July 2 the Japanese light cruiser *Yubari* and nine destroyers had carried out an intensive but ineffective bombardment of Rendova—all the shells landed in empty jungle—and intelligence reports indicated that a similar raid was likely for the night of the third. Ainsworth was therefore directed to take his ships to sea to locate and engage any enemy force attempting to hit the American positions on Rendova. TG 36.1 was on its way back out of Tulagi by 2:45 that afternoon.

As soon as the last vessel cleared the harbor-defense boom, Ainsworth ordered his command to adopt the usual formation—*Honolulu* leading the other two cruisers in line astern, with the destroyers ranging around the larger vessels in a circular antisubmarine screen. The task group skirted south of Savo Island and the Russells at a speed that allowed the ships to reach a point about 20 miles south of Rendova's southwest tip by 10:15 p.m. The formation then turned north and proceeded up the island's west coast, remaining about 15 miles offshore and using radar and the reports of orbiting Black Cat reconnaissance planes to probe the night for the rumored Japanese ships. No enemy units were found, however, and after spending just over three hours west of Rendova Ainsworth ordered TG 36.1 to retire along its original course. By 11:00 a.m. on July 4 the ships of the task group were once again at anchor in Tulagi.

The second Independence Day of America's war in the Pacific was a busy one for the men aboard *Strong* and the other ships of TG 36.1. At 1:00 p.m., as his crew was busy refueling the destroyer and taking aboard additional ammunition, Wellings left for a conference aboard *Honolulu*. Once Ainsworth's subordinate commanders had gathered in the cruiser's wardroom, the admiral handed out copies of a three-page operations order that outlined the plan for the night's "festivities." It was in some ways a familiar document, in that the bombardment of Vila-Stanmore would be conducted in essentially the same way as the May 12–13 attack. The task group would enter Kula Gulf in line astern, with DesRon 21's Captain F. X. McInerney leading in *Nicholas*. *Strong* was to be second in line, followed in order by *Honolulu*—Ainsworth's flagship—*Helena*, *St. Louis*, *O'Bannon*, and *Chevalier*. Given that the northwest end of the gulf had been heavily mined in order to deter Japanese transports attempting to reach Vila-Stanmore, TG 36.1's approach would be from the northeast, staying close to the coast of New Georgia. Once past the most northerly headland on that coast, Visuvisu Point, the ships would cut across the gulf toward the southwest and then turn almost directly south as they neared Kolombangara. *Nicholas* and *Strong* would conduct a radar and sonar search for possible enemy interference and only engage the targets in and around Vila-Stanmore once *Honolulu* opened the bombardment. The remaining vessels were to fire as their guns came to bear—with two Black Cats providing aerial spotting—and at the same specified point each ship would turn directly east and engage the targets at Bairoko (Enogai had been taken off the target list when reconnaissance showed no sign of the suspected gun battery).[16] Having fired the allotted number of rounds, the task group—still in line astern—was to retire to the north, pass Visuvisu Point to starboard, and head back down the Slot to Tulagi.

Near the end of the briefing Ainsworth emphasized that the landings on Rendova had undoubtedly alerted enemy forces throughout the Kula Gulf area, that those forces expected to be attacked at any time, and that Japanese submarines could be encountered at any time.[17] With these dangers in mind, Ainsworth set specific priorities for *Nicholas* and *Strong*—designated Pup 1 and Pup 2, respectively—as they led the column into the gulf. The two destroyers were to screen the cruisers against enemy submarines and torpedo boats, silence shore batteries and knock out searchlights, and bombard troop concentrations.[18]

Ainsworth concluded the briefing by pointing out that the cruisers and their accompanying destroyers would be sharing the constricted waters of Kula Gulf with fourteen other American vessels, the ships of the Rice Anchorage landing force. Designated Task Unit 31.1.11, that flotilla consisted of three groups. Seven World War I–vintage *Wickes*-class destroyers serving as troopships and the escorting *McCalla* constituted the transport group, the high-speed minesweepers *Hopkins* and *Trever* and the destroyer *Ralph Talbot* made up the mine group, and the screening group consisted of the destroyers *Gwin*, *Radford*, and *Woodworth*.[19] While the landing force was to be nominally part of TG 36.1, it would act independently—a fact that understandably concerned Ainsworth, given that when his seven vessels began their retirement following the bombardment mission they would pass close to the ships putting ashore Colonel H. B. Liversedge's 2,200-man Army-Marine landing force at Rice Anchorage. Should TG 36.1 or the other groups of ships be forced to maneuver radically in response to weather conditions, the sea state, or an enemy attack, the already con-fined waters of Kula Gulf could well become far too busy.[20]

A crowded stretch of ocean would not be the night's only chal-lenge, however. At nearly the same time Ainsworth was briefing his captains on the bombardment mission, another admiral—this one wearing the uniform of the Imperial Japanese Navy—was outlining to *his* subordinates a plan that would make Kula Gulf a far busier and vastly deadlier place than TG 36.1's commander feared.

5

DEATH BY LONG LANCE

THOUGH THE JUNE 30 AMERICAN LANDING ON RENDOVA HAD COME AS A SUR-prise to the Japanese—they were, as one postwar account put it, "completely baffled" by the assault[1]—they had known for some time that Allied forces would inevitably move against New Georgia and had been planning accordingly. Following the evacuation of Guadalcanal, the IJN had been landing reinforcements at Vila-Stanmore, and by July 1 there were approximately 10,500 Japanese army and naval infantry troops under Major General Noboru Sasaki divided between there and the area around Munda.[2] The two senior Japanese commanders in the region—General Hitoshi Imamura of the 8th Area Army and Vice Admiral Jinichi Kusaka of the Southeast Area Fleet, both headquartered on Rabaul—did not believe that number was sufficient, however, and on the morning of July 4 they agreed that 4,000 additional IJA troops would be transported to Kolombangara aboard IJN destroyers. The first echelon of soldiers, they agreed, would go that very night.[3]

The man tasked with translating their intent into action was Rear Admiral Teruo Akiyama, the fifty-three-year-old commander of the IJN's Destroyer Squadron 3. An able officer with extensive experience both afloat and in important staff positions in Tokyo, Akiyama determined that the first "Rat Express" mission—as the Japanese referred to the nocturnal reinforcement runs—would be led by Captain Kunizo Kanaoka, commander of Destroyer Division 22.[4] His flagship for the night's run to Vila would be Commander Kiyoshi Kaneda's 3,700-ton *Akizuki*-class destroyer *Niizuki*, which had entered operational service barely three months earlier and was one of the most modern warships then in the Japanese fleet. Armed with eight 3.9-inch dual-purpose guns, twelve 25mm antiaircraft mounts, depth charges, and a quadruple launcher for the excellent Type 93 torpedo, it was fast, well built, and highly capable. And, unlike most IJN destroyers at that point in the war, *Niizuki* was equipped with radar. Its No. 21 Mod 2 set was intended primarily as an air-search system, but could detect surface targets out to a range of about twenty-five miles, depending on sea conditions.[5]

Niizuki's advanced capabilities were not shared by the three other destroyers tapped for the July 4–5 run to Kolombangara, however. *Nagatsuki*, *Satsuki*, and *Yunagi*—captained, respectively, by Lieutenants Commander Tameo Furukawa, Shiro Koizumi, and Masanori Kashima—had all entered IJN service in the 1920s. Obsolete by World War II standards, they were used almost exclusively as high-speed troop transports and would, between them, carry the bulk of the 1,300 IJN troops and fifteen landing-craft loads of food and equipment bound for Vila. But the fact that they were old and dilapidated did not mean the three destroyers were incapable of offensive action; all retained their main-gun and antiaircraft armament, as well as tubes for the Type 93 torpedo—two triple launchers each in *Nagatsuki* and *Satsuki* and three twin mounts in *Yunagi*.[6]

As laid out by Akiyama and Kanaoka, the night's voyage would take the four destroyers southwest out of the Shortland Islands and into the northern end of New Georgia Sound. In line astern with *Niizuki* leading and probing ahead with its radar, the ships would cut eastward toward Choiseul Island and then hug its southern coast until they reached a position almost directly north of Kolombangara. They would then dash across the breadth of the sound, enter Kula Gulf, and proceed south to Vila-Stanmore, again staying close to shore. After unloading their troops and cargo, the destroyers would reverse course and retire with all speed so as to be back in the Shortlands by dawn. The weather was predicted to be overcast, with rain squalls and moderate winds, and the combination of clouds and the setting of a new moon earlier in the evening would make for an unusually dark night. The two senior Japanese officers likely considered the conditions ideal for the night's business, though they would also have realized that the darkness and dirty weather could just as easily conceal enemy forces.[7]

The loading of the reinforcement troops—most of them artillerymen and combat engineers—went entirely as planned, and *Niizuki* led the column to sea on the 165-mile passage to Vila-Stanmore at 4:40 on the afternoon of July 4. The weather, as predicted, soon turned sour, and by nightfall the four Japanese destroyers were being lashed by rain as they plowed their way through swells that broke in foaming white water over their bows. While the bucking and rolling could not have been pleasant for the soldiers packed tightly into every bit of free space aboard the ships, Kanaoka and his captains would almost certainly have welcomed the protection offered by the roiling waves—then, as now, even large ships can be hard to discern by eye in rough seas. More important, from the Japanese officers' point of view, in heavy weather shipborne radars of the period were often unable to isolate target vessels from the background "clutter" at and just above sea level.

Yet *Niizuki*'s radar managed to do just that. At approximately 12:15 a.m. on July 5, as the four Japanese destroyers were moving cautiously down the northwestern edge of Kula Gulf about 3 miles off Kolombangara, Kanaoka and Kaneda were told that *Niizuki* had detected presumably hostile surface contacts 14 miles to the southeast. The sudden appearance of what could only be enemy ships came as a shock to the Japanese officers, though their consternation was somewhat mitigated when *Niizuki*'s radar indicated the targets were continuing to move deeper into Kula Gulf rather than turning to engage. Minutes later the stress level aboard the Japanese ships must have skyrocketed, however, when the darkness and scudding clouds ahead of them were lit by the flashes of large-caliber naval guns. The deep, guttural rumble of explosions quickly followed, and within seconds the men on *Niizuki*'s bridge would have realized that Vila-Stanmore—not them—was the focus of the Americans' attention.

That realization forced Kanaoka to make a split-second decision. As tactical commander of the reinforcement mission, his overarching responsibility was to put the troops and equipment ashore—they were vital to the defense of Munda and the rest of the New Georgia group, and any failure to get them onto the beach at Vila-Stanmore could well contribute to an eventual Allied victory in the central Solomons. Yet the presence of what appeared to be a major American naval force just miles away dramatically changed the situation. Kanaoka's four vessels would likely not survive an encounter with a larger and more powerful surface-combatant group, and the loss of the men and matériel aboard the Japanese destroyers—not to mention the destruction of the warships themselves—would not serve the emperor or the increasingly hard-pressed IJN. And, of course, there was the small matter of the reinforcement group's designated landing place being subjected at that very moment to what was obviously a furious bombardment.

Given these circumstances, Kanaoka's decision would not have been a difficult one to make. Choosing discretion over valor, at least in the short run, he ordered his ships to retire. But he also did what any self-respecting destroyer sailor in any navy would have done under similar conditions—he ordered a parting shot at the enemy. As *Niizuki* turned back to the north—at roughly 12:28 a.m.—four Type 93 torpedoes leaped from its tubes, quickly followed by six from *Nagatsuki* and four from *Yunagi*.[8] The fourteen Long Lances hit the water in showers of spray and plunged deep before coming back up to running depth. Driven by two contrarotating screws, each torpedo surged to nearly 60 miles an hour, streaking southward toward the American ships. While Kanaoka must have realized that dispatching the weapons was probably futile—there'd been no time to determine an accurate prelaunch bearing on the maneuvering targets, which in any case were hidden by darkness and scudding clouds—he also would have been confident that should any of the nearly thirty-foot torpedoes hit an enemy vessel, the result would almost certainly be catastrophic.

With his lethal fish in the water, Kanaoka turned his flotilla for home, eager to make it back to the Shortlands before the rising sun brought out prowling Allied aircraft. Eleven miles to the south, Hugh Miller felt his ship change course, completely unaware that *Strong* had just turned into the path of disaster.

THE SEVEN SHIPS OF TASK GROUP 36.1'S BOMBARDMENT ECHELON had begun their departure from Tulagi at 3:40 on the afternoon of July 4, with the four destroyers adopting a screening formation around the three cruisers in line astern. The journey up the Slot had passed without incident, and as the evening turned into night, the weather deteriorated as predicted. Intermittent rain squalls washed over the darkened warships, and twelve- to fifteen-knot winds from the south-west blew spray in long tendrils from the crests of passing swells.[9]

Just before 11:30 the task group passed New Georgia's Visuvisu Point, moved into column formation, and started southwest across Kula Gulf. The two leading destroyers probed the darkness with radar and sonar as the task group turned parallel to the east coast of Kolombangara. Though the seas had calmed somewhat, the wind and rain continued unabated, and atop *Strong*'s flying bridge Hugh Miller— clad in oilskins and wearing a collared kapok life preserver and steel helmet—repeatedly wiped the lenses of his binoculars as he scanned the surrounding sea. He paid particular attention to the waters off the ship's port side, understanding that an attack by a Japanese surface craft or submarine would likely come from the open expanse of Kula Gulf rather than from the less than two-mile-wide strip of water that by now separated the destroyer from the jungled hillsides of Kolombangara.[10]

Briefly startled by the sudden crashing of *Honolulu*'s guns—a quick glance at his watch showed it had opened fire four minutes early— Hugh turned his binoculars toward shore and watched as the cruiser's exploding rounds threw the tall coconut palms masking Vila-Stanmore into sharp but momentary relief. As the other cruisers and trailing destroyers opened fire, the entire southern tip of Kolombangara seemed to jump with the impact of thousands of 5- and 6-inch shells. The occasional flare of a bright fireball showed where an ammunition or fuel cache had been hit, and searchlight beams would suddenly stab upward as the Japanese sought to illuminate the Black Cats they could hear circling above the target area. When the searchlights revealed the aircraft's positions, Hugh would quickly instruct the gun crew next to him on the flying bridge and those along the ship's starboard side to fire at the point of origin. He knew the chances of knocking out a light at that distance were slim, but the streams of 20mm rounds "his boys" sent arcing toward the Japanese positions were certainly capable of doing significant damage to anyone or anything they might encounter.

Hugh was still watching the flash of impacts on Vila-Stanmore when *Strong*'s sharp turn to port made him grab the nearby railing for support. At the same instant the sky a thousand yards ahead lit up as *Nicholas* opened fire on targets in and around Bairoko Harbor, now bearing to starboard as the two leading destroyers completed the turn east across the bottom of the task group's planned U-shaped track. Hugh opened his mouth as wide as he could to equalize the massive pressure wave that seconds later engulfed him as his own ship's 5-inch guns opened up. The closest of the ship's two forward turrets, Mount 52, was canted hard to starboard barely thirty feet below and in front of him, and the earsplitting roar that signaled the departure of each round from its barrel reverberated in the pit of his stomach. As the acrid, throat-clogging stench of gunpowder wafted about him, Hugh left the starboard rail and stepped to the left side of the flying bridge 20mm mount so as to regain his night vision and renew his scan of the ship's "sea side."

Strong's machine-gun officer stood facing out toward Kula Gulf for the remainder of the destroyer's six-minute bombardment of the Bairoko Harbor targets, but then turned forward as the ship's 5-inch guns fell silent. Almost immediately, *Strong* began a turn directly north, following *Nicholas* onto the task group's retirement course. At that point Hugh was joined by gunnery officer Al Curran, who had climbed down from the ship's Mark 37 director.

At about the same time, one deck below the two officers, Sonarman 2nd Class Jack Haley picked up an extremely loud noise that he couldn't immediately classify. He put the sound through to the speakers mounted on the walls of the chartroom so executive officer Fred Purdy and others in the area could hear it, at the same time saying that the noise might be coming from a spread of fast-moving torpedoes. When Purdy asked him in which direction the sound was loudest, Haley replied that the strongest returns seemed to be coming from Rice Anchorage, from *Strong*'s port bow, and from a point aft and to starboard of the destroyer's track. The executive officer considered this for a moment, then said the sound must be coming from some submerged device being used in the landings at Rice Anchorage. He then walked through the ship's bridge and out onto the open starboard-side bridge wing, apparently to confer with Gus Wellings, who was peering through binoculars toward Rice Anchorage.[11]

Barely ten feet above *Strong*'s captain Al Curran and Hugh Miller were standing just to the left of the 20mm mount, whose crewmen were focusing their attention dead ahead. Curran suddenly pointed to a long, thin, phosphorescent wake coming directly at the ship from the port bow. Hugh immediately saw the incoming torpedo—as did the port-side lookout—but before any of the men could scream a warning, the Long Lance slammed into the ship ten feet below the waterline, its 1,000-pound warhead detonating in a blinding flash and thunderous roar.

As Kunizo Kanaoka had anticipated when he decided to launch a spread of unaimed torpedoes from eleven miles away, the chance hit was immediately catastrophic.

The Long Lance struck at 12:43 a.m. at a point almost directly in line with *Strong*'s forward funnel, blowing a thirty-by-twenty-foot hole in the ship's port side and a smaller one on the starboard side and completely severing the keel. The deck plating above the impact point disappeared, and the collapse of the midships deckhouse dropped the forward quadruple torpedo-tube mount into the interior of the mangled hull. The explosion obliterated the watertight bulkhead separating the destroyer's forward fireroom from the forward engine room and killed all but one man in both spaces, including engineering officer Del Downer. Seawater flooded in and then surged through the damaged bulkhead separating the forward engine room from the aft fireroom. *Strong* immediately went dead in the water and took on a fifteen-degree list to starboard, and as it settled it began to sag amidships.[12]

When the torpedo exploded, Curran, Hugh, and the other men on the flying bridge were thrown to the deck and had trouble getting up because of the ship's immediate list. Once on their feet the two officers clambered down the now steeply inclined ladder leading to the starboard bridge wing, where they found a shaken but unhurt Wellings surrounded by several officers and a handful of enlisted men. *Strong*'s captain was issuing a string of orders in a calm voice—he sent communications officer Benjamin Frazier Jetton and his assistant, Bill Hedrick, to destroy the ship's code machine and classified files; told Milt Hackett and Don Regan to work their way to the fantail on opposite sides of the ship to check conditions aft of where the torpedo had hit; and directed several of the others to find "Doc" Horne and help him care for the injured. Then, turning to Hugh, Wellings told him to find damage-control officer Jack Fulham and get his report on the extent of the destruction.[13]

Though Hugh had discarded his oilskins and helmet after joining the group on the bridge wing, he had retained his kapok life preserver and the sheath knife attached to his uniform belt. He was also still wearing the pistol belt required for all of the ship's officers while at general quarters. In addition to a holstered .45-caliber Model 1911A1 automatic and two extra seven-round magazines, the belt carried two pouches that comprised Hugh's survival kit. These contained first-aid items, chocolate bars and malted-milk balls, fish hooks and a spool of line, a signaling mirror, and a small compass. Hugh briefly considered removing the unwieldy belt while he searched for Fulham, but decided against it and set off with the pistol and other items still firmly secured around his waist.

Hugh found Fulham amidships, and the young officer's report was discouraging. The flooding was spreading into the after fireroom and engine room, the main deck on the starboard side was under water, and the entire port side of the ship from the torpedo's impact point aft to the 20mm mounts was a mass of tangled wreckage. *Strong's* midships sag was increasing, and Fulham was certain that there was no way to prevent its sinking. An unknown number of men had been killed in the explosion, and there were others still trapped belowdecks.

There were a few bright spots, however. While the flooding of the firerooms had knocked out the ship's electrical power, emergency generators had kicked in immediately. This provided power to all but one of the 5-inch turrets, which were capable of firing in local control, as well as ensuring that the ship's primary radio remained usable. Quick thinking by assistant engineering officer Ralph Trost and his men had ensured the bleed-off of steam pressure from the ship's boilers, which prevented them from exploding as they were submerged in seawater. Though ruptured feed lines were spreading a thick coat of fuel oil over the aft end of the ship and the surrounding water, there had been only one minor fire—in an electrical panel—and it had been quickly extinguished. More important, perhaps, Don Regan—who had been officer of the deck when the torpedo hit—had managed to pull several severely injured men from the aft engine room, and others throughout the vessel were also helping to get their injured shipmates onto the main deck.[14]

Hugh returned to the bridge and relayed Fulham's assessment to Wellings. *Strong's* captain had hoped the ship could be kept afloat and had even sent Milt Hackett and Jack Howard forward to the bow to begin rigging a towline. But Fulham's report made it clear that the destroyer was dying and that it would not remain on the surface for long. Wellings then made the hardest decision thus far in his naval career—it was time to abandon *Strong* to its fate. He dispatched Hugh to ensure the evacuation of the Mark 37 director and all the gun mounts and then sent Purdy forward to notify the men rigging the towline of his decision. But before each man left the bridge, Wellings made it clear that he did not want anyone to go over the side until he specifically ordered it. His reasoning was simple: He didn't want his crew drifting all over Kula Gulf, and keeping the men together would make a rescue operation easier. And perhaps the most compelling reason for Wellings's order was his complete confidence that Ainsworth would do everything in his power to send a ship to take off *Strong*'s crew before the destroyer sank.

Wellings's confidence was not misplaced.

THE FIRST INDICATION AINSWORTH AND HIS OTHER CAPTAINS RE-ceived that something had happened to *Strong* came eight minutes after the torpedo hit. At 12:51 the task group commander radioed DesRon 21's McInerney, in *Nicholas*, asking if his "boys"—the destroyers—were all right. *O'Bannon*'s Don McDonald quickly responded that his vessel was fine, but McInerney's query to *Strong* went unanswered. A minute later he tried again, but when he still got no reply he notified Ainsworth that he couldn't raise *Strong*. The task group commander then radioed *Chevalier*'s Commander Ephraim R. "Eph" McLean, asking if he could raise the missing ship, but he couldn't. Then, at 12:55, MacDonald announced that *Strong* was now off his starboard quarter and that *Chevalier* was also nearing the stricken destroyer. Ainsworth ordered MacDonald to "stand by *Strong* and give us a full report" and then told McLean to "check with [Wellings] to see that he is all right." Seconds later, after communicating with the damaged ship by blinker light, McLean told Ainsworth that "*Strong* needs aid." By this point the mortally wounded destroyer was settling fast, and, as if that weren't enough to deal with, Japanese artillery had begun firing at it from positions around Enogai Inlet and star shells lit the sky.[15]

True to his word that he would always send help if his destroy-ers got into trouble, Ainsworth ordered *Chevalier* and *O'Bannon* to render all possible assistance to *Strong*. The two ships engaged the Japanese guns ashore, and McLean began maneuvering his vessel to come alongside the damaged destroyer's port side. As *Chevalier* was moving in, *O'Bannon* crossed behind it; when McLean started backing down his ship's engines to move it into position, *Chevalier* struck *O'Bannon* a glancing blow. The contact knocked *Chevalier*'s starboard depth-charge rack and smoke-screen generator out of commission, though at that moment McLean had other collisions to worry about—his ship was rapidly closing the distance with *Strong*. At 12:56 *Chevalier*'s bow crashed into the damaged destroyer's port side at an angle of about thirty degrees, the hulls of the two ships forming a narrow V. The collision tore a gash in *Chevalier*'s starboard bow that was two feet high and ten feet long, but it was above the waterline and caused no immediate concern. *Strong*, on the other hand, was rolled farther onto its starboard side by the impact, making it difficult for men to stand upright on the deck without bracing themselves.

Chevalier's arrival may have been abrupt and inelegant, but it was welcome nonetheless. Down on *Strong*'s bow Hackett, Howard, and several others scrambled to their feet and grabbed lines thrown from the other ship and secured them around the base of the forward 5-inch mount. At that point they were joined by Regan and Purdy, the latter relaying Wellings's orders that it was time to abandon ship. Men who could make it to the bow were able to walk off the doomed destroyer and onto *Chevalier*, while others jumped into the water and made for the cargo nets now hanging from the rescue vessel or for the life rafts and floater nets that had been put over *Strong*'s sides.[16]

As men were beginning to transfer to *Chevalier*, Hugh reported back to Wellings on the bridge that the gun director and mounts had been evacuated and their occupants told to muster on the forecastle if they could make it before the ship went under. Wellings thanked Hugh for his efforts, told him it was time to get off the ship, then turned to Jetton. The young communications officer reported that he and Hedrick had thrown the code books and other classified material over the side in weighted bags, and then said he and his assistant were going to do a final sweep of the radio room and nearby spaces to ensure that all their personnel were out. Jetton and Hedrick hurried off, just as Purdy returned to update his captain on the transfer of men to *Chevalier*. His report completed, the executive officer turned and started down the ladder that would take him back to the main deck.

Just before Purdy's head disappeared from view, Wellings called out, "Fred, be sure to get aboard *Chevalier* yourself before she casts off from alongside."

Purdy looked up at his good friend and commanding officer, smiled, and replied, "Don't worry about me Captain."[17]

Hugh followed Purdy down the ladder, ended up on the crumpled port-side deck plating, and began working his way toward where Purdy had rejoined Hackett, Howard, and the others near the forward 5-inch turret. At that moment, up on the bridge, Wellings was listening to Eph McLean, who was shouting to him from *Chevalier*'s starboard bridge wing.

"Gus, I think everyone who was topside is either aboard or in the water alongside," McLean yelled through a megaphone. "I better cast off and get out of here in a minute or two, before I am hit and crippled with all your men on board."[18]

The danger that *Chevalier* might be hit by enemy fire was very real. There were enemy aircraft circling in the vicinity, and the Japanese guns at Enogai had increased their rate of fire—indeed, a dud round slammed into the 40mm mount on *Strong*'s fantail as the men were conversing—so Wellings reluctantly agreed with McLean's assessment. Less than a minute later *Chevalier* backed away from *Strong* after having taken aboard 234 enlisted men and 7 officers in barely ten minutes. Then, as if to underscore the validity of McLean's concerns, a string of bombs landed less than seventy-five yards off *Chevalier*'s stern. The explosions opened a leak in the destroyer's hull and caused minor injuries to some of the sailors—both rescued and rescuers—on the ship's fantail.

None of the men gathered near *Strong*'s forward turret had heard the exchange between Wellings and McLean, and all were caught unaware by *Chevalier*'s abrupt departure. Regan was still holding onto one of the lines connecting the two destroyers and was jerked overboard, while the others scrambled away as additional lines between the ships snapped and whipped back toward *Strong* with enough force to cut a man in half. Once the scything hawsers had stopped moving, Purdy began working his way aft on the port side, attempting to locate a man who had earlier been yelling for help. The executive officer instead encountered Hugh. Purdy said the ship was only moments away from sinking, told Hugh to go over the side immediately, and then continued his search for the injured crew member.

As Hugh climbed over the railing and started sliding down the canted port side of *Strong*'s hull, he landed atop two young sailors who had served as his lookouts. The men, Seaman 1st Class Benjamin R. "Roy" McElduff and Seaman 2nd Class Edward Deering, had become entangled in one of the lines that had parted as *Chevalier* backed away and were in danger of being dragged under as the destroyer sank. Hugh pulled the sheath knife from his web belt and managed to cut the men free just as the earsplitting shriek of grinding steel signaled that the two halves of *Strong*'s twisted hull had separated and the destroyer was headed for the bottom.

As Hugh was working to free the two trapped sailors, Wellings was just completing a last-minute scan from both bridge wings to ensure that all of his men were clear of the ship. He decided to go down and take a final look amidships and started down the ladder leading to the main deck. By this time the entire starboard side of the destroyer was under water, however, and Wellings was forced to return to the bridge. There he was shocked to find his leading quartermaster, Signalman 1st Class Maurice Rodrigos, sitting in the chart house. When asked why he hadn't gone to the bow and transferred to *Chevalier*, the man—who had been aboard the destroyer since its commissioning—calmly responded, "I am not leaving the ship until you do, Captain."

Convinced that the ship was about to turn turtle, Wellings said, "Let's get off right now before we're trapped inside when she rolls over." The two men, both wearing kapok life jackets, clambered atop the starboard bridge windscreen and stepped into the water. Turning onto their backs, they paddled away from the ship as quickly as they could and were about thirty feet from the hull when the two halves separated and began their plunge into the depths.[19]

As *Strong* broke up, Hugh and the two sailors he'd cut free were plunged into the water. Both of the younger men were wearing light rubber-tube life jackets that provided only marginal buoyancy

and would not keep their faces out of the water should they lose consciousness, and Hugh barely had time to grab hold of their shirt collars, yell "Kick like hell!" and gulp a lung-full of air before the three of
them were dragged down by the suction of their sinking ship. It's impossible to know how far down they were pulled, but by the time they
bobbed back to the surface—thanks to Hugh's heavy-duty kapok life
jacket—Deering and McElduff were both unconscious and bleeding
from their noses and ears because of the intense water pressure.

As he treaded water, gasping for air and trying to clear his nose
and mouth of the fuel oil that coated him and the two others, Hugh
congratulated himself on surviving the sinking and helping to save the
young sailors. Then, without warning, a giant's fist crushed his abdomen and slammed his testicles, his head was almost wrenched from his
neck, and the seas around him roiled and bubbled as though a volcano
were rising from the depths beneath him.

6

ADRIFT IN KULA GULF

W HEN THE LONG LANCE SLAMMED INTO STRONG, MILT HACKETT WAS AT his general-quarters station, the Mark 27 torpedo direc- tor on the aft end of the starboard bridge wing.[1] He was knocked to the deck by the force of the explosion, but as soon as he was able to get to his feet he called his assistant, Al Naphan, on the sound-powered telephone and told him to go aft to check on the condition of *Strong*'s depth charges.

The destroyer was fitted with two stern-mounted depth-charge rails, each of which held eight of the 600-pound Mark 7 weapons. In addition, on each side of the main deck amidships *Strong* had three K-gun projectors for Mark 6 300-pound depth charges. While both types of charges had contributed to the April sinking of the Japa- nese submarine *RO-34*, they were potentially just as lethal to *Strong* should they explode aboard ship. In order to prevent their prema- ture detonation, each type of depth charge was fitted with three safety systems.

Both charges shared the first—a "safe" setting on the depth-selection dial on the exposed end of the mechanism that actually initiated the explosion of the charge. Known as a firing pistol, this cylindrical device had an inlet valve in the center of the dial. When the charge entered the water, the increasing hydrostatic pressure ultimately caused the pistol to plunge toward the center of the barrel-shaped weapon, where it encountered the smaller booster charge. That device had its own inlet valve, and when the water pressure reached the correct point—one identical to that set for the pistol—the booster was also driven toward the center of the depth charge. When the two moving parts met, the booster detonated, which in turn set off the main explosive. The Mark 7 had a knobbed cover over the pistol's inlet valve and a pronged safety fork over the booster's valve; both were sheared off as the weapon rolled off the rack, arming the depth charge. The Mark 6 had the same valves at either end, but because the lighter depth charge was launched by the K-gun rather than being rolled from the stern rack, the method for arming the weapon was slightly different. Once the charge had been fixed to the arbor—the metal tube to which the depth charge was attached for firing—the flat safety cap over the pistol inlet valve had to be removed by hand. The same person who removed the cap then pulled the booster safety fork free using a short line, and seconds later a strong tug on the K-gun's firing lanyard sent the Mark 6 on its way.

Despite these safety systems, it was not unusual for both types of depth charge to be jarred off "safe" by the vibrations caused by the firing of a ship's own guns or the impact of an enemy torpedo or shell. It was therefore standard procedure aboard *Strong* and most other U.S. destroyers that depth charges were not set until an enemy submarine was located. This in no way impaired the weapons' usefulness, however, because the eight Mark 7s in each of the two stern racks could be set and dispatched in a matter of minutes, and with enough training a three-man K-gun crew could prepare and fire a nine-charge pattern in just twenty to twenty-five seconds.[2]

As an additional safety measure, *Strong*'s depth charges were routinely checked after any sort of severe jarring to the ship. Naphan had dutifully examined all of the weapons following the cessation of the Bairoko Harbor bombardment and had just completed that task and was returning to his general-quarters station atop the aft torpedo mount when the destroyer was hit by the Long Lance. The explosion lifted the young officer several feet into the air, and when he slammed back down the rear edge of his steel helmet cracked against a deck fitting. The blow momentarily stunned him, but he struggled to his feet and plugged his headphones back into the outlet near the torpedo mount. Seconds later he got Hackett's call about repeating the safety checks on the depth charges, disconnected the headset, climbed down a ladder to the main deck level, and started aft. As he made his way toward the ship's stern he encountered a young sailor lying on the deck. Naphan reached out to give the man a reassuring pat on the head when, to his horror, he discovered that the entire top of the sailor's skull was gone.[3]

Naphan hurried on and within minutes made another ominous discovery: not only had the Long Lance's impact knocked most of the charges on *Strong's* port side off "safe," but the depth-setting dial on several had even been rotated to the fifty-foot mark. He reset all of the charges as quickly as he could, but ran into trouble when he tried to move from the fantail racks up the starboard side toward the K-guns. In the harsh glare of the Japanese-fired star shells floating above the ship, Naphan could see that some of the Mark 6 charges had been knocked from the ready-reload racks next to the launchers, but he could not reach them because the decks were already awash as *Strong* began to buckle in the middle. Naphan obviously had to report this ominous development, and, after finding that the sound-powered telephones on the after part of the ship had gone dead, he worked his way through the partially collapsed main deckhouse to the ship's port side and started forward. He located the torpedo officer on the bow near Mount 51 and passed the news about the status of the depth charges. Hackett thanked him and then ordered Naphan across to *Chevalier*. The young man was one of the last to cross to the rescue ship before it backed away, and his news about the suspect starboard Mark 6 charges never reached those who most needed to hear it: the

men already in the water or those who soon would be as the destroyer
began its plunge into the depths of Kula Gulf.

AS *STRONG*'S AFT END SANK THE ONRUSHING WATER SLAMMED INTO
one of the Mark 6 depth charges Naphan had been unable to see. The
turbulence most probably tumbled the weapon against the nearby
K-gun and along the deck, in the process dislodging the safety cap over
the pistol inlet valve and pulling the lanyard attached to the weapon's
booster safety fork. The earlier explosion of the Long Lance torpedo
had apparently knocked the depth-setting ring off "safe"—likely rotating it to either thirty or fifty feet, as had happened on the port-side
weapons—for within about ninety seconds after being submerged, the
Mark 6 exploded.

The detonation of the weapon's 300-pound load of TNT instanta-
neously sent a spherical shock wave racing outward at some five thousand feet per second. Given that such a wave was intended to open
the seams of a submerged submarine's reinforced steel pressure hull
and either sink the vessel immediately or force it to the surface to be
engaged with gunfire, the effect on a human body was infinitely more
destructive. Anyone on or just below the surface of the water within
fifty to seventy-five feet of the depth charge would have simply disin-
tegrated when the shock wave hit, between 1/2,000th and 1/10,000th
of a second after detonation.

The farther someone in the sea was from a depth charge when it
went off the better, of course, though out to a distance of between
three hundred and five hundred feet—depending on the temperature
of the water—serious injury was almost inevitable. As one wartime
publication dispassionately observed, while the fluid-filled hollow
viscera (bladder, renal pelvis, gallbladder) usually escaped injury, "gas-
filled organs are particularly susceptible to damage because the static
pressure wave passing through the body changes to a wave of kinetic
energy at gas/fluid interspaces, with consequent disruption at such
points."[4] Other typical immediate "immersion blast" injuries included
serious damage to the intestines, widespread hemorrhaging, and broken ribs or limbs. Severe concussion (today's traumatic brain injury)

often led survivors of immersion blasts to suffer mental disorienta-
tion, halting speech, persistent drowsiness, amnesia, and personality
changes.[5]

By the time the United States entered World War II, all new sailors
were being instructed on how to prevent immersion-blast injuries,
training that had been developed as a result of British experience
during the first years of the conflict. The best ways to avoid what
many seaman called the "saltwater enema," they were told, was to get
back to the surface as soon as possible after entering the water, quickly
move away from their sinking vessel, turn on their backs, keep their
legs firmly together, and clench their buttocks.

Unfortunately, Hugh Miller and most of the other *Strong* crewmen
who went into the water as the destroyer was breaking up had no time
to prepare themselves for the massive physical assault they were about
to endure.

HUGH, EDDIE DEERING, AND ROY MCELDUFF WERE APPROXI-
mately one hundred feet from the depth charge when it went off and
in the worst possible position—upright, with most of their bodies
submerged. The two young sailors were still unconscious, and Hugh
was tightly gripping their collars while furiously treading water.

All three of the men would have been killed instantly had it not
been for the fact that *Strong*'s sinking hull sections were between them
and the explosion. The destroyer's tangled mass diverted some of the
lethal shock wave, though what remained was more than enough to
cause immediate and intense pain. As the sea around the trio erupted
in a mass of oily bubbles, Hugh realized he'd lost all surface feeling in
his legs, though he was still able to kick them; hardly had that thought
registered when three more depth charges detonated in quick succession.[6] While the explosions were somewhat deeper and farther away,
they were no less punishing—Hugh immediately lost consciousness.[7]

When he came to, probably after no more than a minute, Hugh was
surprised to find that he had kept his grip on Deering and McElduff,
both of whom were still unconscious. At the same instant, however,
Hugh made three far less positive discoveries: his abdomen felt as

though he'd been hit with a sledgehammer, he was swallowing oily seawater, and his legs had gone from merely numb to paralyzed. His kapok life jacket did not have enough buoyancy to keep him and the two others afloat if he could not also kick, and Hugh was fighting to keep his head above water. All three men were in imminent danger of sinking, and there was only one thing Hugh could do. Briefly releasing his grip on McElduff, he reached down and struggled to unfasten his pistol belt but retained the sheath knife attached to his uniform belt. He hated to discard the .45 and the pouches of survival supplies attached to the web belt, but he thought that getting rid of even that much weight might help keep him and the two sailors from going under.

And he was right. As the belt dropped away Hugh rose a little higher in the water, and he reached out to renew his grasp on McElduff's collar. Slowly easing himself backward until he was floating with his legs outstretched, Hugh did his best to pull the two sailors into the same position on either side of him. He concentrated on trying to move his legs, and after a few minutes of painful effort the still-numb limbs responded. Hugh began kicking gingerly, heading toward the sounds of men yelling that they had room on their floater net. The sudden burst of a Japanese star shell overhead revealed the refuge—essentially a cargo net with spools of buoyant cork on all the strands of rope—to be barely fifty feet away, though Hugh's internal injuries and the swells through which he was moving himself and the two sailors ensured that covering the relatively short distance became an exhausting ordeal.[8]

By the time helping hands began pulling the three men onto the floater, Hugh was physically drained and wracked by such savage abdominal pain that he was writhing in agony, moaning out loud, and teetering on the edge of consciousness. As his vision dimmed he saw Milt Hackett leaning toward him, a morphine syrette in his hand. Hugh barely felt the prick of the short needle as it slid into the skin of his upper arm, and seconds later he sensed himself hurtling headfirst into a deep, dark, and very quiet hole.[9]

When *Strong* broke up three of the officers who had aided in the evacuation to *Chevalier*—Milt Hackett, Fred Purdy, and Jack

Howard—were still in the vicinity of Mount 51. As the ship lurched Howard yelled, "Here she goes, jump!" But there was no need to leap, because the destroyer sank out from beneath the men.

Hackett was initially pulled down by the suction, but fought his way back to the surface and found himself just feet from a floater net. Though not as good as one of the destroyer's balsa wood and canvas life rafts—occupants of a floater had to lie prone and were constantly immersed in water—the net was buoyant enough to support a dozen men and was better than remaining in the open sea. That was especially true in Hackett's case, for he had just pulled himself onto the net when *Strong*'s depth charges began detonating. Though shaken by the blasts, he was not injured, and he began calling out to other men in the water. Over the following minutes he pulled several individuals onto the floater—including Hugh, Deering, and McElduff—but was deeply concerned when he saw no trace of Purdy or Howard.[10]

Nor did Hackett see Don Regan, who had been yanked over the side when *Chevalier* pulled away from *Strong*. The torpedo officer needn't have worried about his younger colleague, however. Regan and Seaman 1st Class Jewell Garret, the sailor who had been crossing to the rescue vessel when it backed off, both ended up hanging from one of the lines that had briefly connected the two destroyers. The line did not immediately snap, and when Regan looked down he saw *Strong*'s undamaged captain's gig floating nearby. He and Garrett dropped into the water and swam to the twenty-six-foot whaleboat. Hampered by his injured hip, Regan had to be helped aboard by the young sailor. Once they got the motor started they began crisscrossing the flotsam-covered waters above *Strong*'s final resting place, picking up as many survivors as the boat could hold.[11]

One person not pulled aboard the captain's gig, however, was the sunken destroyer's captain himself. Soon after Wellings and Rodrigos had stepped into the sea from *Strong*'s starboard bridge wing and begun swimming away from the doomed vessel, the first depth charge went off. The two men were on the same side of the ship as the explosion but more than four hundred feet from the point of detonation and on their backs. They were not killed, though both suffered significant immersion-blast injuries and Wellings was knocked unconscious. When he came to several minutes later, he was being helped onto an empty floater net by the man he later described as his "loyal and efficient quartermaster," Rodrigos.[12]

It is unclear how many *Strong* crew members climbed onto or were pulled aboard floater nets, life rafts, the motor whaleboat, or pieces of buoyant wreckage. We do know with certainty, however, that for many—Hugh Miller foremost among them—the ordeal was just beginning.

And they were on their own.

IN SENDING *O'BANNON* AND *CHEVALIER* TO *STRONG*'S AID, AINSWORTH had kept the promise he'd made to all his destroyer captains that he would send help if they got into trouble. But as task group commander the admiral also had to consider the safety of his other ships. He assumed that *Strong* had been hit by a submarine-launched torpedo and had no desire to expose his flotilla any longer than was absolutely necessary to the possibility of a second attack. After telling the captains of both *Chevalier* and *O'Bannon* to take their time and "get everybody" off the sinking destroyer, he directed them to rejoin the task group "outside"—meaning back in the Slot. Ainsworth's assumption that Japanese subs were lurking nearby seemed to be validated minutes later when *Radford*—one of the Destroyer Division 23 vessels supporting the Rice Anchorage landings—reported a sonar contact that was presumed to be a submarine and moved in to drop depth charges. Yet even then the task group commander was thinking of his "boys"; as *Nicholas* and the cruisers raced northeast at twenty knots, Ainsworth notified DesRon 23's Commander John Higgins aboard *Gwin* that *Strong* had been torpedoed and was sinking and directed him to have his ships make a final sweep for survivors before they departed the gulf.[13]

At roughly the same time that radio exchange was taking place, it began to look as though a second destroyer might be in danger of sinking in Kula Gulf. While the valiant actions of Eph McLean and his men had led to the rescue of the majority of *Strong*'s crew, *Chevalier* had not gotten away unscathed. Its bow had been mangled by the intentional collision with *Strong*, the explosion of a jammed 5-inch/.38 round had demolished its Mount 53, and the string of Japanese bombs that fell astern of it as it was backing away from the sinking ship had caused further damage. Then, as if it had not absorbed enough punishment, *Chevalier* was severely buffeted by the same depth-charge explosions that ravaged the *Strong* crewmen in the water.[14] The rescue vessel's bow was lifted by the detonations, then settled down again with a heavy shudder. All of *Chevalier*'s electronics—radar, sonar, and radios—went dead, and minor flooding was reported in several lower spaces. The destroyer's engines were unharmed, however, and McLean determined that, given the damage his ship had sustained, the fact that it was fully illuminated by star shells and that the fire from the Japanese shore batteries on Kolombangara and Enogai was becoming dangerously accurate, it was time for *Chevalier* to leave.

At 1:27 a.m. McLean radioed Ainsworth with a report of the damage and said he was going to retire from the scene. *Chevalier* then turned to the northeast with *O'Bannon* in trail, and as the two destroyers built up speed they passed small groups of survivors in the water. Though it went against everything they believed in as Navy officers, McLean and MacDonald could not stop to pick up the men—in the savage calculus of war the tactical situation in Kula Gulf had changed significantly in the time that had elapsed since *Strong* was hit, and the chance of saving a few additional men was no longer worth risking further damage to, or especially the loss of, either one of the withdrawing destroyers. But they did what they could; as the ships sailed past Rice Anchorage, both captains repeated Ainsworth's request that the vessels of DesRon 23 pick up any survivors they might find. Then *Chevalier* and *O'Bannon* raced to rejoin the rest of TG 36.1.[15]

As soon as *Nicholas* and the three cruisers had emerged from Kula Gulf, Ainsworth had ordered a turn to the northwest, intending to conduct a radar sweep of the waters immediately north of Kolombangara. By this point, however, Kanaoka's four Rat Express destroyers were well on their way back to the Shortlands and beyond the range of TG 36.1's radars. Seeing no targets for his ships' guns, Ainsworth ordered the task group to reverse course and head back down the Slot.

As the formation steamed past the entrance to Kula Gulf, *Chevalier* and *O'Bannon* emerged and took up their usual screening positions, though *Chevalier*—its decks packed with *Strong* survivors—was soon having difficulty keeping up. At about dawn the destroyer *Jenkins* joined the group, and Ainsworth directed its captain to escort the heavily laden and limping *Chevalier* the remainder of the distance to Tulagi. The rest of TG 36.1 plowed on, bound for Santo—though a change of orders would soon send them back for what would turn out to be yet another disastrous night in Kula Gulf.[16]

By 9:30 in the morning on July 5, the 234 sailors and 7 officers McLean and his crew had rescued from *Strong* were disembarking from *Chevalier* into the landing craft that would carry them the final few hundred feet to the beach, where trucks and ambulances waited to take them for medical examinations and debriefings. And one of the key questions the survivors would be asked was, "What happened to the others?"

AFTER WELLINGS AND RODRIGOS CLAMBERED ONTO THE FLOATER net, they spent several minutes catching their breath and taking stock of their injuries. Both men had taken "a terrific beating," as Wellings later wrote, though the exploding depth charges seemed to have been harder on him than on his chief quartermaster.[17]

The two men determined that making for Rice Anchorage was their only hope and began trying to paddle the floater in that direction. Over the next few hours they didn't get far, though they did manage to take aboard three other survivors: Ensign Keith Sherlie, Machinist's Mate 1st Class Melvin Du Bard, and Seaman 1st Class Edward Rock. All three of the new arrivals were slightly injured but in good spirits, and Wellings was delighted when Sherlie produced a watertight bag containing all of the ship's pay lists. The young officer's foresight would allow *Strong*'s survivors to be paid as soon as they reached safety without having to wait for the reconstruction of their pay records. That was, of course, assuming Sherlie and the four others managed to survive themselves.

The men were paddling in the direction of Rice Anchorage, but the current was against them and they weren't making any headway. They could see the destroyers supporting the landings firing at the Japanese shore batteries, and as Wellings later recalled he knew they had to attract the American ships' attention before the vessels withdrew from the gulf. One of the sailors they'd pulled from the water had a working flashlight, so the men in the boat took turns signaling toward Rice Anchorage. They got no response until they'd drifted to within a mile of Visuvisu Point, when an American destroyer suddenly loomed up ahead, coming straight at them. The men signaled wildly with the flashlight and broke out in cheers when they realized the warship was slowing and putting nets over the side.[18]

The rescue ship was *Gwin* of DesRon 23, and by the time it had the floater safely alongside Wellings was so weak that Du Bard had to carry him up the cargo net. *Strong*'s former captain was rushed to the destroyer's wardroom, where *Gwin*'s medical officer gave him morphine and two units of blood plasma. The ship then got under way and accelerated toward the Slot and, ultimately, Guadalcanal.

Wellings and his companions were lucky to have been spotted and taken aboard by *Gwin*—it and the other vessels of the Rice Anchorage support force had orders to be out of Kula Gulf by 6:00 a.m. Even more fortunate, however, were Regan and those with him in *Strong*'s gig. He and Garret had picked up sixteen other survivors and then set off for Rice Anchorage. Regan determined that rather than run the risk of having the U.S. warships mistake the crowded gig for a Japanese torpedo boat or barge, the wiser course of action was to make for Visuvisu Point and attempt to signal the friendly vessels as they departed the gulf. He and the others quite possibly passed the floater carrying Wellings and the others without seeing it, for the gig was well out into the Slot when, at 7:05, Garret spotted a U.S. destroyer coming up astern. One of the men quickly broke out the semaphore flags carried in the boat and signaled the ship, which turned out to be *Ralph Talbot*. The destroyer hove to, took Regan and the other survivors aboard, and then shaped a course for Koli Point on Guadalcanal.[19]

AFTER INJECTING HUGH MILLER WITH MORPHINE, MILT HACKETT carefully took stock of the situation aboard the floater net. In addition to himself and Hugh, there were five other men—Deering, McElduff, Yeoman 1st Class Lewis Summers, Seaman 1st Class Robert E. Moeller, and Metalsmith 2nd Class Frank Alby. Hackett alone was uninjured, though after regaining consciousness McElduff appeared to be less seriously hurt than he'd first appeared. The others had a variety of major injuries and were either unconscious or delirious, and everyone on the net was covered with fuel oil. Though Hugh was the senior man, he was obviously in no condition to make decisions, so Hackett took command.

While the net was not the ideal "vessel" on which to drift about in the open sea, it was not entirely without its benefits. Attached to several of the floats were circular metal cans, twelve inches in diameter and fourteen inches long, that were watertight and had screw tops. Inside each can was a compass and several signaling mirrors; such emergency rations as cans of fresh water and tins of meat, hard crackers, chocolate bars, and malt balls; and small first-aid kits that included bandages, salves for burns, and the morphine syrettes.

Given their precarious circumstances and the threat of being spotted by the Japanese, Hackett undertook his inventory in the dark with only the occasional flare of a star shell for illumination. These sporadic bursts of ghostly light also revealed other survivors nearby, and in the hours following *Strong*'s sinking Hackett and his group were joined by sixteen men on two other nets and two damaged rafts. Among the new arrivals were badly injured Al Oberg and slightly burned Jack Fulham, Hackett's shipboard roommate, who paddled up wearing a kapok life jacket and pushing a piece of wooden wreckage bearing Officer's Cook 2nd Class Ezra Sisson, who had a horribly mangled leg.[20]

With Hugh still unconscious Hackett remained the senior man in the now expanded group of twenty-three survivors. All but five were injured, and it seemed obvious to the young officer that several would die without immediate medical attention—which would be available only from the ships supporting the Rice Anchorage landing. Hackett knew the troop transports and their escorts would be leaving Kula

Gulf before first light and decided that the only hope for all of the survivors was to send the uninjured men for help. At about three in the morning he ordered four sailors—Motor Machinist's Mate 1st Class Richard Shepard, Fireman 3rd Class Gilbert Salter, and Seamen 1st Class Ephrain Bird and Robert Eudy—and Jack Fulham to join him in the least damaged raft. Hackett used one of the compasses to establish a bearing toward Rice Anchorage, some ten miles to the east, and he and the others then set off.

Within minutes Hackett realized they had no chance of intercepting the ships of the landing force before they left the gulf and determined that the only possible course of action was to try to reach the U.S. troops ashore. With only two paddles shared among the six men, the raft's progress was painfully slow, and a freshening wind and increasing swells weren't helping either. After more than an hour of strenuous effort the raft had traveled less than a mile from the floater nets—which were invisible in the dark—and Hackett was rethinking the wisdom of attempting to paddle across the gulf when he and the others on the raft heard what sounded like the motor of a small boat. Their spirits soared at this apparent sign of imminent rescue, but their joy turned to panic when they realized that the boat was approaching from the direction of Japanese-held Kolombangara. Hackett ordered everyone into the water, where the men clung to the sides of the raft as they strained to make out whether the approaching craft was friend or foe.

The answer wasn't long in coming. Not having seen the raft or the men in the water next to it, the power boat surged past, and a machine gun mounted on the craft's bow opened fire. Tracer rounds arced off in what seemed from Hackett's perspective to be the direction of the floater nets. The Americans were sure that the men they had left aboard the nets not long before had just been killed and fully expected the enemy boat to circle back and finish them off as well. To their intense relief the craft did not return, instead increasing speed and heading back in the direction from which it had come.

After remaining in the water a few minutes longer to make sure the threat had actually disappeared, Hackett and the others hauled themselves back aboard the raft. Using the two paddles and their hands, they resumed the arduous voyage toward Rice Anchorage, happy to

be alive but seething with anger over the apparent cold-blooded mur-
der of their injured and helpless shipmates.[21]

WHOEVER THE JAPANESE HAD BEEN SHOOTING AT, IT WASN'T HUGH
Miller and the men huddled around him.

That the enemy did not have the opportunity to machine-gun the
grouped floater nets and remaining life raft was likely the result of
several factors. First, once TG 36.1 had left Kula Gulf, the Japanese
had stopped firing star shells, and the resultant stygian darkness had
helped conceal from the enemy's view many—though not all—of
those who went into the water following *Strong*'s demise. Second, the
nets and raft rode very low in the water, making them difficult to see,
especially since while searching for targets the crew of the Japanese
boat had used only a small flashlight rather than a spotlight for fear
of attracting the potentially lethal attention of an orbiting Black Cat.
Third, the currents in Kula Gulf are relatively strong and fast, meaning that most anything that floated off the sinking destroyer would
have quickly been carried away from the spot where it went down.
And fourth, there is the factor that no one in war ever discounts—
sheer dumb luck.

Whatever the reason, Hugh and the others with him went unnoticed by the Japanese, and by dawn on July 5 the connected floaters
and raft had drifted many miles to the north. The men could occasionally make out the towering form of the extinct volcano that was
Kolombangara's dominant feature, but no amount of paddling would
have changed the course of the heavy, low-lying nets—even if the men
had wanted to make landfall on the enemy-held island. As the day
wore on it seemed as though the group would be swept even farther
north, perhaps even out into the Slot, but again caught in a powerful
current they were pulled back to the southeast.

At some point during the night Hugh had regained consciousness.
He'd woken up vomiting a mixture of fuel oil and seawater, and his
abdomen was painfully distended. He was passing small amounts of
blood from his rectum, and finding it difficult to breathe he rightly
assumed that the concussion of the exploding depth charges had dam-

aged his lungs and diaphragm. But Hugh quickly became aware that there were others aboard the nets and raft in even worse shape. Deering, Oberg, Summers, and Alby were all ashen gray and apparently comatose; Sisson's leg had been almost completely severed (though a tourniquet, likely applied by Fulham, had kept the man from bleeding out); and several men were continually vomiting gouts of tarry blood. But the worst off, perhaps, was twenty-one-year-old Bobby Moeller. The young seaman had been extremely close to one of the detonating depth charges, and his internal injuries were so extensive and so immensely painful that he could not keep himself from screaming—when he stopped to draw what breath he could, he would tearfully apologize, then begin shrieking anew.

Hugh realized, as Hackett had, that the only chance of survival for the injured men around him—and in all likelihood for himself—was immediate medical attention. And, like Hackett, Hugh understood that their only hope was to send some men ashore to make contact with the U.S. forces at Rice Anchorage. While the remaining raft was in bad shape, it might still make it to the beach, but who to crew it? The healthiest of the survivors had departed with Hackett; those left were all injured to some extent, and the trip to New Georgia would be a grueling one. In the end, Hugh tapped McElduff and one other man for the mission. The pair took to the raft in midmorning, struggling mightily to keep the damaged balsa wood and canvas craft heading in the right direction despite their injuries and the strong current.

The raft's departure left Hugh and fourteen others on the floater nets. Every one of the men was suffering from internal injuries caused by the depth charges, and several—most notably Sisson—also had severely damaged limbs. And as if their injuries weren't enough for the men to contend with, by midday on July 5 the previous night's clouds and rain squalls had given way to oppressive heat and piercingly bright sunshine. The nets and those on them were still covered in fuel oil, which in the harsh light turned to the consistency of tar. Scrape as the men might, they could not get the congealed oil off their skin or out of their hair. The heat also increased their thirst, and Hugh had to institute a rationing system to preserve their limited supply of fresh water—one mouthful per man every two hours. There was no need to similarly apportion the emergency rations, however, since most of the men—Hugh included—could not keep anything solid down.

Like several of his companions, Hugh slipped in and out of consciousness for most of the day. He also passed more blood, and his breathing was still labored. By the time darkness fell on July 5, he was starting to think that he might not make it through the night and was surprised when he awoke hours later with the morning sun on his face. Summers was not so lucky, however. He had never regained consciousness, and as the occupants of the nets began to stir they realized the young sailor had died during the night. Hugh felt that it was his responsibility to somehow mark the man's passing; after asking for a moment of silence—a request that was more easily fulfilled now that Moeller had lost consciousness and was ominously quiet—Hugh spoke the words of the Lord's Prayer as best he could given the damage to his lungs and diaphragm. Then several of the men removed Summers's life jacket and pushed the body over the side.[22]

The impromptu burial at sea cast an understandable pall over those on the nets who were still conscious. In pain, constantly wet, their exposed skin broiled by the sun, the men had little to do but contemplate the odds of their own survival. Hugh and the others must each have wondered which of them would be the next to be consigned to the waters of Kula Gulf, and the coming of night—the second they would spent adrift—would only have sharpened their anxiety, for they all knew that the enemy preferred to operate under the cover of darkness.

Then, just before two in the morning, it must have seemed that their worst fears were about to become reality. A deep rumble from somewhere to the north sounded at first like the engines of a large vessel coming their way but then, a few anxious seconds later, resolved into the unmistakable sound of large-caliber guns firing from the direction of the Slot. Barely had that realization dawned when a series of detonations lit up the sky just over the horizon in the direction of Kolombangara.

There would indeed be dead men in Kula Gulf that night, but they wouldn't come from the floater nets.

CAPTAIN KUNIZO KANAOKA'S DECISION TO ABANDON THE REIN-
forcement mission to Vila in the early hours of July 5 had been entirely
correct given the circumstances. By reversing course the commander
of Destroyer Division 22 had saved his four Rat Express ships and the
troops packed aboard them from a probable mauling by the American
vessels detected by *Niizuki*'s radar, and he believed that his parting
shot with Long Lances had sunk an enemy cruiser and destroyer.[23]

But as prudent as Kanaoka's withdrawal from Kula Gulf had been,
it also meant that the troops and equipment bound for Kolombangara
had not reached their destination. That delay could well have serious
consequences for the Japanese defense of the newly contested area
around Rice Anchorage or, more important, of Munda—the obvious
next target of an American landing. So, almost as soon as *Niizuki* and
the other three destroyers dropped anchor at Buin in the Shortlands
on the morning following the encounter with Ainsworth's TG 36.1,
Rear Admiral Teruo Akiyama announced to his subordinates that another Rat Express would sail that very night. While the mission was
to be the same—carrying troops and equipment to Vila for onward
movement by barge and landing craft—Akiyama intended it to be a
much larger effort, involving ten destroyers divided into three sections. The admiral himself would be in overall command aboard Kaneda's *Niizuki*, which with *Suzukaze* and *Tanikaze* would form the
Support Unit that would screen and, if necessary, defend the ships of
the First and Second Transport Units. The former would consist of
the destroyers *Hamakaze*, *Mikazuki*, and *Mochizuki* and the latter of
Amagiri, *Hatsuyuki*, *Nagatsuki*, and *Satsuki*. Between them the seven
transports would embark some twenty-four hundred troops and 180
tons of ammunition, food, and medical supplies.

The Reinforcement Group, as Akiyama's combined armada was
designated, sortied from Buin at 5:00 on the afternoon of July 5. The
ships followed the usual route for the first leg of the 165-mile trip to
Vila, staying close to the south coast of Choiseul Island. Shrouded by
darkness and developing rainstorms, the Japanese ships were not detected by the Black Cats that routinely patrolled the northern reaches
of the Slot, nor did Allied coastwatchers on the various islands catch
sight of the passing destroyers. The fact that Akiyama's convoy was

not spotted on its way to Kolombangara ultimately was of little import, however, for intelligence analysts on Admiral William Halsey's staff in Nouméa had assumed that the Japanese would of necessity run a large "Vila Express" as soon as one could be assembled. This assumption, and Halsey's decision to act on it, resulted in the message sent to Ainsworth as he was leading TG 36.1 back to Santo.

Received aboard *Honolulu* at about 3:00 p.m., the transmission directed Ainsworth to take his task group back to Kula Gulf to intercept an expected Japanese reinforcement attempt. The message also informed Ainsworth that the destroyers *Jenkins* and *Radford*—both then in Tulagi—would replace the sunken *Strong* and damaged *Chevalier*. Because TG 36.1 was at that moment southeast of Guadalcanal in the Solomon Sea, Ainsworth ordered an arcing turn to the north into Indispensable Strait and then west into the Slot. This maneuver accomplished the necessary course reversal while also allowing *Jenkins* and *Radford* to join the armada as it steamed between Santa Isabel and the most northerly of the Florida Islands.

By the time the American task group reached the area just to the north of Visuvisu Point, the Japanese Reinforcement Group had entered the northern end of Kula Gulf and was steaming south in column. At 12:26 a.m. Akiyama ordered the three ships of the First Transport Unit to sheer off toward the southeast coast of Kolombangara for the final run to Vila. The remaining destroyers continued south, and at 1:06 a.m. *Niizuki*'s radar detected several large vessels moving from east to west across the top of the gulf. Thirteen minutes later the Japanese column reversed course and headed north, and at 1:43 the Second Transport Unit also headed toward Vila to offload. The three destroyers of the Support Unit continued north with *Niizuki* in the lead, its radar operators still trying to determine how much of a threat the unidentified ships presented. Minutes later Akiyama recalled the Second Transport Unit, having decided that even heavily laden with troops the four destroyers would be needed if a fight developed.

Barely thirteen miles to the north the ships of TG 36.1 had already moved from cruising formation into battle array. *Honolulu*'s Sugar George radar had initially detected the Japanese ships at 1:36, and within minutes Ainsworth realized he was dealing with more than one group of enemy vessels. Several course changes brought the American cruisers and destroyers into optimum position, and at 1:57 the first 5- and 6-inch rounds shrieked toward the enemy. Their targets were the three destroyers of the Support Unit, now less than four miles away and turning in to attack.

It is one of those ironies of war that destruction came to *Niizuki* as suddenly and unexpectedly as it had to *Strong*. Mere seconds after Akiyama, Kaneda, and those with them on the destroyer's bridge saw the flash of the enemy's guns, the men were dead, blown apart by the same American salvo that instantly reduced their once-proud vessel to a mass of twisted steel. Pounded by more than a dozen high-explosive shells, *Niizuki* immediately lost steerage and went dead in the water as fires broke out both above and belowdecks. Though its death throes were eerily similar to *Strong*'s—as it went down, secondary explosions from detonating ammunition, rather than depth charges, filled the air with shrapnel—the end result for *Niizuki* was far worse than for the American destroyer it had helped to sink. While most of *Strong*'s crew survived, all but a handful of the 300 officers and men aboard the Japanese vessel perished.

The fight at the top of Kula Gulf was not one-sided, however. Even as *Niizuki* was dying, the other two ships of the Support Unit— *Suzukaze* and *Tanikaze*—launched swarms of Long Lances toward the American warships. Though most missed, three slammed into *Helena* within the space of less than four minutes, blowing off the bow, knocking out the propulsion and steering, and breaking its back amidships. The cruiser slowly jackknifed, with the after part of the hull rising almost to the vertical and what was left of the forward section assuming a forty-five-degree angle. Less than twenty-five minutes after the first hit, *Helena* disappeared beneath the oil-covered water.

The main part of the Battle of Kula Gulf, as the engagement came to be known in American naval history, lasted less than forty minutes but was significant in several ways. The sinking of *Helena* was a blow to the Americans, of course, but TG 36.1 had largely succeeded in its assigned task of preventing the Japanese from landing reinforcements at Vila. Barely 850 of the 2,400 embarked troops and only about a third of the ammunition and supplies had been put ashore before the captains of the surviving Rat Express ships had chosen discretion over valor and headed back to Buin. *Niizuki*—the most advanced Japanese warship in the Solomons—had been sent to the bottom, taking with it several hundred men and two of the most capable destroyer commanders in the IJN, Kaneda and Akiyama. And, finally, *Nagatsuki* had run hard aground during the night battle and was located and destroyed by American aircraft the following day.[24]

WITHIN MINUTES OF REALIZING THAT *HELENA* HAD GONE DOWN, Ainsworth ordered *Nicholas* and *Radford* to search for survivors. The two ships recovered the majority of those who had lived through the cruiser's sinking, though the return of Japanese destroyers to the area in the early hours of July 7 ultimately forced the American warships to suspend their search and head down the Slot. Before departing, however, *Nicholas* and *Radford* put volunteer-manned whaleboats into the water to continue the hunt for survivors. This effort was supplemented by the dropping of life rafts and life jackets by aircraft and by the individual heroism of many of *Helena*'s crew. With the final recovery of men cast away on Vella Lavella and other islands, all but 168 of the cruiser's 1,188-man complement were rescued.[25] As comprehensive as the *Helena* rescue effort was, however, it was of no aid to those *Strong* survivors not picked up by *Chevalier*, *Gwin*, or *Ralph Talbot*. The cruiser had gone down at the "top end" of Kula Gulf, far to the northwest of *Strong*'s final resting place.

That said, some members of the sunken destroyer's crew had managed to make their way ashore even before *Helena* met its end. Hackett, Fulham, and their companions, for example, had landed on the coast of New Georgia on the afternoon of July 5. They were befriended by natives, ultimately joined up with U.S. forces at Rice Anchorage, and were finally evacuated to Tulagi aboard the destroyer *Crosby*. On July 6 a quintet of *Strong* survivors also washed up on New Georgia, though they did not encounter the Hackett group. The five—enlisted sailors Garold Ballenger, William Gardener, Robert Gregory, Clell Kimball, and Frank Wolter—were also ultimately able to locate an

American unit with the help of local guides, but not before making a grisly discovery.

While out searching for fresh water, Gardner and Gregory discovered the decomposing body of Fred Purdy lying facedown on the beach. *Strong*'s executive officer had not simply washed ashore; tracks in the sand indicated that he had been able to crawl out of the water and up past the surf line. The body was wearing a torn life jacket and was covered with oil, but there was no immediate indication of the cause of death. A closer look at the tear in Purdy's life jacket revealed that it had been caused by a piece of shrapnel—or perhaps by a Japanese machine-gun bullet. The two young sailors carefully went through Purdy's pockets, removing his wallet and identification card, which they carried back to camp and presented to Wolter, the senior man among them. He was later able to turn the effects over to an Army chaplain at Rice Anchorage.[26]

A less tragic outcome awaited two other *Strong* crewmen, Siggy Butler—the radar operator who first detected the submarine *RO-34* on April 5—and Fireman 1st Class Robert McGee, who engineered both their own rescue and that of a downed Army pilot. When their ship went down the sailors had ended up in a raft, in which they spent four days adrift in the gulf. They eventually washed ashore on New Georgia, north of Rice Anchorage, and though both men were suffering from immersion-blast injuries and severe oil ingestion, they were able to spend a few hours each day foraging in the heavy jungle for food and fresh water while avoiding Japanese patrols. During one such foray, on July 13, the young sailors were startled when a voice emanating from a nearby thicket whispered, "Hey, you Americans!" Seconds later a tall, lanky Caucasian man wearing a torn flight suit limped slowly into view.

The apparition turned out to be an Army Air Forces pilot, twenty-five-year-old 1st Lieutenant Edward B. Whitman Jr. of the Guadalcanal-based 339th Fighter Squadron. Two days earlier he had been part of a combat air patrol over Rendova when he and fellow aviators engaged a force of twenty Zeroes. Whitman was able to down one of the enemy aircraft before his P-39 Airacobra was disabled by 20mm fire and he was forced to bail out. When his parachute opened, his harness snapped against his face, fracturing several bones in his right cheek. Worse was to come: Whitman's parachute snagged the top of a one-hundred-foot tree, and he had to cut himself free from his harness and begin climbing downward. While still some twenty-five feet above the jungle floor Whitman slipped and fell, breaking his left arm. He'd spent two nights in the jungle eluding Japanese search parties before hearing a whispered conversation between McGee and Butler and, taking a chance, revealed himself to them.

As Whitman later wrote in a letter to Gus Wellings:

> *The two lads from [your] ship, Butler and McGee, fell to with a will and did everything possible to ease my pain and gave me what little rations they had managed to get from an abandoned Army rubber landing boat. Both were in poor physical condition from having swallowed large quantities of oil while in the water after their ship went down. . . . Despite his weakened physical condition, not once did I hear [Butler] complain or express any other opinions than that he was planning to keep going until we were picked up or he passed out. . . . McGee grew noticeably weaker, as did Butler, but [he] refused to allow himself to be dominated by this physical weakness, and through sheer willpower did all the work necessary . . . and generally maintaining an extremely high state of morale.*[27]

Butler's determination and refusal to give up ultimately saved all three of the men. In order to avoid Japanese patrols they rowed the recovered rubber boat out into Kula Gulf, paddled south toward Bairoko Harbor, and on July 15 were rescued by Marines in a landing craft. As Whitman summed up in his letter to Wellings, Butler's actions during the ordeal in the New Georgia jungle "left only the deepest admiration and respect in my mind for this sailor which will never leave me as long as I live. I do not feel that it is possible to commend him too highly. His conduct and behavior were in the highest traditions of the armed forces of the United States."[28]

Whitman's letter, in addition to a later corroborating statement by McGee, led Wellings to recommend that Butler be awarded the Navy Cross for his actions while cast away on New Georgia. In the end, the intrepid Butler received the Navy and Marine Corps Medal in recognition for his valor and "heroic conduct" during the eleven days that he spent adrift and ashore before he and his companions were rescued.[29]

Yet another *Strong* survivor was soon to embark on an odyssey behind Japanese lines that would eclipse the eleven-day sojourn of McGee and Butler by more than a month.

THE FLURRY OF RESCUE ACTIVITY THAT FOLLOWED THE SINKING OF *Helena* did not, unfortunately, result in the recovery of Hugh Miller and the others with him. The men had consolidated on one floater following the departure of McElduff and his companion, hoping that they would reach friendly forces and spur a rescue attempt. But no friendly ships had steamed into view; no search aircraft had dropped supplies or lifeboats. It became clear to Hugh over the following days that neither of the two groups of men sent off toward Rice Anchorage in search of help had apparently succeeded in finding any. The logical assumption was that Hackett, McElduff, and the others had either been captured or killed by the Japanese before locating American forces.[30]

Nor did death ignore those aboard the floater net. Several men—Moeller, Alba, Sisson, and others whose names are unclear—succumbed in the days following the departure of McElduff and his companion. Hugh said the Lord's Prayer over each of the dead before their bodies were committed to the sea. By the night of July 8 the floater's occupants included just seven men out of the original twenty-three: Hugh, Oberg, Deering, Fireman 1st Class Francis Armbruster, Seaman 1st Class Floyd Lawrence, Seaman 1st Class Daniel Mullane, and another young sailor whose name has been lost to history. He, Oberg, and Deering were unconscious, and Hugh was still in bad shape. Though Armbruster, Lawrence, and Mullane were also suffering from oil ingestion, they were in better condition.

Drifting in the darkness, the floater rising and falling on the swells, Hugh and the three conscious sailors all must have realized that they and the others were doomed if rescue did not come soon. Though emergency rations remained—oil in one's stomach greatly reduces appetite—water was by now in desperately short supply. As the senior man Hugh keenly felt his responsibility for the others' welfare, yet what more could he possibly do? They had no way to maneuver the unwieldy floater net, nor was there any way to attract the attention of friendly forces. They were, in the end, utterly and completely at the mercy of the sea.

And then, just after midnight on July 8, the sea saved them.

7

CAST UPON A HOSTILE SHORE

Hugh Miller wasn't sure what woke him up. He'd been asleep—or, more likely, unconscious—for several hours. Then something, the sound of waves on a beach or of palm fronds rustling in the wind or the earthy smell of rotting vegetation, roused him, and despite the inky darkness he knew there was land nearby. Struggling against the pain that throbbed in his abdomen and the nausea that engulfed him whenever he tried to sit up, he reached out to wake Armbruster, Lawrence, and Mullane.[1]

Though each was suffering from oil ingestion, sunburn, and dehydration, the three young sailors were the only ones on the floater capable of any real physical activity. At Hugh's command they went overboard and, finding that they were able to touch bottom with their feet, pulled and pushed the floater net and its cargo of injured men toward the sound of breaking waves. In the early minutes of July 9 the net grounded not on a sandy beach, but against the side of a large mangrove tree standing in a foot of brackish water atop a narrow reef separated from a larger island by a lagoon. The tree might not have been the ideal landing place, but it was a better refuge than a constantly drifting net. Not wishing to cross the lagoon in the dark, Hugh directed Armbruster, Lawrence, and Mullane to secure the floater to the tree with a length of line. That done, the sailors began hefting the injured onto the mangrove's broad and sturdy branches, lashing the men in place with more line. Sadly, as they were preparing to move the young man whose name no one knew, they realized he had died sometime during the night. Not knowing if there was sufficient earth nearby in which to bury him, Hugh issued the by now all too sadly familiar order to remove his life jacket and commit him to the sea. Within moments the body was taken by the currents and disappeared into the darkness.

As tragic as the sailor's death was—he'd passed away just when it seemed that those on the floater might have found safe haven—Hugh had to concentrate on saving the living. Once all the survivors were ensconced in the spreading mangrove and the floater net had been attached to its trunk, he told those who were conscious to settle in for the night and get what sleep they could. When the sun rose they would explore their new home.

THOUGH IT WOULD BE SEVERAL HOURS BEFORE HUGH AND THE others realized it, the tree that had become their refuge sat on the southernmost tip of a small unnamed islet just off the northeastern shore of Arundel Island, barely seven miles southwest of where *Strong* went down.[2] Some sixty yards wide and about two hundred yards long, the islet was one of several separating Stima Lagoon from the open waters of Kula Gulf. Two miles to the east, across the northern end of Hathorn Sound, lay the western tip of New Georgia. Bairoko Harbor, which *Strong* had shelled right before its demise and was still held by the enemy, was a little more than five and a half miles directly east. More ominously, the Japanese complex at Vila-Stanmore was barely five miles to the northwest, just across Blackett Strait, the narrow waterway separating Kolombangara and Arundel.[3]

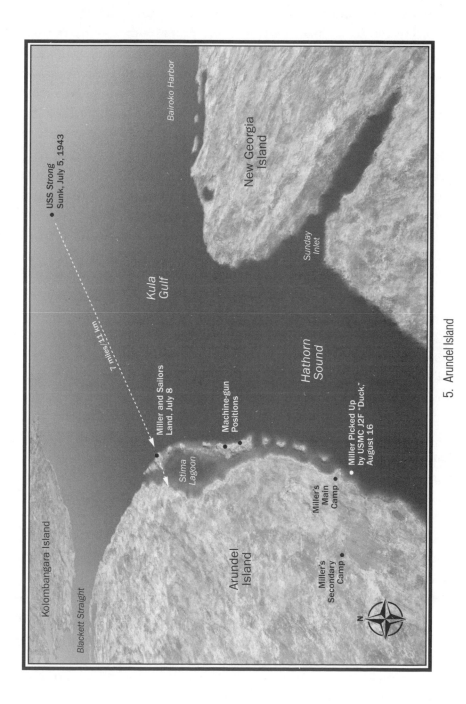

Bairoko Harbor

New Georgia
Island

Sunday
Inlet

USS *Strong*
Sunk, July 5, 1943

Kula
Gulf

Hathorn
Sound

7 miles/11 km

Miller and Sailors
Land, July 8

Machine-gun
Positions

Stima
Lagoon

Miller Picked Up
by USMC J2F "Duck,"
August 16

Miller's
Main
Camp

Miller's
Secondary
Camp

Arundel
Island

Kolombangara Island

Blackett Straight

N

5. Arundel Island

About eight hundred yards across at its widest point, Stima Lagoon was no deeper than six feet at any point, with a sandy bottom and relatively clear water. On its western side it lapped the shores of Arundel, a roughly kidney-shaped island some ten miles long and six miles wide. Its eastern shoreline was fringed by a reef on which were numerous islands and cays—including the one where Hugh and his companions rested in the mangrove tree—which extended south to Diamond Narrows, the channel separating Arundel and New Georgia at the southern end of Hathorn Sound. Of rough coral formation, Arundel was covered with red clay soil and was generally flat except for a few small hills and several coral depressions.[4]

Though mangroves ringed the island, its interior was jammed with wild brush and more orderly stands of coconut palms, the latter planted by Europeans following Arundel's absorption into the British Solomon Islands Protectorate after 1893.[5] The island's western side comprised the Kinda Plantation, while the Arundel (or Nauru) Plantation hugged the southeastern coast. Both estates produced coconuts whose meat was dried and exported as copra to Australia and elsewhere as a source of oil and animal feed. The plantations employed Melanesian laborers—often as little more than indentured servants—and were relatively profitable until the Europeans and most of the native population fled the island following the Japanese landings on Kolombangara in November 1942. That operation was part of the larger mission to seize New Georgia and establish the airfield at Munda, and though Arundel was initially left ungarrisoned it ultimately became a staging base for barges carrying Japanese troops and supplies from Vila to Rendova and Munda. By the time Hugh and his companions fetched up against the mangrove tree, elements of two Vila-based Imperial Japanese Army infantry regiments—the 13th and 229th—and troops of the 7th Yokosuka and 8th Combined Special Naval Landing Forces were based on Arundel.[6] In addition to dealing with the island's nearly incessant rainfall—one hundred to two hundred inches a year—the Japanese troops also had to contend with endemic malaria, dysentery, dengue fever, and a frightening array of fungal infections, all while staying alert for American activity in the southern end of Kula Gulf and in Hathorn Sound.[7]

While that mission might have seemed boring and routine to the Japanese on Arundel Island, they nonetheless carried it out as ordered. The troops established a string of heavily camouflaged observation positions along the island's east side and conducted frequent patrols along the narrow beaches facing New Georgia, searching for any sign of enemy activity. They apparently discovered the bodies of several dead members of *Strong*'s crew—and, possibly, captured men who'd made it ashore alive—and despite the tedium of their duty they kept their eyes open for the Allied invasion forces most must have known were coming.

It is therefore nearly miraculous that they *didn't* discover the small band of Americans lashed to the spreading mangrove.

WHEN DAWN BROKE ON JULY 9 HUGH AND THE OTHERS WERE ABLE to judge the true extent of the small islet. The tide had gone out, and the foot of brackish water that had covered the area immediately adjacent to the mangrove tree in which they'd spent the night had disappeared, revealing a surface of rough coral and pockets of brilliantly white sand. Looking north, the men could see that the islet widened out and grew more substantial, the mounds of brush that covered its surface interspersed with clumps of stunted coconut palms.

After moving Hugh, Oberg, and Deering to a drier sandy area, Armbruster, Lawrence, and Mullane went in search of fresh water. They slowly and carefully traversed the length of the islet, staying low to take advantage of what cover there was. Though they found no water, they did discover fallen coconuts, which they brought back to the group's new "camp." Hugh used his sheath knife to split the thick, fibrous husks and then pierced the nuts' small indented "eyes" so the men could drink the juice. Once the precious liquid was gone, Armbruster used the knife and a heavy piece of coral to crack the nuts open, revealing the rich white "meat" inside. He, Lawrence, and Mullane found the coconut flesh to be more appetizing and palatable than the dry emergency rations in the can attached to the floater net, though Hugh could keep nothing down but the juice. Oberg and Deering were still unconscious, and neither could be roused enough to take anything by mouth.[8]

Still suffering crippling intestinal pain and periods of unconscious-
ness, Hugh determined that the group would stay on their tiny island
for the time being, resting and trying to regain their strength. He and
the three relatively healthy young sailors spent the remainder of that
first day sleeping in what shade they could find, though the abundant
mosquitoes and sand fleas made deep slumber impossible. The insect
problem abated somewhat as darkness fell and an onshore breeze
kicked up, however, and the men drowsed as best they could.

As the night wore on Oberg came back to semiconsciousness,
moaning frequently and thrashing about, feverish and obviously in
intense pain. The young officer's abdomen was hugely distended, and
he was passing gouts of dark, tarry blood from his rectum. Hugh and
the others tried to make him comfortable and attempted to give him
coconut water, but Oberg's condition continued to worsen. Soon after dawn on July 10 *Strong*'s twenty-two-year-old assistant gunnery
officer died as so many of his contemporaries did, far from home and
with only a handful of shipmates to witness his passing. His body
was laid in a shallow grave scraped out by Armbruster and Mullane
using cut-down palm fronds as shovels, and Hugh said the Lord's
Prayer over his friend.[9]

Oberg's death and the steady worsening of Deering's condition
underscored the need for the small band of survivors to move on in
search of help. In the early afternoon Hugh directed the three sailors to
retrieve the floater net from the base of the mangrove tree, cut it down
to a more manageable size, and lash several coconuts to it alongside the
cans containing the emergency rations and what was left of the fresh
water. After dragging the net into Stima Lagoon, Armbruster and the
others carefully lifted Deering and Hugh aboard and then pulled the
unwieldy craft away from the islet. Mullane and Lawrence took up positions on the forward corners of the floater and used sections of palm
fronds as paddles, while at the rear of the net Hugh kicked weakly
with his legs. Armbruster, the largest and most physically capable of
the group, entwined one of his feet through the forward strands of the
net and swam forward, pulling the floater behind him.

The distance to Arundel was about five hundred yards, and though
the lagoon's waters were calm the mini voyage still took two hours.

During that time the floater and its occupants would have been clearly visible from the air or from shore, but their luck held and the men made it across without being spotted by the Japanese. Dragging the net up onto a narrow strip of beach, Armbruster, Mullane, and Lawrence carried Hugh and Deering into the cover of nearby scrub trees. The three then collected the watertight cans of fresh water and emergency rations and the coconuts they'd brought from the islet and stashed them near the two injured men. Not wanting to leave the floater for the enemy to find, the sailors rolled it up and carried it into the tree line. Then, at Hugh's direction, they used their palm-frond "paddles" to sweep the beach clean of their footprints and other signs.

The group had landed amid coconut palms of the former Arundel plantation, but no fallen nuts were evident close to the beach and Hugh sent the sailors in search of both those and fresh water. They returned fairly soon, saying they'd found a location that offered both, and once again Armbruster, Lawrence, and Mullane moved the two injured men and the group's meager supplies. The new spot was a small clearing several hundred yards from the beach, centered on a tiny freshwater spring. Nearby was a compact lean-to built of palm fronds, beneath which the men discovered a few rusted ration tins, two empty Japanese beer bottles, and a ragged blanket. While it was obvious that enemy patrols used the lean-to as a resting spot, Hugh's ability to "read" the bent branches, flattened grass, and other woodland signs—a skill he'd learned so many years before during his long expeditions in the woods with Uncle Jim—revealed that the shelter had been visited as recently as the day before. It was obvious that the survivors could not stay in the immediate vicinity, but Hugh didn't want them to get too far from the spring, either. Another brief reconnaissance by Armbruster and the others revealed a safer location about three hundred yards away, so after only a few hours at the first site the group moved on to the second.

The transfer to the new camp required two of the healthier sailors to carry Deering, whom they'd wrapped in the tattered blanket, while the third helped Hugh. He was having great difficulty walking—the pain in his gut forced him to move forward in an awkward hunch—and it took some time to reach the second site. It was a small clearing surrounded by fallen coconut logs and scrub brush, with standing trees providing overhead cover. As far as Hugh could tell in the fading light, it was an adequate place to spend a few days, far enough from the lean-to and the beach that a Japanese patrol would be unlikely to stumble upon it but with ready access to coconuts and the freshwater spring. After pulling together palm fronds as a bed for Deering, the others settled in for their first night on Arundel Island.

Having spent so much time in the woods as a child, Hugh was not daunted by the need to "sleep rough" on a tropical island. He made himself as comfortable as he could considering the still agonizing pain in his abdomen and turned his ear to the noises that seem to fill any tropical forest when darkness falls. Above the sound of cicadas he could discern the slight difference between the rustling of a passing lizard and the hurried scuttling of a rat. He could identify the soft fluttering in the trees above as the wings of bats setting out to feed and knew from the various croakings in the underbrush that several types of frogs and toads were nearby. Armbruster had spent much of his childhood in Florida hunting and fishing with his father and was also at ease with the sounds of the surrounding forest, as was Georgia farm boy Lawrence. Brooklyn-born and -raised Mullane, on the other hand, was most definitely out of his element, a confirmed big-city kid likely imagining a landscape filled with the venomous reptiles and insects, lurking carnivores, and other unnamed terrors that had populated the back-lot jungles depicted in the movie serials of his youth. He needn't have worried; other than the occasional scorpion or bad-tempered coconut crab, Arundel held few natural terrors.

But then there were the Japanese. During that first night on the island, Hugh and the others occasionally heard men moving through the underbrush, often no more than a hundred feet away. The enemy troops, engaged in regular patrols on established paths through the forest, did not seem concerned with noise discipline. Their voices carried easily to the ears of the hidden Americans, as did the tantalizing aroma of their cigarettes. Hugh decided that the soldiers had not yet found any sign of the rolled-up floater net—if they had, they'd be sweeping the area in force and with far greater determination—and he congratulated himself that after reaching the new camp site, he'd sent

Armbruster back to brush away any sign of their movement from the freshwater spring.

The night passed without incident, and on the morning of July 11 Hugh dispatched the three young sailors to the spring to fill the beer bottles and collect a few coconuts. Still suffering intensely, Hugh himself was barely able to move and could only lay on his bed of fronds and try not to cry aloud as wrenching intestinal spasms forced him to pass more dark, clotted blood. Just feet away Deering lay wrapped in the castoff Japanese blanket, his breathing shallow and labored and his face ashen gray and beaded with sweat. He had not regained consciousness, and the others had not been able to get any water into him. Though Hugh could not know the true extent of the man's injuries, it was all too obvious that Deering had been catastrophically traumatized by the detonating depth charges and was fading quickly. His condition continued to deteriorate throughout the two days the group spent at their concealed camp, and early on the morning of July 13 Hugh was awakened by Eddie's feeble voice calling, "Mr. Miller, Mr. Miller." Before Hugh could crawl across the few feet that separated them, Deering died.[10]

After saying the Lord's Prayer over the young man's shallow grave—scraped into the forest floor by Frank Armbruster using cut-down fronds—Hugh told the others that it was time they moved on. He explained that from looking at charts aboard *Strong* he knew that Hathorn Sound got so narrow at its southern end that it might be possible to cross from Arundel to New Georgia by simply wading across a few hundred feet of shallow water.[11] If that were possible, he said, they'd be that much closer to the U.S. forces in and around Munda, and their chances of being rescued would increase significantly. Armbruster, Lawrence, and Mullane were skeptical of the idea, however, pointing out that Hugh was not in any condition to walk the four or five miles through heavy foliage that would be necessary to reach the potential crossing point. Moreover, they argued, if such a place did exist, the Japanese would know of it too and would likely have it covered to prevent Allied forces from advancing across it from New Georgia.

Both arguments made sense, of course, but Hugh reminded the sailors that their current location was none too secure, either. They

knew the Japanese were active in the vicinity, and should enemy troops
find the rolled-up floater net or any other sign of the Americans' presence, there would be little chance of remaining undetected. Though
as an officer he could simply have ordered his young companions to
abide by his wishes, like any good leader Hugh knew that in many
perilous situations collective agreement yields better results than does
rigid adherence to military hierarchies. By explaining the situation as
he saw it with the polished persuasiveness of the attorney he'd once
been, Hugh convinced his companions that moving on was a better
idea than staying put. Moreover, he said, he was feeling better and
would have no trouble "going the distance" to the potential crossing
point—all he needed was a walking stick.

Hugh's insistence that his health was improving was disingenuous,
to say the least. In reality, he was unable to keep down any solid food,
was still passing blood, and was actually increasingly convinced that
without adequate medical attention, he would likely die within days.
His primary goal now was simply to get "his boys" as close to safety
as possible before he succumbed to his injuries. Hugh therefore determined to keep his worsening condition to himself as much as he could.
So, when the four men gathered their meager supplies and broke camp
on the afternoon of the thirteenth, he set off at the best pace he could
manage, relying on the walking stick Armbruster had cut for him.

Unfortunately, the trek south proved even more punishing for
Hugh than the sailors had predicted. The men obviously could not
walk along the shore for fear of being spotted by the Japanese, so they
stayed within the tree line. They had to climb over every toppled log
they encountered, as well as having to ford several small streams and
trudge across the occasional coral pit and stretch of swampy ground.
Though Hugh started the journey with resolve, the sailors soon were
helping him along, and by the time the sun went down the group had
traveled less than two miles. As the others made camp and gathered
coconuts, Hugh stood motionless, leaning heavily on his walking stick
and trying to catch his breath. He moved slowly to a fallen log and sat
down heavily; as he did so his guts heaved, and he involuntarily passed
a huge gout of blood, soaking the legs of his tattered trousers. Armbruster rushed to his side, leading him to a makeshift bed of leaves

and palm fronds and then helping him sip water from one of the beer bottles.

As he lay there, his head spinning, his pulse hammering in his ears, and his intestines convulsing, Hugh felt himself falling yet again into a dark and silent abyss.

THROUGHOUT THE NIGHT OF JULY 13 AND INTO THE AFTERNOON of the fourteenth, Hugh lay deathly still upon his leaf and palm-frond "bed," drifting into and out of consciousness. His skin had taken on the same gray pallor that Deering had worn in the hours before his death, and during the brief moments when Hugh was lucid and able to open his eyes he could see the concern—and the uncertainty—in the eyes of Armbruster, Lawrence, and Mullane. The young sailors took turns watching over him, giving the injured officer sips of water and swatting away the clouds of flies and mosquitoes that hovered around all of them.

Sometime during the night of the fourteenth or very early on the morning of the fifteenth, Hugh awoke, brought to sudden consciousness by the sound of men moving through the underbrush only about a dozen yards from where he lay. He carefully turned his head toward where his young companions were sleeping, whispering a prayer of thanks that none of the sailors snored. He did not try to waken the men, knowing that any attempt to do so might startle them into making a noise that would alert the nearby Japanese patrol to their presence.

As the enemy troops moved on, Hugh, unable to go back to sleep, undertook a slow and methodical evaluation of the situation in which he and his companions now found themselves. They'd been incredibly lucky thus far, having evaded detection and made their way a fair distance toward the potential crossing place at Diamond Narrows. Moreover, the three sailors were in relatively good health and had been able to find fresh water and edible coconuts with which to bolster their emergency provisions. On the downside, however, the longer the men lingered on Arundel, the greater would be their chances of discovery and capture by the Japanese—a fate that no American serviceman wanted to suffer, given the enemy's well-documented tendency to torture and then execute prisoners. And the simple, unavoidable fact was that Hugh was slowing "the boys" down—their laudable desire to nurse his injuries was putting them in increasing jeopardy. After praying for divine guidance, Hugh came to a momentous decision: if his physical condition did not significantly improve by morning, he would order the men to press on without him.

Unfortunately, the dawn of July 15 brought no relief from the pain that had dogged Hugh since *Strong*'s depth charges had battered him ten days before. If anything, his symptoms had gotten worse. His abdomen was grossly distended, and the slightest touch on its surface caused waves of nausea to roll over him. He was still occasionally vomiting oil, now with small amounts of blood mixed in, and could not keep any solid food down. Hugh could also tell that he was running a high fever, and he felt utterly weak. But worse was yet to come, for when he asked Lawrence to help him sit up, Hugh discovered that he could neither move nor feel his legs. Slumping back down, he knew with crystal clarity that he was completely done in and simply could go no farther. It seemed all too obvious that he was dying, and despite his best intentions he would not be shepherding "his boys" to safety—they would now have to find it on their own.

Having made up his mind, Hugh asked the three men to prop his head up with the Japanese blanket and then gather around him. With a supreme effort of will he then slowly reached out, cleared the leaves from a small patch of dry ground, and picked up a twig. Dragging it over the dirt he sketched out a simple map of the southeastern end of Arundel, Diamond Narrows, and the western shoreline of New Georgia. Pointing to the spot he believed might offer the best crossing route, Hugh then told the sailors they were to go on without him. All three immediately protested, saying they would carry him if necessary. Hugh pointed out that they were endangering themselves by staying with him and that their only hope for survival was to make the crossing and link up with American forces advancing northwestward from Munda. When the sailors continued to argue against the plan, Hugh summoned what little strength he had left, lifted his head to look each of the men in the eyes in turn, and announced in as firm a tone as he could muster that he wasn't making a suggestion; he was issuing an order, and he expected it to be obeyed.

Put in those terms, Armbruster, Lawrence, and Mullane could do nothing but whisper their assent. Their chagrin at the thought of leaving Hugh to die alone—or, worse, to fall into the hands of the Japanese—only intensified when he told them to take his shoes (Mullane was barefoot, having lost his own footwear in the sinking), the large sheath knife, and what remained of the emergency rations. In return he asked them to camouflage him as best they could with fallen fronds and to leave him with one of the rusted ration tins, a few husked coconuts, and the water-filled beer bottles. At that point Lawrence kneeled down to hand Hugh a one-and-a-half-inch piece of a broken penknife blade, saying that in the absence of the sheath knife, "the lieutenant" might need it to poke through the eyes of the coconuts to get to the water inside them. Hugh thanked him and then pointed at Armbruster. As the senior enlisted man and most experienced woodsman of the three, he said, Frank would be in charge, and the other two were to follow his orders.

Having gathered their meager supplies, the sailors each took a moment to shake Hugh's hand and then slowly walked away. Just before they disappeared into the surrounding woods, Armbruster turned back and waved. He looked for a moment as though he might say something, but then rejoined his companions.

Sadly, Hugh's hopes for the men's survival were ultimately in vain. None of the three was ever seen again.[12]

8

——— ALONE AMONG ENEMIES ———

THE SAILORS' DEPARTURE HAD A PROFOUND AND IMMEDIATE EFFECT ON HUGH, producing waves of helplessness and depression that he had never before experienced. And understandably so: He was now utterly alone on an island occupied by a cruel and implacable enemy, and he was completely incapable of defending himself. He was in intense pain and was unable to stand upright, let alone walk. His ragged uniform was still covered in viscous oil and swaths of dried blood, and clouds of mosquitoes and biting flies tormented him. He had not been able to eat anything in ten days, and once his water was gone and his few coconuts empty of their juice, the hot and humid climate would ensure his inevitable dehydration. Any way he looked at it, his situation was hopeless, and the only foreseeable outcome was his death—from his injuries, from starvation, or, worst of all, as a result of what the Japanese would certainly do to him if he fell into their hands.

In the end, it was sheer exhaustion that finally quieted the chaotic storm of thoughts swirling in Hugh's head. A few hours after the sailors' departure, he slipped into deep and undreaming sleep, oblivious to the world around him. Until, that is, he came suddenly awake in the early afternoon because his unconscious mind had registered the subtle crackling of leaves and swishing of branches caused by a Japanese patrol moving through the underbrush nearby. Aware that his labored breathing might be audible to the enemy troops, Hugh attempted to hold his breath despite the pain the effort caused in his lungs and bloated abdomen. After the patrol moved on, he lay there, again contemplating the hopelessness of his situation. Then, just as he was about to drift off sometime in the early evening, another enemy patrol passed within thirty or forty feet of Hugh's well-hidden position. Again he tried to hold his breath, though this time the effort caused even greater pain than he'd experienced earlier in the day, and he almost blacked out.

While the enemy soldiers again passed without discovering him, Hugh was by this point convinced that he was so close to death that there was no point in trying to conserve his meager supply of fresh water. Deciding that if he was going to die, he wouldn't die thirsty, he first drank the juice from the coconuts the sailors had left him and then emptied both of the Japanese beer bottles as quickly as the roiling pain in his gut would allow, as though he were a condemned man and the precious liquid his final meal. Then, pulling the tattered blanket over his face to ward off the insects, he made himself as comfortable as he could. He passed several hours remembering his earlier life, reliving scenes from his childhood and his times on the gridiron. He thought of his now ten-year-old son, of his parents and brother, of Uncle Jim, and most especially of his wife, Frances. How would she cope when she received the news that he was missing in action? What would her life be like, never knowing what had become of him? Would she accept the fact that he was gone forever and move on with her life or live in hope that he might one day reappear? These thoughts and countless others raced through Hugh's mind, until finally he forced himself to release them and let the images of his loved ones begin to recede. Trying to ignore the pain that still coursed through him, he settled down to await the inevitable, resigned to the fact that he would be dead before the sun rose.

Hugh was therefore understandably surprised and not a little confused when he awoke on the morning of July 16, the sun he had not
expected to see again clearly visible through the trees towering above
him. The dawning realization that he had survived the night was not
necessarily a relief, however, for it was accompanied by pain that
seemed even worse than it had been the day before. And then there was
anger; Hugh realized he had been uncharacteristically foolish to drink
all his coconut juice and water. In so doing, he had condemned himself
to suffer the increasing tortures of dehydration for every minute that
he actually stayed alive. Hugh's despair deepened still further as those
minutes stretched into hours—he lay on his mat of fronds throughout
the day and into the late afternoon, the tropical heat drawing every bit
of moisture from him and leaving his tongue swollen and his lips dry
and cracked. The coming of darkness did nothing to relieve either his
thirst or his pain; indeed, both increased still further after sunrise on
July 17. As his second day alone on Arundel progressed, Hugh began
to think that perhaps the best way to relieve his suffering was to use
the broken penknife blade on himself—a quick slash across his carotid
artery would be preferable to the slow and agonizing death that now
seemed his certain fate.

But thoughts of suicide also triggered something else in Hugh, a
growing realization that he simply did not have it within himself to
just give up and die. That would be the ultimate surrender, the final
admission of helplessness, and, in Hugh's reckoning, cowardice at its
most basic level. He had never been a quitter, had never backed away
from a challenge, and had tried never to give in to his fears, whether
it had been in the forests he'd roamed as a child or on the football
field facing opponents who were invariably larger and stronger than
himself. Both Uncle Jim and Wallace Wade, each in his own way, had
taught Hugh the value of self-reliance and ingenuity, of adaptability
and dogged determination. They had molded him into a person who
faced adversity and persevered despite the odds. He would not, he
could not, let them down now, he lectured himself. He was going to
survive, damn it, no matter what it took.

And the first necessity, he knew, was water—without it he would
never be able to arise from his bed of fronds. Still in considerable pain

and unable to move, he knew that the only way he was going to be able to refill his empty Japanese bottles was if it rained. At that point Hugh again prayed, fervently and sincerely. As darkness fell he made a promise to both God and himself; if the Lord would give him water, he whispered, he would get to his feet and move. His prayer concluded, he settled back and listened to the familiar sounds of the jungle until he lapsed into a fitful sleep. Then, some hours later, he awakened to the sounds of raindrops hitting the vegetation around him.

What began as a relatively light shower rapidly became a typical South Pacific downpour, and Hugh cupped his hands together to catch as many of the heavy drops as he could. He quickly sipped enough to moisten his cracked lips and parched tongue, then retrieved the empty emergency ration tin and moved a few inches closer to where a narrow stream of rainwater was running off the lower end of a long leaf, almost as if from a faucet. Hugh held his makeshift cup beneath the flow until the tin filled and then greedily drank its contents down in one long pull and was pleasantly surprised when it stayed down. He gulped three more tins, one after the other, then used the vessel to fill both of his Japanese beer bottles. After topping off the tin one final time and setting it aside, he propped himself up against a fallen log, draped the now wet blanket around his equally sodden head and shoulders, and settled down to wait for dawn. Deciding that the good Lord had answered his prayer in spades, Hugh was determined to hold up his side of the bargain: when morning came he would do whatever it took to stand up and move. His mind made up, he soon drifted off to sleep.

While the rainstorm may well have been simply fortuitous— Arundel Island gets an average of 150 inches of rain a year, after all— what happened soon after sunrise verged on the truly miraculous. When Hugh awoke he found, to his astonishment, that the feeling had returned to his legs. He could move both limbs, with the only lingering ill effects being stiffness and an intense tingling sensation running from the small of his back to his toes. After slowly savoring the tin of water he had saved from the night before, Hugh carefully rolled onto his side and lay there for a moment. Though his abdomen was still distended and his breathing somewhat shallow because of the lingering pain in his diaphragm, he decided that his battered body felt better than at any time since *Strong*'s sinking. And the improvement wasn't just physical—he realized that the depression and self-doubt that had plagued him before the storm had completely vanished, replaced by a cautious optimism that he might actually be able to survive his forced sojourn as a castaway on Japanese-infested Arundel Island.

But, ever the realist, Hugh knew that to stay alive he would have to move. And he would have to start *now*.

THOUGH HE KNEW STANDING UP WOULD TAKE SOME EFFORT, HUGH wasn't prepared for how challenging it was simply to get himself off the ground.

The gut-wrenching pain that resulted when he briefly attempted to roll onto his distended stomach made it abundantly clear that he would not be able to push himself up onto his knees that way. After a few minutes of thought he decided on a different tactic. Rolling onto his back, he slowly wriggled his way to the base of a nearby tree, pulling his walking stick along by gripping it between his bare feet. With his hands palm down on the ground, he pushed himself up the trunk until he was in a sitting position. Then, after shifting both hands to the top of the walking stick, he pushed steadily downward with his biceps and used his shoulder blades to "walk" his back upward inch by inch until he was able to get his feet beneath him. Then it was a matter of slowly pushing farther up the tree until he was finally standing upright. Hugh didn't have the chance to revel in his accomplishment, however, for he was immediately engulfed by waves of nausea and an intense lightheadedness that very nearly made him faint.

When the jungle around him finally stopped spinning and the gorge that had risen in his throat subsided, Hugh reached out with the walking stick and lifted his tattered blanket off the ground. He'd earlier rolled it up like a sleeping bag and tied it with a length of vine, and now he wedged it beneath one of his arms. The Japanese beer bottles, each topped off and stoppered with wadded leaves, were in either of the front pockets of his uniform pants, and the broken pocket-knife blade was in one of his shirt pockets. With all of his worldly possessions thus stowed, Hugh pushed himself away from the tree and haltingly shuffled into the surrounding bush. He intended to move back north to the spring he and the three sailors had discovered and remembered the distance as roughly a mile and a half. With luck, he thought, he could make it to the water source in two or three hours.

Within minutes, however, it became painfully obvious that the journey would take far longer. Having earlier given his shoes to Danny Mullane, Hugh now was forced to walk barefooted, and his feet were soon lacerated by the coral shards, rocks, thorns, and wood splinters that littered the forest floor. He could cover only thirty or forty yards at a time before he'd have to find a log to sit on so he could attempt to clean out the wounds, rinsing them with some of the water from the beer bottles. In one sense, however, these first-aid stops were a blessing: Hugh was still dealing with fairly serious and painful internal injuries, had not eaten since his ship went down, and tired quickly. The frequent halts helped him to catch his breath and, perhaps more important, gave him a chance to utter brief self-motivational pep talks.

About halfway to the freshwater spring Hugh encountered yet another challenge—a wide salt flat that he didn't remember crossing when he and the sailors were first making their way south. To go around the obstacle in order to remain under cover would add hours to his journey, and since the tide was out and the flat was relatively dry Hugh decided to go straight across it. He would be completely exposed the whole time, but it was a risk he was willing to take if it meant reaching the spring before nightfall. Hugh moved back into the trees and stood silently for a few minutes, scanning the surrounding area and listening for any sound that might indicate a threat. Sensing nothing, he stepped out into the open and gingerly took a few steps. Though the soles of his feet immediately began to sting as the residual salt found its way into the numerous cuts, he pressed on with all the speed he could muster. He had just reached the halfway point when he heard a low rumble coming from behind him. The noise quickly swelled into the unmistakable sound of an aircraft engine, and Hugh, caught in the open with no chance of reaching cover, could only lean on his staff and pray the machine would prove to be friendly.

Hugh Barr Miller Jr. was born in 1910 in Tuscaloosa, Alabama, and by the time he reached fourteen he was an expert outdoorsman and outstanding athlete. In high school he played on each of the organized sports teams, but his first love was football. His gridiron skills helped win him a spot on the University of Alabama's varsity team despite his relatively slight stature. *(Courtesy Fitzhugh Miller)*

Led by famed coach Wallace Wade, on January 1, 1931, the Crimson Tide trounced the Washington State Cougars 24–0 in the Rose Bowl. Hugh Miller was among those who took part, participating in several plays as a guard. It was his last game for Alabama; he moved on to law school and marriage to Anne McComb Gayden. *(Courtesy Fitzhugh Miller)*

Seen here just after his September 29, 1941, commissioning as an ensign in the Naval Reserve, Hugh Miller was initially assigned as an aide to the assistant commandant of the Seventh Naval District in Key West. In the spring of 1942 a chance meeting with a senior officer set in motion a chain of events that would ultimately help "the lawyer" go to sea. (*Courtesy Fitzhugh Miller*)

The future USS *Strong* (DD-467) takes shape on the ways at Bath Iron Works (BIW). Hull number 193 was among the first six of an eventual 31 2,100-ton *Fletcher*-class destroyers constructed by the Maine shipbuilder, and by the time Hugh Miller first saw his new ship it had been under construction for 366 days. (*National Archives*)

Following its launching on May 17, 1942, *Strong* was moved to BIW's fitting-out basin for completion. Seen here tied up inboard of sister ship *Chevalier* (DD-451), *Strong* has not yet received the gun turrets, torpedo tubes, and 20mm and 40mm cannon that will turn it into a lethal ship of war. *(National Archives)*

This builder's plate, attached to the aft bulkhead of *Strong's* bridge during the ship's construction, was its "birth certificate" and a point of pride for the destroyer's crew. *(National Archives)*

Flanked by senior officers from the First Naval District, on August 7, 1942, Lieutenant Commander Joseph H. "Gus" Wellings—the man who engineered Hugh Miller's transfer from a desk job in Key West to sea duty aboard a destroyer—reads the orders officially assigning him as the newly commissioned USS *Strong*'s captain. *(Naval War College Library)*

Gus Wellings poses for an official photograph on the day of *Strong*'s commissioning. A 1925 graduate of the U.S. Naval Academy, the Boston-born officer had already enjoyed an interesting and varied career that included time afloat on the battleships *Utah, Florida,* and *California* and the destroyers *King* and *Tillman*; two years as a Navy ROTC instructor at Harvard; and duty as the assistant naval attaché at the U.S. embassy in London. A superior leader, he was a friend and mentor to Hugh Miller, in whom he saw the makings of a fine wartime naval officer. *(Naval War College Library)*

Handpicked by Wellings to be *Strong*'s executive officer, 1933 Naval Academy graduate Lieutenant Frederick W. Purdy had been serving aboard the battleship *California* when it was damaged during the Japanese attack on Pearl Harbor. As Wellings's second in command, Purdy would be both the destroyer's navigator and its chief administrator, handling personnel issues and many other bureaucratic chores on his captain's behalf. *(Naval War College Library)*

Strong's officers pose for an official portrait on the day of the destroyer's commissioning. Wellings is in the center of the bottom row, with Purdy immediately to his right and chief engineer Lieutenant Marvin I. Rosenberg to his left. Hugh Miller, the ship's 20mm and stores officer, is to Purdy's right. *(National Archives)*

Upon its September, 1, 1942, completion of the yard period in Boston, *Strong* was assigned to Commander, Destroyer Force Atlantic, for a seven-week shakedown period. The vessel is seen here in Massachusetts Bay, underway for the Naval Torpedo Station in Newport, Rhode Island. Note that while its armament is clearly visible, Navy censors have blotted out radar antennas, radio aerials, and other mast-mounted systems. *(National Archives)*

Kentucky-born William C. "Bill" Hedrick was commissioned an ensign in the Naval Reserve at Chicago's Northwestern University in October 1942 and joined *Strong* two months later during the ship's New York yard period. Assigned as an assistant communications officer, he was also a talented writer and poet and kept a detailed journal of his time aboard the destroyer. *(Courtesy Tambrie Hedrick Johnson)*

This photo, taken in New York in December 1942 following *Strong*'s return from North Africa, shows the two forward 5-inch/.38-caliber mounts and, to either side of the after mount, the two canvas-shrouded forward 20mm cannon. Behind and slightly above the after turret are the circular windows of the ship's pilot house, directly above which is the box-shaped Mark 37 gun director. The canvas-enclosed area beneath the director is the ship's flying bridge, Hugh Miller's personal battle station. The numbers on this non-censored image indicate new systems added to the destroyer in New York; No. 2 indicates the "stovepipe" antenna for the IFF (Identification Friend or Foe) system. *(National Archives)*

Taken on the same day as the image on the preceding page, this photo shows two of *Strong*'s three aft 5-inch/.38 mounts. Just visible above the higher turret are the twin barrels of one of the ship's two twin 40mm cannon. The other 40mm gun is just out of the picture to the right, as are the destroyer's stern-mounted depth-charge rails. The circular objects on the main deck to the left of the aft deckhouse are 300-pound Mark 6 depth charges in their ready-access stands; the K-gun projectors from which the weapons were fired are just forward. *(National Archives)*

King Neptune and his retainers hold court beneath *Strong*'s aft-most 5-inch/.38 mount during the January 10, 1943, crossing the line ceremony. As Gus Wellings later wrote, "the Jolly Roger was broken at the top of the mast and after a very colorful parade his Royal Highness held court and awarded sentences to all the pollywogs." *(Courtesy Milton Hackett)*

Neptune's royal barber closely cropped the hair of all pollywogs, which included all but four of *Strong*'s officers. In this photo, taken on the destroyer's flying bridge, Gus Wellings is standing, center, wearing a white shirt. Fred Purdy stands immediately to the captain's right, and a well-shorn Hugh Miller kneels directly in front of Wellings. *(Courtesy Milton Hackett)*

Strong picked up Lieutenant Colonel Edward N. Fay in Bora Bora and transported him to New Caledonia, where the 47-year-old Army Quartermaster Corps officer was to help organize the service's logistics operations in Polynesia. Gus Wellings called the gregarious Fay "a grand shipmate," and Hugh Miller and "Colonel Eddie" remained friends for life. *(Harry Ransom Research Center, James A. Michener Collection, University of Northern Colorado)*

Strong delivers mail to *Honolulu* via highline just days before the destroyer's July 1943 sinking in Kula Gulf. Note that the ship's 5-inch/.38 mounts are pointed skyward in air-defense mode. Also visible is the raised platform built out from the rounded front section of the ship's bridge to house an additional 20mm cannon, as well as the 20mm mount added to the flying bridge just forward of the Mark 37 director. Hugh Miller is standing immediately to the right of the gun on the flying bridge. *(National Archives)*

Ground crewmen prepare to load bombs aboard a Grumman TBF of Marine Torpedo Bombing Squadron 143 (VMTB-143) on Guadalcanal. This may be the actual aircraft flown by First Lieutenant James R. Turner on August 16, 1943, when he spotted Hugh Miller on Arundel Island and initiated the rescue effort that saved the red-bearded castaway. *(National Archives)*

Ungainly looking though it may have been, the Grumman J2F Duck amphibian was an excellent air-sea rescue platform. After being picked up from Arundel Island, Hugh Miller made the journey to Munda in the cramped passenger compartment built into the aft end of the aircraft's main float, directly below the rear cockpit. His only view of the world was through the small window visible just behind and below the trailing edge of the Duck's lower wing. *(National Archives)*

Following his rescue, Hugh Miller displays the *hinomaru yosegaki* flag he took from the body of one of the first enemy troops he killed on Arundel Island. Carried by the majority of Japanese military personnel in World War II, these flags were symbols of good luck given to men before they deployed. Inscribed with patriotic slogans, religious sayings, and good wishes for health and success in battle, the flags were often worn wrapped around the body. *(Courtesy Fitzhugh Miller)*

Major Vernon A. Peterson, Major Goodwin R. Luck, and Master Technical Sergeant John J. Happer pose for a photo next to the J2F Duck in which they carried out the rescue of Hugh Miller. Years later all three men would be surprise guests on the episode of "This Is Your Life" honoring the "Castaway of Arundel Island." *(National Archives)*

Twenty-nine-year-old Associated Press war correspondent Arthur Burgess was the first reporter to relate Hugh Miller's story in print. The article—slugged "Ex-Rose Bowl Star Saved After Being Missing 43 Days" and datelined August 20, 1943—ran in a variety of Stateside papers and laid the foundation for all subsequent reporting about the "castaway" and his exploits. *(Associated Press, used by permission)*

Wearing the Navy Cross and a Purple Heart with Gold Star that Eleanor Roosevelt has just pinned to his newly issued khaki uniform, Hugh Miller shakes hands with the First Lady as Admiral William "Bull" Halsey (to Hugh's immediate right) looks on. The ceremony—held at the naval hospital in Nouméa, New Caledonia, on September 15, 1943—was conducted at the foot of the bed occupied by Electrician's Mate 2nd Class Willard G. Langley, the sole known survivor of *Strong*'s forward engine room. *(National Archives)*

Crimson Tide football great-turned-movie star Johnny Mack Brown and Hugh Miller pose for photographers in Los Angeles in mid-November 1943. Brown was determined to introduce his Navy Cross–wearing friend to the sorts of people who could put the amazing story of wartime survival in the South Pacific onto the silver screen. In between Hugh's public-relations duties he was feted by some of Hollywood's most influential movers and shakers. *(Courtesy Fitzhugh Miller)*

On November 14, 1956, Hollywood gossip columnist Hedda Hopper reported that John Wayne wanted to star in "Hide and Seek," the prospective movie version of Hugh Miller's story. Producer Bill Hawks said the iconic actor—seen here in Navy uniform in a publicity still for one of his many films—was attracted to the Robinson Crusoe–aspect of the story, likely because of the success two years earlier of Spanish *auteur* Luis Buñuel's film version of the Daniel Dafoe novel. Wayne never made the film, however, and Miller's option ultimately passed to Robert Stack and then to Desilu. *(Courtesy Batjac Productions via Gretchen Wayne)*

Always proud of his Scottish heritage, the former "castaway of Arundel Island" poses in full Highland regalia just months before his death. On June 21, 1978, a burst abdominal aneurysm did what the Japanese had been unable to do. Hugh Barr Miller Jr., holder of the nation's second-highest award for valor in combat and the man whom Bull Halsey had called "the bravest man I ever met," was 68 years old. *(Courtesy Fitzhugh Miller)*

His prayer went unanswered, however, for seconds later a Japanese A6M "Zero" fighter appeared from the southeast. The plane—likely returning from a raid against U.S. forces on Munda or Rendova—was flying fast and very low, barely clearing the tops of the trees. The enemy pilot was probably as startled by the sudden appearance of a gaunt, hunched figure in the middle of the salt flat as Hugh was by the Zero's unexpected arrival, for only a single burst of fire leaped from the fighter's guns. The rounds threw up small parallel gouts of sand and salt as they stitched their way toward Hugh, but the stream of bullets halted before reaching him, and the plane flashed by overhead. Probably leery of being bounced by prowling American fighters, the Japanese pilot did not circle back to check on the effects of his fire, and the roar of the Zero's engine rapidly diminished as the aircraft raced for the relative safety of Rabaul.

Hugh had turned his head to follow the fighter as it roared overhead, and as he did he'd felt simultaneous searing pains on the right side of his neck and on the underside of his left wrist. A quick exam with his fingers revealed that both wounds had been caused by bullet fragments, likely the result of one of the Zero's rounds disintegrating into ricocheting bits after hitting a rock or coral outcrop. Despite some bleeding, neither injury was serious, and Hugh was able to pull out the fragments. He carefully rinsed each site with water from one of the beer bottles and then resumed his trek toward the spring. As he walked he thought of how lucky he'd been—had the Japanese pilot fired a little earlier or later, or a bit farther to one side or the other, or chosen to return for a second pass, Hugh knew he would now be a blood-soaked corpse lying in the middle of the salt flat, just another meal for the crabs.

But as lucky as he had been during the encounter with the Zero, Hugh also realized that his situation had taken a dramatic turn for the worse. When the pilot returned to base he would certainly report the sighting of a Caucasian man on Arundel Island. Thus far, the greatest threat to Hugh's safety had been his accidental discovery by a roving enemy patrol. Now the Japanese would know of his presence, and they were sure to come looking for him.

HUGH REACHED THE FRESHWATER SPRING LATE THAT AFTERNOON.
After checking the area for signs of the enemy and finding none, he
drank his fill and then rinsed his lacerated feet and the bullet-fragment
wounds before moving about forty feet away and pulling together a
bed of brush beneath a fallen log. The day's exertions ensured that he
didn't stay awake long.

When he opened his eyes just after dawn on July 19, Hugh found
that he felt surprisingly well. The minor bullet wounds stung, his feet
still hurt, and his abdomen remained quite tender, but he'd stopped
passing blood and felt better than he had in some time. And, he noticed with amazement, he was actually hungry. After drinking some
water from the beer bottles, Hugh slowly got to his feet and went in
search of fallen coconuts. He found several clustered at the base of a
tree about a hundred yards from his "camp" and carried three of them
back. His mouth watering in anticipation, he set about trying to husk
the nuts using the broken penknife blade.

It was impossible, of course—cutting through the hard and fibrous outer covering had been difficult enough for Armbruster and
the other sailors using the much larger and far sharper sheath knife.
Increasingly frustrated, Hugh first tried hitting the nut with a large
stick, and, when that didn't work, the former gridiron star repeatedly
threw the football-size object against a tree with all the strength he
could muster. When it still did not yield, he decided on a different tactic: carrying two of the coconuts in his folded arms, he walked about
twenty yards to the edge of a small salt flat that was studded with
sharp coral rocks. After scanning for possible danger, Hugh walked
to the closest jagged stone, sat down next to it, and started banging
the first nut against it. Though the makeshift tool worked—after each
strike against the sharp coral, Hugh was able to pull off a strip of the
coconut's sinewy husk—the process was both time-consuming and
tiring. It took some two hours to completely free both nuts, and by
the time he was finished Hugh was so exhausted that he could barely
stagger back toward his camp. Collapsing onto his bed of fronds, he
used the broken penknife blade to poke out the eye of one of the nuts
so he could drink the juice. Then he cracked open the shell with a
handy rock and scraped out the rich white "meat" with the blade and

his fingers. It was the first solid food he'd been able to keep down since *Strong*'s sinking, and after eating as much as he could he laid back and closed his eyes. Just before drifting off to sleep, he decided that he would spend a few days resting and building up his strength before moving on in search of rescue.

Those few days eventually stretched into a week. Hugh's strength and stamina increased dramatically—fueled by a diet of coconut meat and fresh water from the spring—and the pain in his abdomen slowly faded away. Yet not all was entirely well in his world. The need to move about each day in search of coconuts kept the lacerations on the soles of his feet from closing, and the wounds became infected despite his frequent attempts to clean them with water. Almost as galling were the clouds of mosquitoes that followed Hugh wherever he went, inflicting painful bites despite his attempts to ward them off by smearing mud on his exposed face, neck, hands, and feet. And, most seriously, the Japanese had stepped up their patrolling on Arundel, likely in response to the Zero pilot's report of seeing a white man on the island. Though Hugh had remained near the freshwater spring, the increased enemy activity had prompted him to change his sleeping location more than once.

Finally, on July 26, he decided it was time to make a more permanent move. During a foray in search of coconuts the previous day, Hugh had stumbled upon what turned out to be an ideal location for a more permanent "hide"—and it was less than one hundred yards from the spring. A thicket of mangroves lined the inland edge of another small salt flat, on the seaward side of which was a narrow tree-fringed beach fronting the area where the southern end of Kula Gulf met the northern end of Hathorn Sound. At high tide the flat disappeared under two or three feet of water, providing a ready-made moat on that side that enemy troops would not be able to traverse without making a fair amount of noise. The mangroves' massive intertwined roots offered many places to hide should the Japanese come too near on foot, and dense ground cover and the trees' broadly spreading branches screened the site from hostile aircraft, from vessels offshore, and from anyone walking past more than twenty feet away. Hugh quickly "furnished" his new home, using fallen limbs and palm fronds to build a small lean-to beneath a low branch. He then made a bed out of fronds and the Japanese blanket, and, feeling far more secure than at any time since landing on the island, he promptly indulged in a midday nap.

Hugh didn't sleep for long, however, for in the early afternoon, the swelling noise of approaching aircraft roused him. He rose from his palm-frond bed and moved to the edge of the salt pan to get a better look. To his delight the machines were American TBF Avengers, flying at about five hundred feet in very loose single-file formation from the direction of Vila south toward Rendova.[1] Seeing the chance to alert friendly forces to his presence on Arundel, Hugh hobbled out into the open and began frantically waving his arms. Just as he did so, the last aircraft in the group roared overhead. It seemed for a moment as though the Avenger would continue on its way, but then it turned—likely because its radio operator had seen Hugh from his position in the lower fuselage aft of the bomb bay. Though bulky and barrel shaped, the TBF made a surprisingly quick course reversal and circled the salt pan several times, so low that the faces of the pilot and the turret gunner were clearly visible. When the machine eventually leveled off and raced away to rejoin the formation, Hugh was certain that the aviators' account of seeing him on the island would lead to an immediate rescue effort. No such salvation was forthcoming, however; the TBF either was brought down by hostile action or suffered some sort of mechanical problem, for it never returned to base.[2]

Though hours and then days passed with no sign of deliverance, Hugh never lost the conviction that he would eventually be rescued. But he had also come to the conclusion that friendly forces would have to come to him, rather than him somehow making his way to them. While his health was improving, his feet were in no condition to make the trek down to Diamond Narrows. Moreover, the crossing was likely the focus of increased Japanese attention, and even if Hugh could get there he stood little chance of making it across to New Georgia without being detected and either taken prisoner or killed outright. So he resolved to stay on Arundel and build up his strength and endurance in preparation for the rescue he believed was inevitable.

Hugh also made another key decision. As long as he remained on the island, it was his duty to do whatever he could to gather useful information on the Japanese forces operating in the vicinity. Any details he could amass—the designations and strengths of units, the locations of heavy weapons and strongpoints, the timing of patrols—would be of immense operational value to the Allied intelligence officers planning the eventual invasion of Arundel.

But Hugh realized that his intelligence gathering could well have more immediate value. Nearly every night he'd so far spent on the island had been punctuated by the low throbbing of many poorly muffled engines chugging along just offshore. He knew instinctively that the sound came from landing craft and small boats ferrying Japanese reinforcements from Vila toward the southern end of Hathorn Sound, and he assumed that from there the enemy troops crossed Diamond Narrows and moved on toward Munda or Rice Anchorage. Realizing that it would be far easier and more effective for Allied forces to interdict the nightly flotillas than it would be to fight the troops they carried once the men were offloaded and had moved inland, he decided to gather as much information as he could about the seaborne traffic. This data—and whatever observations he might be able to make about enemy forces on Arundel—would be of great tactical value to Allied forces operating in and around New Georgia.

The trick, of course, would be staying alive long enough to relay the information.

THOUGH HUGH DIDN'T KNOW IT, HE WASN'T THE ONLY ALLIED seaman determined to keep tabs on Japanese activities near Arundel Island. Just miles away, from a well-camouflaged lair atop a twenty-three-hundred-foot ridgeline on Kolombangara's southwest coast, a thirty-eight-year-old sublieutenant in the Royal Australian Naval Volunteer Reserve (RANVR) was also tracking the movements and dispositions of enemy air, naval, and ground forces in the vicinity.

Arthur Reginald "Reg" Evans was part of the "Ferdinand" organization of coastwatchers activated throughout the Southwest Pacific in 1939 under the authority of the Royal Australian Navy's Intelligence Division. Like most of Ferdinand's members, Evans had lived and worked in the Solomon Islands before the war and was intimately familiar with the terrain and the local peoples. He'd joined the Australian army after the outbreak of hostilities, but his background eventually brought him to the attention of Lieutenant Commander Eric A. Feldt, who ran coastwatcher operations in the Solomons. After undergoing training in Australia in the use of codes and the recognition of Japanese ships and aircraft, Evans was commissioned in the RANVR and dispatched by air to the southeastern end of New Georgia. From there he traveled onward by canoe, moving by night and hiding ashore by day. He passed Munda—so close to the beach that he could hear the Japanese working on the airfield—and paddled up Arundel's east side before landing on Kolombangara's western coast in late February 1943. With the assistance of friendly islanders, he and his native scouts set up a series of lookout posts, and Evans was soon radioing information to a Ferdinand substation on Guadalcanal. From there his reports were passed on to Feldt's headquarters in Townsville, Queensland.[3]

The Japanese became aware of Evans's presence on Kolombangara but were unable to capture him despite repeated attempts, and the lanky Australian continued to provide valuable intelligence about enemy activities in and around Vila and in Blackett Strait and the northern approaches to Hathorn Sound. He also observed the clashes between Allied and Japanese warships in Kula Gulf and reported the sinkings of both *Strong* and *Helena*—though he did not know the ships' names until his scouts encountered some of the cruiser's survivors who had drifted ashore on Kolombangara's north coast. These men, as well as others who washed up on Vella Lavella, were ultimately returned to Allied control thanks to the coastwatchers stationed on both islands.[4] Only weeks later Evans played a vital role in a rescue that was to ultimately have global implications—the recovery of Lieutenant (jg) John F. Kennedy and members of the crew of his *PT-109* following their vessel's collision with the Japanese destroyer *Amagiri* in the waters between Kolombangara and Gizo islands on the night of August 1–2 1943. Without the efforts of Evans and two of his native colleagues, Biuku Gasa and Eroni Kumana, future U.S. president Kennedy and his crew would very likely have been captured and executed by the Japanese.

Although Reg Evans and Hugh Miller were destined never to meet, by deciding to gather information on Japanese activities on and near Arundel the American castaway had effectively joined the Australian in the fraternity of coastwatchers. Unlike Evans, however, Hugh would be completely on his own—no native guides, no radio link to the outside world, and no guarantee that the information he collected would ever be passed on to those who could make use of it.

While Evans on mountainous Kolombangara could keep a godlike eye on the Japanese from his various aeries astride towering ridgelines, Hugh Miller on flat Arundel had a decidedly less panoramic view of his surroundings. The same thick vegetation that helped hide him from enemy patrols also made it extremely difficult to see more than a few yards in any direction, and the only place from which Hugh could monitor activities offshore was from the edge of the tree line bordering the beach. This put him at increased risk of discovery by Japanese troops, who often chose to walk on the sand rather than struggle through the underbrush.

A few days after establishing his new camp among the mangroves, Hugh found the solution to his "elevation problem." A stone's throw from his lean-to he discovered a large coconut palm that had toppled over and become wedged into the V formed by two even larger standing trees whose upper trunks crossed each other. The fallen palm rested at about a forty-five-degree angle—forming the third leg of what resembled a large tripod—and the point where it was held by the two living trees was some thirty feet above the ground. After carefully clearing away the vines and old fronds that wreathed the palm trunk, Hugh was able to slowly shinny up it using his hands, knees, and feet. From the "crow's nest" formed by the interlocking trunks he had a clear view of the surrounding forest, the entire salt flat, and the northern end of Hathorn Sound.

Hugh used his new perch to good advantage during the first two days—and nights—of August. He ascended to the crow's nest several times during daylight in order to keep tabs on Japanese activity on Arundel itself, noting that each day patrols of five or six soldiers moved along paths through the trees during the late morning. Hugh was surprised by the troops' apparent lack of concern about the possible presence of enemy forces, for they talked and smoked as they walked and carried their 7.7mm Arisaka Type 99 bolt-action rifles casually and without fixed bayonets.

Although the view from the crow's nest was not as good in the dark, Hugh was still able to clearly see the enemy landing craft that appeared each night as soon as the sun went down. The vessels had bow ramps and looked to be of two sizes—the smaller about fifty feet in length and the larger some ten feet longer—and the rattling noise and clouds of dark smoke they produced made it obvious that both types were powered by diesel engines.[5] The craft were armed with machine guns, some had what looked like plates of crude armor bolted to their sides, and each boat was packed with troops. The vessels moved southward from Vila and landed at Cutter Point on New Georgia, just north of the entrance to Diamond Narrows and directly across Hathorn Sound from where Hugh had said good-bye to Armbruster and his two companions.

Like the men who patrolled the island in daylight, the soldiers in the landing craft must not have felt themselves to be in much danger, for Hugh could clearly hear them talking and laughing above the sound of the engines. The apparent nonchalance with which the Japanese undertook their nocturnal voyages underwent a dramatic reversal, however, on August 3.[6]

Just after nightfall that evening, as Hugh was carefully climbing up to his crow's nest, he heard the throaty rumbling of what could only be the three Packard V-12 engines of a U.S. Navy eighty-foot PT (patrol torpedo) boat.[7] It was a sound he'd heard many times before *Strong*'s sinking, and his first thought was that it might signal his imminent rescue. With growing excitement he shinnied back down the tree and hurried through the undergrowth as quickly as his injured feet would allow. He intended to get as close to the PT as possible and then attract the crew's attention; with luck, he'd be in Munda or Rendova by dawn.

Unfortunately, Hugh was not the reason for the PT boat's presence off Arundel. The vessel was one of six operating from a forward base in Grasse Lagoon on New Georgia's north coast, their purpose being to interdict the flow of Japanese reinforcements south from Vila into Hathorn Sound and thence to Munda. Though originally intended to attack large warships and merchantmen with torpedoes, the PTs' size, shallow draft, and high speed ideally suited them to "barge busting" with machine guns, 20mm cannon, and whatever other weapons the crew could scrounge and bolt to their boat's wooden deck.

On this night the captain of the vessel that had attracted Hugh's attention was intent on ambush rather than cavalry charge. He'd carefully backed the PT in toward the shore, the stern facing the mangroves and the bow canted slightly to the south so that all guns fore and aft could be brought to bear on any enemy vessel that might appear from the north. The hide position was at the upper end of the large salt flat to the northeast of Hugh's camp, and as he hurried through the forest he heard the telltale rattle of Japanese diesel engines. Just as he neared the edge of the tree line and was about to break out into the salt flat, the PT's guns opened up with a roar, tracers arcing toward the first of two heavily laden landing craft that had just rounded the end of a small coral spit. The yell of savage delight that welled up in Hugh's throat never reached his lips, however, for a hail of automatic weapons fire shredded the foliage around him, and he instinctively dropped to his stomach and rolled behind a fallen log.

As the bullets buzzed over him—the occasional ricochet whining off into the night sky—Hugh guessed, correctly, that the panicked Japanese troops aboard the landing craft were wildly spraying return fire in the PT boat's general direction. Because he was almost directly astern of the American vessel, he thus became the unintended target of their volleys, though the fire quickly slackened and then died as the PT's rounds silenced the Japanese gunners. The lull prompted Hugh to rise to his knees in preparation for the final shuffling sprint toward deliverance, only to be sent sprawling as bullets again lashed the shrubs around him. This time, however, it was not the Japanese sending him to ground. The fire came from the fantail of the PT boat, where a crew member was methodically sweeping the shoreline with a .45-caliber Thompson submachine gun, apparently to discourage any enemy troops ashore from attacking the American vessel from the rear.

Pinned down and with no choice but to stay hunkered behind the protective log, Hugh could only listen as the PT boat raked the Japanese landing craft. The enemy vessels had apparently been carrying drums of fuel in addition to troops, for tracer and incendiary rounds from the American guns had caused huge whooshing detonations that set both craft furiously alight. During brief lulls in the gunfire Hugh could hear the agonized screams of men burning to death, interspersed with the sharp crack of rifle rounds "cooking off" because of the intense heat of the flames.

Some twenty minutes after opening the firefight the PT's guns fell silent as the burning hulks of the two landing craft drifted away, already beginning to sink. Hugh knew that he had only moments to attract the Americans' attention before their vessel roared off toward its home base. Realizing that running toward the craft yelling "Help!" or "Hey, Navy!" would only draw the Americans' fire—doing so was a favored Japanese method of confusing U.S. troops during an attack— Hugh hurried back to his camp and shinnied up the sloped palm tree. Once in his crow's nest he started singing the Marine Corps Hymn at the top of his lungs, counting on the fact that few Japanese knew, or could pronounce, the words. His cleverness did him no good, however, for he was barely through the tune's first stanza when the PT boat's engines came to life. The vessel carefully navigated the shallows and, once in open water, roared off into Kula Gulf at high speed.

Though understandably disappointed that he was not aboard the rapidly disappearing PT, Hugh consoled himself with the scale of destruction the American vessel had inflicted on the Japanese landing craft. Scores of enemy troops had been killed outright, and others continued to shriek in agony on the beach or in the flame-covered water. Hugh felt no sympathy for the dead and dying; they were the same hated foe who had attacked Pearl Harbor and enslaved much of Asia. More personally, they were the enemy who had sunk his ship and killed his shipmates and were now likely hunting him.

No, Hugh quietly vowed to himself, he would not pity the Japanese soldiers and seamen. Indeed, when morning came he intended to see if there was anything the newly dead "sons of heaven" could do for *him*.

A few hours after the PT boat's departure, several addi-tional Japanese landing craft had arrived on the scene of the ambush and recovered abandoned weapons, survivors, and as many of the dead as they could carry. By the time Hugh reached the beach early on the morning of August 4, only a few bodies remained, most of them already drifting out into Kula Gulf, buoyed by their now pointless life jackets.

After carefully scanning for enemy activity, Hugh moved out of the tree line and waded into the shallow water between the beach and the nearest reef. He moved as quickly as he could toward the corpse of a young Japanese soldier that had gotten hung up on a rocky out-cropping, the upper torso out of the water and the legs moving in the gentle swell, almost as though the dead man were swimming. In his haste to reach the body, Hugh stepped into a shallow hole in the sandy bottom and lost his footing, pitching forward into the water and badly cutting his hand and ankle. He struggled upright and, using all the strength he could muster, dragged the corpse off the rock and onto a nearby stretch of sand.

Keenly aware of how vulnerable he was, Hugh hurried to claim his spoils. He first pulled away the protective fabric puttees that spiraled up each of the man's legs from ankle to just below the knee and then unlaced the boots and pulled them off. When both were free Hugh removed the corpse's socks and shoved them deep into his pockets, then tied the boot laces together and slung the footwear around his neck as he undid the buckle on the man's equipment belt. In addition to a long bayonet in its scabbard, the belt bore two hand grenades in a woven-leather carrier and a small pouch containing a bar of soap and several circular tins about an inch and a half in diameter. Hugh hastily hooked the belt around his waist and then rolled the corpse onto its back and pulled off what little remained of its bullet-shredded life jacket so he could go through the small knapsack beneath it. He discovered five tins he took to be rations and pushed them into his pockets with the socks. Finally, certain that he'd recovered everything useful from the dead soldier, Hugh sloshed his way back across the shallow water and into the tree line.

And just in time, as it turned out, for Hugh had barely scurried into the underbrush when a Japanese landing craft rounded the nearby headland. The vessel threaded a narrow passage into the shallow lagoon behind the reef and nosed toward the beach. When its bow grounded on the sand, the forward ramp dropped and five troops emerged. The men seemed fairly relaxed, their mission obviously to locate any further recoverable items from the previous night's debacle. As Hugh watched, the soldiers spread out, shouldered their rifles, and began a desultory search along the beach. Their casual attitude changed abruptly, however, when one of the men spotted the body that had just moments before been the source of Hugh's booty. At the direction of the man who was obviously the group leader, three of the soldiers waded out to where the corpse now lay on the small sand spit.

As the men splashed toward their dead comrade, Hugh realized that he'd made a huge tactical error. In his eagerness to obtain whatever spoils the body might offer—especially boots with which to protect his lacerated, aching feet—he hadn't considered the full implications of his actions. They were quickly brought loudly home to him, however, for as soon as the soldiers saw that the body had been relieved of its footgear and other items, they began shouting excitedly. With a sinking heart, Hugh realized that any possibility of remaining undetected was now irrevocably lost. If the Zero pilot's report of a Caucasian on Arundel had for any reason not piqued the interest of senior Japanese commanders on Kolombangara, the discovery of the looted body certainly would.

Angry with himself for thinking with his injured feet instead of his head, Hugh momentarily considered using his two newfound hand grenades to eliminate the Japanese squad. From briefings on enemy weapons held aboard *Strong* before its sinking, he recognized the four-inch-tall, two-inch-wide devices as Type 97 fragmentation grenades. He remembered that to arm the device, the thrower first pulled the safety pin that protruded from the narrow cylindrical percussion cap projecting from the top of the grenade and then struck the cap against any solid object. The blow activated the fuze, and the grenade's detonation would hurl shrapnel in all directions. Anyone within twenty feet of the explosion would almost certainly be killed, while serious injuries were likely out to forty feet.

Though Hugh knew that his football-throwing skills would allow him to accurately hurl the 1-pound grenades a good thirty to forty yards, he also remembered warnings about the unreliability of the weapons' fuzes. Though set for four and a half seconds, they were said to frequently detonate early, and sometimes not at all. Moreover, the fuzes made a clearly audible popping noise when activated and then hissed and smoked for most of the grenade's time in flight. What finally dissuaded Hugh from tossing the weapons at the enemy troops, however, was the fact that both had been submerged in seawater since the night before, and he seriously doubted that either would explode.

While Hugh was contemplating his attack, the Japanese troops had re-formed on the beach, their rifles now unslung and pointing inland. They seemed hesitant to enter the forest, though, likely unwilling to confront an enemy of unknown number. After a few moments of intense debate, the men reboarded their landing craft—leaving the body of Hugh's benefactor behind—and quickly motored back into open water. Although relieved by their departure, Hugh was certain that they and many of their comrades would soon be back—and they would definitely be looking for *him*.

9

BACK IN THE WAR ————————————————

UPON RETURNING TO HIS CAMP, HUGH DRANK DEEPLY FROM ONE OF HIS water-filled beer bottles and then settled down to examine his new possessions.

He first untied the bootlaces and set the footwear and socks in a patch of sunlight to dry and then placed the two grenades nearby, hoping the warmth would revitalize their undoubtedly soggy fuzes. Hugh then eased the bayonet from its scabbard, smiling as the razor-sharp sixteen-inch blade revealed itself. He closely examined the weapon—a vast improvement on the broken penknife that had been his only tool for nearly a month—then whetted it on a handy rock and used the pointed tip to open one of the small ration cans. Having not had a decent meal in the weeks he'd been on Arundel, Hugh's mouth was watering at the thought of tucking into whatever might be in the tin. His hunger faded considerably, however, when he removed the lid and discovered a greasy, gelatinous, and foul-smelling mass of what appeared to be preserved meat. Unable to discern exactly what type of meat it might be, he reluctantly fingered a wad of it into his mouth and almost gagged at its lumpy consistency and rancid flavor. He nonetheless forced himself to chew the unidentifiable mass slowly before swallowing it, telling himself that as bad as it was, it would provide far more protein than he had so far been getting.

After choking down the remainder of the mystery meat, Hugh drank water and coconut milk until the foul taste in his mouth abated. Then, turning to the small pouch attached to the Japanese soldier's equipment belt, he removed the bar of rough soap and set it aside for later use. He then pulled out one of the small circular tins, removed the close-fitting lid, and discovered the container was filled with a strongly lemon-scented salve. Puzzled at first, he quickly realized that the cloud of mosquitoes and sand flies that had been his constant companion since the day he first set foot on Arundel had vanished and correctly assumed that the balm was some sort of insect repellent. He rubbed it on all of his exposed skin, noticing as he did so that in addition to whatever insect-repellent properties the cream might have, it also eased the irritation of previous bites and soothed the pain of the sunburn on his arms and neck. And, to his relief, the strong lemon scent helped offset the aroma of rotting meat that had enveloped his small camp after he'd opened the ration tin.

Having decided that the socks and boots had dried enough, Hugh pulled them off the log and examined them. The socks were woven of thin wool and, to his surprise, fitted him almost perfectly when he eased them carefully over his injured feet. The boots, he noticed, were made of tanned leather and had rounded tips rather than the split-toe "tabi" design that he'd heard was common in the Japanese military. He pulled the boots on and laced them up, relieved that they were only slightly tight when he stood and walked a few paces. He was still admiring his new footwear when the by now unmistakable sound of a low-flying American TBF gave him his first chance to run across Arundel's punishing terrain in something other than bare feet.

Hugh sprinted toward the nearby salt flat, excitedly repeating out loud his now daily mantra, "This is my day! This is my day!" He reached the open area just as the torpedo bomber roared in from the direction of Munda, obviously following the shoreline of Hathorn Sound. Hugh wildly waved his arms and jumped up and down, and the TBF snapped into a tight turn and circled the salt flat as the pilot obviously looked him over. The aviator must have liked what he saw, for on the next pass he pushed his cockpit canopy open and motioned toward the aircraft's tail. As Hugh watched, an access hatch in the TBF's side popped open, and the plane's radio operator tossed out a small parcel. The man's aim was good, for the package landed just feet from where Hugh was standing. He quickly scooped it up and then turned to wave at the already disappearing aircraft.

Hugh hurried back to his camp, settled down cross-legged with his back against a log, and carefully examined his unexpected gift from above. The package consisted of a ragged piece of T-shirt bound tightly with a short length of thin copper wire. After unwinding and removing the wire, Hugh folded back the fabric as though he were opening a much-anticipated Christmas present. Inside he discovered three smaller items, each also wrapped in a piece of T-shirt. The first was a standard-issue compression bandage, the type used by medics to staunch the flow of blood from an open wound. When Hugh found that the second item was a small bottle of iodine, he immediately set the package aside, pulled off his boots and socks, and liberally painted the bottom of each lacerated and festering foot with the liquid disinfectant. Though the fluid stung mightily as it entered the sores on his feet, Hugh knew that it would help prevent a possibly fatal infection of the kind that seemed to invade any wound suffered in the tropics.

As pleased as he was with the first two items in the air-dropped package, Hugh was overjoyed when he unwrapped the final one. A rectangle of about two by four inches, its waxed covering was labeled "U.S. Army Field Ration D," and within were four ounces of hard chocolate. Hugh read the list of ingredients as though it were a love letter from his wife: chocolate, sugar, skim milk, cocoa butter, and oat flour. His mouth again watering, he reverently unwrapped the cake of chocolate and slowly savored each of the six square segments. It was the most nutritious meal he'd had since the evening before *Strong's* sinking, and it certainly went down easier than the Japanese tinned meat. Hardly had Hugh finished the bar when he felt a surge of energy as the dense carbohydrates began hitting his malnourished system, and it struck him that eating the bar all at once had been a mistake—if he'd rationed himself to one square every other day as a supplement to coconut meat and the putrid Japanese rations, he could have kept up his strength for far longer.

Still, the energy rush produced by the single Ration D bar would come in handy soon enough.

HUGH SPENT THE REMAINDER OF AUGUST 4 ANXIOUSLY WAITING for some sign that the low-flying TBF had reported seeing him and that some kind of effort was under way to retrieve him.[1] When it became obvious that no rescue was immediately forthcoming, he reluctantly resumed his usual routine. After replenishing his water supply and collecting coconuts, he ascended to his crow's nest to keep watch on the Japanese. There was no offshore resupply activity or obvious patrolling that night, however, and after several hours of fruitless watching he came down from his perch and turned in for the remainder of the night.

Though Hugh usually awakened with the sun, on the morning of August 5 it was the rumble of artillery that brought him to consciousness before first light. Over the preceding few days the sound of heavy-caliber American gunfire from the direction of Munda had been steadily growing in both intensity and duration, but that morning it seemed to have swelled into a continuous gut-thumping cacophony. Afraid that the noise would prevent him from hearing the Japanese patrols he was certain would be coming after him, he spent the day in his crow's nest, scanning for any sign of trouble. Hugh was both puzzled and relieved when no enemy troops appeared, and as night fell he decided to work his way up the island to the point where the landing craft normally put the patrols ashore. Doing so would offer him a better chance to discern the enemy's intentions and allow him more time to respond accordingly. Shod in his new boots and with the belt bearing the bayonet and hand grenades cinched firmly around his waist, Hugh set off through the moonlight-dappled forest.

Though not unexpected, the sight that awaited him on the beach was decidedly alarming. Instead of the ten or twenty men who constituted the usual evening patrols along Arundel's east side, some one hundred Japanese troops were already milling about on the sand. As Hugh watched from cover, officers and noncommissioned officers (NCOs) formed the soldiers into smaller groups and dispatched them inland and southward toward Diamond Narrows. Finally, only five men were left on the beach, and as Hugh watched with mounting concern their leader started them in a direction that would ultimately take them almost directly toward the crow's nest camp. The Japanese moved forward in a wide line that resembled a row of "beaters" trying to flush game, and Hugh withdrew, moving stealthily from cover to cover and always keeping at least one of the soldiers clearly in view.

As Hugh retreated he considered the irony of his position. A hunter all his life, he had used this very same technique to drive his quarry toward a waiting band of shooters. He knew that another line of Japanese was likely waiting on Arundel's west side to kill or capture him should he break cover and realized that his only hope was to neutralize the five-man "beater" team. To do that he would have to use one or both of his hand grenades. And there was only one way to guarantee that all five of the Japanese would die: he would have to get them into a group tight enough to fit within the grenade's lethal blast radius. Even as that thought formed in his head, the perfect location for the ambush came to him. Should the Japanese "beaters" continue in their current direction, they would encounter a line of thick thorn bushes that was too wide to easily bypass. With luck, the man in charge would take the soldiers through a gap in the thorns together rather than risk sending them one or two at a time.

Hugh steadily fell back before the advancing patrol, crossing through the narrow passageway in the thorn bush while the Japanese were still some thirty yards away. On the other side he chose a position about seventy feet from the opening, behind a log and with a relatively unobstructed line of sight to the moonlit kill zone. As Hugh waited for the enemy to appear, he removed the two grenades from their carrier and closely inspected their now dry cylindrical percussion caps. He gently straightened the flared ends of each weapon's pin and then sat back expectantly, wondering if the Japanese would actually appear.

The answer wasn't long in coming. Within minutes the enemy soldiers emerged through the opening, moving carefully but—as Hugh had hoped—within an arm's length of each other. Taking a deep breath, Hugh pulled the pin on one of the grenades, smacked the top of the percussion cap against a rock, stood up quickly, and hurled the hissing, smoking weapon in his best Crimson Tide passing style. The grenade arced cleanly through the trees, thumping to earth almost exactly in the middle of the startled troops. Hugh dropped to the ground just as the device exploded, and to his intense relief the sound of the detonation was largely lost in the pervasive rumble of the U.S. artillery battering Japanese positions around Munda.

Knowing intuitively that a second grenade wouldn't be necessary, Hugh jumped up and ran to within a few feet of the crumpled bodies. A quick glance at the carnage the grenade had inflicted convinced him all five men were dead, but rather than risk discovery by any enemy troops who might be close enough to have actually heard the explosion Hugh left the bodies where they lay and retreated back into the jungle. He'd previously set up a fallback position in the tangled roots of a large banyan tree and had stocked it with coconuts and water, and he spent the night there.

It was not a restful stay, however. Hugh was kept awake by his anxiety about being discovered by a roving Japanese patrol, but also by his need to come to grips with the stark fact that he had just deliberately killed five human beings. They were the enemy, of course, and while aboard *Strong* Hugh had participated in operations that led directly to the deaths of many Japanese soldiers and sailors. But the grenade attack was something very different. Far more intimate than a shore bombardment, the ambush had forced Hugh to almost literally look into the eyes of the enemy that he was about to destroy and to watch as the men moved inexorably toward their deaths. While he had perhaps not always been as devout a Christian as his mother might have hoped, Hugh was most definitely a man of faith, and he could not simply shrug off his taking of human lives. He therefore spent most of the night reliving the attack in his mind, absorbing the reality of it, examining his conscience, and, ultimately, accepting the moral responsibility for his actions. By the time dawn broke, Hugh was at peace with himself and ready to face whatever the new day presented.

The first order of business that morning of August 6 was to return to the scene of the ambush and see what useful items he might be able to recover. After a circuitous and wary approach proved that no live Japanese were lying in wait, Hugh cautiously approached the tangle of bodies. In daylight the scene was far more frightful than it had been in moonlight. The single fragmentation grenade had landed almost exactly in the center of the group of soldiers, with none of the men being more than two or three feet from the explosion. The blast had done horrific damage to three of the bodies, all but dismembering them and ruining the equipment they had been carrying. The other two corpses—one of which belonged to the NCO who had been in charge—were in somewhat better condition. Hugh quickly relieved the latter men of their small haversacks, each of which contained tins of food, a shelter half, dry socks, a straight razor, a light rain poncho, clay pipes and wads of rough tobacco, and what looked to be small religious amulets. He pulled the bayonets and grenade carriers from the men's belts and added them to one of the haversacks. These were the only weapons he was able to recover, however, for the explosion that killed the five men had rendered their rifles useless.

Once he'd secured all the serviceable booty from the two relatively intact bodies, Hugh started going through their uniforms in search of items that might later be of use to Allied intelligence officers. Both had been carrying bank notes, coins, personal photos, and what looked like letters from home, but the NCO's pockets were also a treasure trove of official-looking documents—what Hugh took to be pay accounts, orders of some kind, and a small notebook with numerous entries. He also discovered a folded Japanese flag covered with handwritten characters, which he assumed was some sort of good-luck totem.[2] After stuffing the documents and flag into one of the haversacks, Hugh used his bayonet to remove the rank insignia from each man's collar—red rectangles with a single horizontal yellow stripe for the NCO and red rectangles with two yellow stars for the other man.[3]

Hugh assumed that when the members of the patrol did not return to their rally point, other troops would come looking for them, and to throw the search teams off the scent he decided to bury the five dead men. A few yards from the scene of the attack, he found a circular depression screened by bushes. After deepening it with his bayonet and several cut-down palm fronds, he dragged the corpses into the hole, tossed in their ruined rifles and the other unusable pieces of gear, and then covered everything with the excavated dirt and several layers of fallen branches, fronds, and underbrush. He then did his best to sweep away any sign of the patrol's presence and of the ambush, obliterating boot prints and covering the pools of blood with soil. Hugh knew the hurried effort wouldn't have met Uncle Jim's strict standards for eliminating "sign," but it would have to do.

The job completed, Hugh set off with the straps of the well-filled haversacks over either shoulder. As he walked he felt optimism growing within him, and to his surprise he realized it was a result of his attack on the Japanese patrol. He'd had no choice, of course, when it came to engaging the enemy troops—if he hadn't, they would certainly have discovered his camp—and he knew that taking the soldiers' lives in such a direct and brutal manner had changed him in ways he hadn't yet begun to fully understand. But the ambush had also fundamentally altered the circumstances of his forced sojourn on Arundel. He was no longer just a castaway on an island crawling with enemies; he had become as much a predator on the hunt as he had been prey on the run. No matter what his ultimate fate might be, he could take immeasurable pride in one simple fact: he was back in the war.

WHILE THE REPORTS OF A MYSTERIOUS CAUCASIAN ON ARUNDEL Island and the subsequent disappearance of the five-man patrol undoubtedly gave Japanese commanders some cause for concern, they had much larger issues with which to deal.

On the afternoon of August 5—hours before Hugh Miller tossed the grenade that began his one-man war on Arundel—American forces had finally overrun and secured Munda airfield. Having determined that he could no longer hold New Georgia, General Noboru Sasaki had then ordered the majority of his remaining troops to evacuate to Baanga, a long, narrow island just west of Munda and south of Hathorn Sound, and to Kolombangara. Skeleton units had established a defensive line that ran roughly from Bairoko Harbor southwest toward the southern end of Diamond Narrows and were doggedly trying to slow the American advance. Nor were Japan's military misfortunes confined to the jungles of New Georgia: on the night of August 6–7 four Japanese destroyers carrying supplies and some nine hundred troops to Vila were intercepted in Vella Gulf, west of Kolombangara, by six American destroyers under Commander Frederick Moosbrugger. Three of the Japanese vessels were sunk, with the loss of more than twelve hundred sailors and soldiers.[4]

One result of the fall of Munda and Sasaki's subsequent decision to withdraw the bulk of his forces from New Georgia was an increase in American naval activity in the southern end of Kula Gulf. The ongoing evacuation of Japanese forces from Bairoko to Kolombangara and a growing effort to ship reinforcements from Vila to Baanga ensured that the waters off Arundel's east coast remained a rich hunting ground for Tulagi-based destroyers—and especially for the PTs from Lever Harbor. The August 4 attack on the landing craft moving south along Hathorn Sound had shown just how devastatingly effective the American torpedo boats could be at disrupting the nocturnal missions that were fast becoming the only way the Japanese could move men and matériel south from Vila. In an attempt to neutralize the danger presented by the PTs, senior Japanese leaders on Kolombangara requested an increase in the number and frequency of nighttime sorties over Kula Gulf by Rabaul-based floatplanes and ordered the establishment of defensive positions along the eastern side of Arundel Island.

Hugh first noticed the increased enemy activity just before nightfall on August 7. He had moved from his crow's nest camp to a position near the beach where two nights earlier he'd watched the large Japanese force come ashore. His original intention had been to monitor the activity of any additional search parties that might land that evening, but instead he found dozens of troops constructing fighting positions at several points along the shoreline facing Kula Gulf and

Hathorn Sound. The men were digging shallow foxholes that they encircled with stacks of sandbags before emplacing a heavy machine gun in each position and then camouflaging the site with fronds and underbrush. The enemy troops were obviously planning to engage any American PT boat that might attempt to repeat the inshore ambush that had proved so successful three nights earlier.

The establishment of the machine-gun posts put Hugh in a quandary. He knew that the Japanese would undoubtedly continue to search for him and that the best way to guarantee his own survival was to stay deep in the jungle and do anything he could to remain unnoticed until he was rescued. Yet the new fighting positions were obviously a direct threat to the PT boats seeking to interdict the nighttime flow of Japanese reinforcements, and Hugh knew it was his responsibility as a naval officer to do everything in his power to disrupt the enemy's plan. His skills as a woodsman had allowed him to evade and then attack the five-man patrol, and he was convinced that he could find a way to engage the new positions with equal success.

Hugh spent the remainder of the night of August 7–8 watching the activity on the beach, noting that each completed gun emplacement was manned by four troops—the machine gunner, his two assistants, and one rifleman. The positions were roughly three hundred yards apart, and Hugh realized that they were not mutually supporting—each of the guns was sited to fire directly out to sea through a gap in the sandbags and could not be trained more than a few degrees to either side. More puzzling was the fact that none of the foxholes had overhead cover. The Japanese obviously did not expect the emplacements to be engaged by either artillery fire or aircraft, nor did they seem concerned by the possibility of an infantry attack. And Hugh's assumption that the gun positions were intended only for nighttime use against marauding American PT boats was borne out just after dawn on August 8, when a landing craft grounded on the beach and dropped its ramp. The Japanese troops gathered up the machine guns and quickly boarded the boat, which then backed away and set off in the direction of Vila.

After returning to his camp for a few hours of sleep, Hugh decided to spend the daylight hours "beachcombing," as he'd begun thinking of his forays in search of Japanese bodies that might provide useful items. Not wanting to follow a routine the enemy might be able to discern and take advantage of, he went northwest rather than east. The hike took longer than he'd anticipated, and it wasn't until mid-afternoon that he reached a beach facing Blackett Strait and Ferguson Passage. His efforts were soon rewarded, however, for there were three life-jacketed corpses resting on the sand. After carefully scanning the area for signs of trouble and finding none, he quickly retrieved several hand grenades, a few more tins of meat, some additional containers of the lemon-scented insect repellent, and a handful of official-looking documents. He also noted that these men were apparently naval infantry—though they were dressed in army-style drab-green uniforms, their helmets were emblazoned with small anchors.[5]

By the time Hugh returned to his camp, night had fallen. Exhausted by his cross-country trek, he decided to sleep for a few hours before setting out toward the new beach gun positions. His normally reliable internal "alarm clock" failed him, however, because when he awoke on August 9, the sun was high in the air. Though upset with himself for sleeping so long, he realized that the night's rest had done him good. He felt wonderfully refreshed and spent the remainder of the day doing "chores"—gathering coconuts and fresh water, sweeping the area around his camp to remove any sign of his presence, and, in late afternoon, treating himself to a bath in one of the freshwater springs using the soap he'd taken from the first Japanese corpse he'd found.

Just after darkness fell Hugh left camp, a bayonet on his belt and a haversack over his shoulder carrying several hand grenades and a water-filled beer bottle stoppered with a wad of leaves. He was determined to raise a little hell with the machine-gun emplacements on the beach, though he wasn't yet sure how he could engage them with the grenades and get away alive. The answer was not long in coming, however. As he huddled down behind a log some sixty feet behind one of the enemy foxholes, Hugh realized three things in quick succession. First, the sound of gunfire from New Georgia was much louder than usual—he rightly assumed that American forces had taken Munda and were hammering Japanese holdouts in and around Bairoko. Second, he noted that artillery was also firing from somewhere to his south, either from the ex-treme end of Arundel or, more likely, from Baanga, and that the rounds were on their way toward the American positions around Munda. And third, above the rumble of the guns he could discern the welcome sound of Black Cat engines—the PBYs were clearly aloft, either spotting for the American gunners or out to raise a little hell of their own.

Hugh was still carefully observing the gun position in front of him when one of the Black Cats roared in low from the south, barely two hundred feet off the ground and paralleling the beach. The PBY crew was obviously "trolling" for an enemy reaction, and they quickly got one. One of the Japanese positions just to the north of where Hugh was hiding opened fire on the American patrol plane, an incredibly foolish act on the part of the gunner since by the time he pulled the trigger, the PBY was already well past him. Minutes later the Black Cat returned, this time coming in from a different direction with the twin .30-caliber guns in its nose turret pumping rounds in the general direction of the now revealed Japanese position. Bullets were not the only form of death raining from the sky, however. As the PBY thun-dered overhead, two 24-pound "parafrags"—parachute-retarded frag-mentation bombs—dropped from the aircraft's wings. Small canopies blossomed behind the devices, causing them to slow dramatically and fall almost straight down and allowing the quickly disappearing Black Cat to avoid being caught in the ensuing detonations. The bombs straddled the Japanese machine-gun nest, the twin explosions failing to knock out the gun but undoubtedly giving the foxhole's occupants something to think about.

While the PBY may have just missed its target, the attack showed Hugh how he could engage the Japanese positions without giving himself away. He knew that the American aircrew's report of enemy machine-gun posts along Arundel's east coast would draw other Black Cats, and all he had to do was wait for one of the nocturnal marauders to overfly the stretch of beach in front of him. As the plane passed, he would hurl a grenade into the closest foxhole, and, with luck, the explosion and subsequent destruction would be blamed on a PBY at-tack. He was still pondering the beauty of the plan when, just after midnight, the swelling sound of twin radial engines announced that another Black Cat was incoming. Hugh drew a grenade from his haversack, pulled the pin, smacked the top of the detonator on the log in front of him, and, as the PBY soared unseen overhead, stood and unleashed a "pass" that would have made Coach Wade proud. The hissing grenade dropped squarely in the center of the Japanese gun position and exploded with a flash. Hugh realized that the sound of the detonation had been drowned out by the noise of both the passing PBY and the rumble of artillery on New Georgia, and as he hurried back toward the safety of his crow's nest camp he knew he'd found the ideal way to strike out at the enemy and survive the experience.

As he'd done following his attack on the five-man patrol, Hugh let the night pass before investigating the extent of the damage he'd inflicted. On the morning of August 10 he made his way back to the scene of the previous night's action and, after determining that no Japanese troops had been left behind, carefully examined the foxhole that had been his target. The grenade's explosion had scattered the encircling sandbags and palm-frond camouflage, and while there were no bodies the sand in and around the hole was marked by patches of soaked-in blood. To Hugh's disappointment there were also no weapons—the machine gun and the soldiers' rifles had all been removed—nor was there any other useful equipment. Still, it was obvious that the grenade had caused casualties, and Hugh consoled himself with the fact that every Japanese soldier removed from the battlefield reduced the enemy's overall combat effectiveness.

Though eager to carry out another nocturnal attack, Hugh realized that the Japanese were certain to become suspicious if every night they lost a gun position to what appeared to be a direct hit by a blind-bombing PBY. He therefore spent the nights of August 10 and 11 simply observing the Japanese emplacements, trying to determine how many were spread out along Arundel's east side and attempting to fix their positions in his mind. On August 12 he went back on the offensive, attacking the gun immediately to the north of his first target. Again he waited for a Black Cat to fly overhead before "passing" the grenade, and when he reconnoitered the area the following day the results were the same as those of his first assault—a lot of blood but no bodies, no usable weapons, and, fortunately, no indication that the Japanese were aware they were losing men to an American castaway rather than to the aircraft that were becoming increasingly common in the night skies.

Early on the evening of August 13 Hugh headed out of his camp in the direction of the Japanese gun emplacement directly to the south of the one he'd attacked the night before. He was not planning on launching another assault so soon and intended only to spend a few hours doing reconnaissance. As soon as the beach came into view his plans changed, however, for he saw a group of about fifteen Japanese soldiers debarking from a landing craft. Since the machine-gun positions he could see were already fully manned, it was obvious that new arrivals had come to look for him. Indeed, even as he watched the soldiers broke into two sections and started inland, one group to Hugh's north and one to his south. Repeating the tactic he'd employed with the five-man patrol days earlier, Hugh steadily retreated while keeping at least one of the troops in sight at all times. This time, unfortunately, the Japanese searchers seemed intent on conducting a much more thorough search. The two patrols crossed each other's paths several times—a tactic meant to ensure that their quarry could not pass through the gap between them—and two men from each group trailed the main line by twenty-five or thirty feet in order to surprise anyone who might break cover once the main body of searchers had passed. The soldiers displayed excellent noise discipline and moved easily through the dense undergrowth, suggesting they were far more experienced than the troops conducting the earlier searches. Although Hugh managed to evade detection throughout the night, several times individual Japanese soldiers passed within yards of him—and at least twice he didn't hear their approach until they were almost on top of him.

Just before dawn on August 14 the troops suspended their search and returned to the beach to board the landing craft that were also embarking the machine-gun crews. Though relieved by the departure of the Japanese search team, Hugh was also quite shaken by the night's events. For weeks he had evaded the enemy patrols with relative ease, in the process becoming somewhat contemptuous of the soldiers' obvious inexperience and lack of familiarity with how to operate in the forest. He'd begun to think of those earlier pursuers as the second or even third string, in football terms, but he was forced to admit that the men who had come after him just hours before were obviously the varsity squad. Had the search effort been stepped up because of his attacks on the gun emplacements, he wondered, or had the Japanese just decided that the mysterious Caucasian on Arundel Island had eluded them long enough? In the end, it didn't really matter either way, Hugh admitted to himself, for the result would be the same. He might be able to outwit the "varsity team" for a few more days, but sooner rather than later he would make a mistake and the Japanese would kill him—or, worse, they would capture him and spend days or even weeks interrogating him before the blade of a samurai sword or a bullet to the head ended his torment.

Though Hugh had long since accepted the possibility of his own death—whether at sea or on the island—the idea of being taken alive by the Japanese frightened him more than anything he'd so far experienced in the war. The only way to keep the fear from paralyzing him, he knew, was to continue to take the fight to the enemy no matter the odds against him. Despite the near certainty of failure and an agonizing death, he would go on doing whatever he could to hurt and confound the Japanese, and that included more attacks on the machine-gun positions. He decided to launch another grenade assault that night, both to further erode the enemy defenses on Arundel's east side and, he hoped, to finally acquire a working rifle. The hand grenades had stood him in good stead, but if he was going to have to fight it out with Japanese troops he wanted to be able to hit them from as great a range as possible.

By nightfall Hugh was again within sight of one of the machine-gun positions, this one well to the south of the two he'd previously attacked. The rumble of artillery fire from both New Georgia and Baanga had lessened considerably, and it took some time for Hugh to move to within about sixty feet of the enemy emplacement without being heard. So intently did he concentrate on moving slowly and carefully, in fact, that Hugh did not hear the approach of a Black Cat—he had barely settled in behind a fallen log when the PBY roared overhead. Not knowing if he'd have another chance, Hugh quickly stood, pulled the pin on a grenade, smacked it against the log, and hurled it toward the soldiers huddled around their machine gun. The throw was rushed, and the grenade landed not in the center of the emplacement but to one side, the sandbags absorbing some of the deadly fragments when the device exploded.

To his horror, Hugh saw that two of the four men in the emplacement had survived the grenade's detonation. One man was standing upright, obviously dazed, while the other was writhing on the edge of the foxhole, screaming in agony. Knowing he had no choice, Hugh tossed a second grenade, which killed the standing man but did not silence his wounded companion. A third grenade finally stilled the soldier's shrieking, but both of the final explosions had been clearly audible—the Black Cat had long since left the area, and the Japanese in the neighboring positions would know beyond doubt that they were under attack from the rear. When that realization hit him, Hugh turned and bolted into the forest, his fear so great that he sprinted like a wild man, arms and legs pumping as though he were headed for the touchdown of his life and his breath ragged in his throat. He ran until he reached his secondary camp beneath the banyan tree and then burrowed as deeply as he could between the massive roots, his heart pumping and his hands shaking so much he was barely able to pull his bayonet from its scabbard.

Hugh's fear was well founded, for in the hours that followed his fumbled attack on the gun emplacement numerous Japanese patrols scoured Arundel looking for him. Several times soldiers came within yards of Hugh's hiding place, where he huddled still as death, his bayonet in one hand and a grenade in the other. He spent a sleepless and terrified night hunkered down within the protective banyan, and it wasn't until well after daylight on August 15 that he was able to regain his composure.

Upon emerging from his sanctuary, Hugh gulped down water from the two bottles he'd cached and then slumped against a log to take stock of his situation. He was, he admitted to himself, well and truly screwed. The Japanese now knew beyond doubt that he was the source of the unexplained nocturnal attacks, and they would tear the island apart looking for him. Hugh's entire arsenal now consisted of just a few remaining hand grenades and a couple of bayonets, and unless he could get his hands on a rifle—or, better yet, a machine gun—

he wouldn't have a hope of staying alive for more than forty-eight hours. He realized that despite the very real danger he'd be discovered by the Japanese, he had no choice but to make his way back to the beach to see if the previous night's attack had netted him a firearm.

His decision made, Hugh steeled himself for whatever might come. Again he clipped one of the bayonets to his belt and shouldered a haversack bearing his last grenades and then set out for the beach with more trepidation in his heart than he had known at any time during his sojourn on Arundel. The journey took longer than usual, for he was especially careful in his movements, stopping every few minutes to listen for any sound that might indicate the presence of the enemy. He was frankly surprised that he made it to the previous night's observation position without being detected, and by late afternoon he was laying silently behind a log, peering out at the grenade-blasted foxhole. When he was certain there were no Japanese lying in wait, he dashed into the open and ran hunched over to the edge of the emplacement, only to find that—as with his previous attacks—the only thing remaining in the empty fighting position was bloodstained sand. Bitterly disappointed, Hugh retreated into the trees and settled in to decide whether to attempt another attack.

In the end, the decision was not Hugh's to make. As night fell several landing craft grounded on the beach before him, disgorging not only the usual machine-gun crews but also some sixty additional troops who immediately formed into search parties and headed into the bush. Hugh managed to fall in behind one of the patrol lines, noting that the soldiers were only a few feet apart and seemed to be probing every clump of bushes with their bayonets. They were definitely part of the "varsity squad," or at the very least of the same caliber, and Hugh was still trying to decide his next move when he realized with a jolt that another search team was coming up behind him. He was barely able to make an end run around this second group before the troops swept past him, his alarm at their sudden appearance compounded by the fact that they moved through the underbrush in almost total silence and it was only his "woodsman's sense" that had warned him of their approach.

To Hugh's chagrin, the second line of troops was even more thorough than the first. The men were not overlooking anything, thrusting their bayonets into the underbrush and stopping occasionally to obviously listen for any sound that might be out of the ordinary. Hugh was still pondering his next move when the soldiers in the second sweep line did something he had never seen before—with no obvious command they suddenly reversed course and started moving directly back toward him. He had no choice but to retreat, anxiety squeezing his chest and his breathing rattling in his throat. He had fallen back less than a half mile when to his horror he realized that a third line of troops was moving toward him—he was caught between two lines of soldiers and had no time to do anything but drop into a shallow depression between a fallen log and a small mound of earth. He hurriedly covered himself with fallen leaves and then pulled two of his last grenades from the haversack and waited, terrified, as the Japanese searchers came inexorably closer.

That he was not discovered Hugh could only credit to divine intervention. The third line of enemy soldiers passed within feet of him, one man actually poking his bayonet into a clump of dirt not eighteen inches from Hugh's face. Yet the Japanese moved on without discovering their quarry, and Hugh spent several hours huddled behind the protective log, grenades at the ready in case the searchers doubled back, before slowly making his way to the crow's nest camp. Exhausted by the night's events, he soon fell into a fitful sleep.

By the time Hugh awoke the sun was well up in the sky, and he judged the time to be about eight o'clock. Gathering his "towel"—the slogan-bearing flag he'd taken from the dead enemy NCO—two hand grenades, and a bayonet, he set off for the nearby spring. He gulped down as much of the fresh, clear water as he could and was washing his face when he heard the unmistakable drone of an approaching TBF. Hugh leaped up and ran out onto the closest salt flat, wildly waving the flag and jumping up and down. For a moment he thought he'd missed his chance, but then the American torpedo bomber banked suddenly, came back toward him, and looked for a moment as though it were lining up for a strafing run. Hugh was about to run for cover when the aircraft abruptly pulled up, waggled its wings, and did a quick circle above him. The pilot cranked back his canopy, gestured something Hugh couldn't decipher, and then wracked the TBF into a tight turn to the east.

As he watched the tubby aircraft depart, Hugh was filled with a sense of relief. For some reason he couldn't fathom, he was sure that this was the day he'd been waiting for since the moment he and his companions had grounded on Arundel Island. He knew in his heart, in a way he could never have expressed, that today was the day of his deliverance.

And, as fate would have it, Hugh Miller was right.

10

BACK TO THE WORLD

WHILE AUGUST 16, 1943, WAS TO BE A TURNING POINT IN HUGH MILLER'S life, the day had thus far been nothing but ordinary for the man who spotted the castaway of Arundel Island.

First Lieutenant James R. Turner, a lanky twenty-two-year-old from Tyler, Texas, and a member of Marine Torpedo Bombing Squadron 143 (VMTB-143), had taken off early that morning from Guadalcanal. His mount was a Grumman TBF that had just been overhauled, and the day's mission was to conduct what the unit's *War Diary* termed a "local test hop." The flight was to be more than a brief post-maintenance check ride, however. Turner and his two crewmen—turret gunner and navigator/radio operator—were also to use the mission to further familiarize themselves with their squadron's large operational area.[1] After taking the big Avenger up the Slot as far as Kula Gulf, they would turn southwest in the general direction of Arundel before heading east over Munda and from there along the south coast of New Georgia back to Henderson Field. Given that the five-hundred-mile flight would be conducted in what was still very much a combat theater, Turner's aircraft carried a full load of ammunition for its wing and turret machine guns, though its cavernous bomb bay was empty except for an auxiliary fuel tank.[2]

The first half of the flight passed without incident. Turner flew the briefed route up the Slot and then into the often busy airspace over Kula Gulf, though on this particular day things were quiet. He gave the east coast of Kolombangara a wide berth, wary of the antiaircraft emplacements around Vila, but after passing the eastern entrance to Blackett Strait Turner banked toward the northern end of Arundel and took the TBF down to barely four hundred feet above the waves. His intention, he later said, was to sweep down the island's east side and try to spot any Japanese barges that might be nestled in among the mangroves. To improve the chances of locating the enemy craft, Turner throttled back the Avenger's huge Wright R-2600 engine, lowered the wing flaps, and trimmed the aircraft slightly nose down to keep it level. Cruising just barely above the torpedo bomber's stall speed, the young pilot and his two crewmen scanned the shoreline of Arundel as it passed below them.

As the TBF droned southwestward Turner's radio operator was peering out the rear-facing ventral position when he saw a figure flash past below. The sailor called out the sighting to Turner over the intercom, saying he thought he'd seen a Japanese soldier gesturing from the center of a small salt flat. Marine that he was, the pilot could not resist the opportunity to engage the enemy, and he immediately wracked the Avenger into as tight a turn as he dared at such a low altitude and speed. As the aircraft came around Turner switched on the Mark 8 gunsight fixed to the top of the instrument panel just behind the windshield and then pulled the charging handle that armed both wing-mounted .50-caliber machine guns. His finger already on the trigger, Turner leaned slightly forward and peered through the sight in search of his target.

He had just spotted the wildly gesticulating figure on the ground when he realized that the man definitely did not look Japanese. Even from a distance and at some seventy miles an hour, Turner could clearly see that the "enemy soldier" had a red beard. The pilot pulled the Avenger into a shallow turn, at the same time telling his turret gunner not to fire on the man, whom he had immediately decided must be a downed Allied flyer. As the TBF came back around toward the salt flat, the pilot slid back his canopy and leaned out, flashing a thumbs-up signal toward the man below and then tapping the side of his leather flying helmet to indicate that he would radio for help. Turner then eased the Avenger's throttle forward and pulled the stick back to gain altitude, and when the aircraft reached about five hundred feet he retracted the flaps and turned southeast.[3]

The course change resulted from the fact that almost as soon as he had indicated to the red-bearded mystery man that help would be summoned by radio, Turner decided *not* to broadcast news of the discovery. He knew the Japanese monitored American signals traffic and was concerned that if the enemy overheard the transmission, they would be able to capture the man before help arrived. Moreover, if prematurely alerted that a rescue mission was being organized, the Japanese might also set a trap for those coming to the castaway's aid. Turner determined that it would be safer for all concerned to report the sighting in person, and the closest place to do that was the airfield at Munda—barely twelve miles and scant minutes of flying time away.

Other than being nearby, however, Munda had little to recommend it. The Japanese-built airfield had been declared fully secured only two days earlier, and Seabees were still filling in the last of the many bomb craters that pockmarked the strip and adjacent taxiways. Despite the damage, the field was already crowded with American aircraft; a Marine J2F-5 Duck biplane amphibian carrying Brigadier General Francis P. Mulcahy, commander of the 2nd Marine Air Wing (MAW), had landed near midday on August 14 and was followed hours later by the first twelve of an eventual twenty-four F4U Corsairs of Marine Fighter Squadron 123 (VMF-123). Though the fighters had flown their first mission from Munda on August 15, the field was still sporadically being shelled by Japanese artillery firing from Baanga. That fact, combined with the crowded conditions, had prompted Mulcahy to close the runway to any aircraft but the Duck and the Corsairs, except in an emergency.[4]

From Turner's point of view, the need to inform higher headquarters of the presence of a downed pilot on Arundel definitely qualified as an emergency, and he said as much to the Munda approach controller. That officer agreed, and the TBF—the first of its type to land at Munda—was soon parked in one of the crude revetments the Seabees had bulldozed into the thick vegetation just off the taxiway.[5] Within minutes of touching down, Turner was recounting the sighting of the red-bearded castaway to Majors Vernon A. Peterson and Goodwin R. "Roy" Luck, two air operations officers on Mulcahy's staff. Though the young TBF pilot didn't realize it, few aviators in the Marine Corps were as well qualified to conduct the rescue flight as were the two Minnesotans standing before him.

St. Paul native Luck and Peterson, of Minneapolis, had both joined the Marine Corps Reserve in the early 1930s. After flight school the men had pursued their civilian aviation careers—Peterson with Eastern Airlines and Luck as an aeronautical engineer—while also flying Marine biplane fighters and other types during monthly reserve drills and annual summer training. Called to active duty after Pearl Harbor, both had been assigned to the 2nd MAW and accompanied Mulcahy when he was tapped to be Commander, Air (ComAir) New Georgia. Indeed, it was Luck who piloted the J2F-5 Duck that carried the general to Munda on August 14.[6]

But ferrying senior officers around the Solomon Islands was not the Duck's primary purpose. Soon after Mulcahy and his staff arrived on Rendova in June 1943 in preparation for the assault on New Georgia, Luck and Peterson had approached the general with a plan to establish a small-scale air-sea rescue operation. They pointed out that until the Munda airfield could be secured and rendered usable, Guadalcanal-based Allied pilots operating over New Georgia and the islands around Kula Gulf would need to be rescued if their aircraft were shot down or suffered catastrophic mechanical failure. The two staff officers suggested that by keeping both a Duck and a high-speed motorboat on call at all times, they could provide the vital rescue cover, and Mulcahy agreed. The general signed the necessary directives, and on July 3 a Navy pilot flew the J2F-5 from Guadalcanal to Rendova. Since Luck had amassed hundreds of flight hours in Ducks during his prewar reserve time, he became the chief—and only—pilot in the newly authorized rescue unit, while Peterson was in charge of mission support. This latter task included finding 100-octane gasoline for the J2F-5's Wright R-1820 Cyclone engine—fuel that was sometimes donated by Rendova-based PT boats, including on at least one occasion John F. Kennedy's *PT-109.*

Galvanized by Turner's report of the "downed airman" on Arundel who "looked like Rip Van Winkle," Luck and Peterson immediately set about planning the rescue.[7] The former would pilot the Duck, while the latter served as lookout in the rear cockpit. Master Technical Sergeant John J. Happer—who volunteered to go along in case the well-worn aircraft had any mechanical problems—would ride in the cramped passenger position behind and below the pilot's seat and scan to either side of the J2F-5's path through the small windows set into both sides of the fuselage just aft of the lower wing.

A review of the latest intelligence reports on Japanese activity in the area convinced the trio that a roundabout approach made the most sense. After takeoff from Munda, Luck would head due west, flying just above the waves until the J2F-5 passed the southern tip of Baanga. A wide turn to the north would take the Duck along Arundel's west coast, and at a point about three quarters of the way up the length of the island Luck would turn due east and fly at treetop level until reaching Hathorn Sound in the approximate area where Turner had sighted the mystery man. If he was still there—and if the three Marines aboard the amphibian determined they were not flying into a trap—Luck would land the aircraft, and Peterson would row ashore in the J2F-5's two-man dinghy to collect the presumably debilitated castaway. Once both men were back aboard, the Duck would take off and fly straight down Hathorn Sound and Diamond Narrows until again reaching the southern tip of Baanga and then turn hard to port and head for Munda. Luck calculated that, if all went well, the thirty-seven-mile round-trip flight should take less than an hour.

The plan was a good one, the men agreed, though they realized they were not quite as prepared as they might have been. For one thing, though each aviator carried a holstered pistol, they would have no way to defend themselves should they be bounced by Japanese fighters—the Duck's rearward-facing .30-caliber machine gun had been removed from the aft cockpit before the aircraft left Guadalcanal, and there had been no opportunity to find a replacement. Moreover, the compressed-air cartridges used to inflate the dinghy had been expended earlier, and Peterson would have to employ a hastily scrounged bicycle pump to blow up the rubber craft when the time came. A final potential problem arose from the fact that the Duck's engine was not equipped with an electric starter. After landing in Hathorn Sound, Luck intended to shut the power plant down so the characteristic throaty rumble of the big Cyclone wouldn't draw the attention of nearby enemy troops. That meant that once the "downed airman" had been brought aboard, Luck and Happer would have to hand-crank the engine's inertia starter to coax the R-1820 back to life. Should the starter fail to do its job, or, worse, should the men lose the hand crank overboard before the engine caught, the aircraft would literally be a sitting—and extremely vulnerable—Duck.

Their preparations complete, the three Marines climbed aboard the aircraft and just before ten in the morning—barely ninety minutes after first hearing about the castaway on Arundel—Roy Luck lifted the J2F-5 off the Munda runway and pointed the nose west. Turner, standing by the side of the runway, watched the amphibian depart and fervently hoped that the rescuers would find the red-bearded man before the Japanese did.

FOLLOWING THE TBF'S DEPARTURE IN THE DIRECTION OF MUNDA, Hugh Miller had remained on the salt flat, afraid that if he went back into the shelter of the trees for even a moment, the aircraft would return for a final check, its crew wouldn't see him, and, concluding that Hugh was likely the bait in some sort of Japanese trap, the aviators would call off any rescue attempt. So he stayed out in the open, despite the danger he might be seen by an enemy patrol, broiling in the tropical sun for what seemed an eternity.

Hugh had just started to think that help wasn't coming when the sound of an aircraft engine came to him from the west. He could tell immediately that it was not the TBF returning, because the engine had a completely different pitch. Indeed, it almost sounded like one of the Japanese floatplanes that occasionally operated from Blackett Strait, and Hugh was about to sprint for cover when the Duck came into view.[8] He recognized the type immediately and started jumping up and down and waving his arms. The amphibian did a quick circle around him and then landed into the wind just offshore. Hugh ran to the water's edge as the Duck taxied closer to shore, and when Luck was as close to the beach as he could safely get he cut the airplane's engine and ordered Happer to throw out the anchor. Just as the burly sergeant did so, Hugh turned and hurried back into the forest to gather up the Japanese documents and other items he knew would be of value to Allied intelligence. Unaware of his intentions, the trio aboard the J2F-5 momentarily wondered if they'd been lured into a trap, though Hugh's speedy return—his arms encompassing two well-filled haversacks—put their minds at ease.

Peterson had begun inflating the rubber dinghy almost as soon as the Duck touched down, and when Hugh reappeared on the beach the Marine officer shouted that he would row in to get him. Some forty feet of water separated the aircraft from the shoreline, and it took Peterson several tense minutes to guide the rudderless dinghy to the beach using one of its two small aluminum oars. When the craft grounded on the sand, Hugh handed Peterson the haversacks, telling him they contained important information, and then pushed the raft back into the water before jumping aboard. The Marine handed him the second oar, and the two men paddled as quickly as possible back toward the Duck.

Luck and Happer had begun hand-cranking the plane's inertia starter as soon as they saw the dinghy leave the beach, and by the time the craft bumped up against the plane's main float the engine was running smoothly and Luck was back in the pilot's seat. Peterson and Happer held the dinghy securely as Hugh climbed up and into the rear cockpit. He turned and took the two haversacks from Happer, who told him to drop them through the floor hatch into the small passenger compartment in the main float. Hugh did so and then clambered down behind them and settled into the narrow for-ward-facing seat. Moments later Peterson joined him, pulling the now deflated and folded dinghy after him. Happer climbed into the rear cockpit above them and was fastening his seat belt when he saw Luck gesturing to him. In their hurry to get aboard the plane and take off before they were discovered, none of the men had pulled in the anchor, which was now caught on a coral spur. The pilot stood up in his cockpit, turned around, and tossed Happer a six-inch hunt-ing knife—something Luck always carried in case the small life raft that formed his seat cushion accidentally inflated in flight. Happer quickly slashed the rope connecting the anchor to the airplane, and Luck gunned the Duck's engine.

As the aircraft picked up speed, the wing floats and the front half of the main float came free of the water, and after what seemed to Hugh to be a surprisingly short takeoff run the sturdy amphibian lifted into the air—though not very far. Luck kept the J2F-5 at less than fifty feet for most of the short flight back to Munda, gaining altitude only once he passed the southern tip of Baanga. On approach to the airfield the Marine pilot dropped the Duck's flaps and gear and with the ease re-sulting from many years of practice put the amphibian smoothly onto the runway just after noon. Although Luck usually parked the aircraft just off the taxiway in order to ensure a quick departure during rescue flights, on that day something prompted him to run the Duck into one of the protective revetments. It would soon prove to be a fortunate change of habit.

Hugh had spent most of the brief flight from Arundel deep in thought, replaying in his mind the events of the past forty-three days. It was only as Luck and the others were helping him out of the Duck that the former castaway allowed himself to accept that he was safe, that he really had been rescued and was no longer alone on an island teeming with enemies. Through the grace of God—and by relying on the woodland skills he'd learned from Uncle Jim so many years before and the relentless determination and drive drummed into him by Wal-lace Wade—Hugh had survived. Yet he knew that many of his friends and shipmates had not, and as he slowly climbed into the back of a waiting Army "deuce and a half" truck he was suddenly overcome by the grief and sense of loss he had not allowed himself to feel while he was on the island.[9] As the vehicle moved off, bearing Hugh and his two haversacks to a nearby aid station, tears coursed down his sunburned cheeks and into the red beard that had helped bring about his salvation.

THE RIDE WAS BRIEF, FOR THE TRUCK'S FIRST STOP WAS A FIELD DISpensary a few hundred yards from the runway. The facility was operated by the medical section of ACORN 8, a unit that included the 73rd Naval Construction Battalion and an aviation base unit—the former was tasked with repairing and improving the original Japanese runway and constructing the necessary support facilities, while the latter included the men who actually operated the airfield.[10] The dispensary was treating all Navy and Marine personnel in the Munda area until the scheduled October completion of the larger USN Base Hospital No. 11.

The story of Hugh's sojourn on Arundel Island had preceded him, and as soon as he was helped down from the back of the truck—still clutching his haversacks—he was whisked into the large tent that served as the dispensary's triage area. A corpsman recorded that Hugh's blood pressure, pulse, and temperature were all within acceptable limits, and Lieutenant Commander John H. Ward Jr. then conducted a thorough examination. An internist by training, the physician was particularly interested in his new patient's account of the immersion-blast injuries he'd suffered during *Strong*'s death throes. Though Ward determined that most of the intestinal ill effects of the depth-charge explosions seemed to have dissipated, he believed that the continuing leg weakness and calf-muscle cramps Hugh mentioned were likely tied in some way to the detonations' effect on his lower spine. Ward also noted that Hugh's ear canals were partially plugged by dried fuel oil, and he retained light to moderate patches of the tarry substance on his face, neck, shoulders, and abdomen. While the lemon-scented Japanese insect repellent had prevented all but a few minor bites, the coral lacerations on Hugh's feet and the wounds on his wrist and neck from the ricocheting bullet fragments were all

infected, despite the iodine he'd applied to them. He was also suffering from boils on his lower back and buttocks. The most obvious
result of Hugh's time as a castaway, however, was that his weight
had dropped by forty pounds—not an unexpected result, Ward dryly
noted, given the patient's recent diet.[11]

Upon completion of the exam Ward found a spare uniform for
Hugh to wear and told him he had visitors; in walked Turner, Luck,
Peterson, and Happer. The aviators had brought along a large metal
canteen cup filled with bourbon and a tray from the nearby mess
tent piled high with food. The men passed the cup around, and the
whiskey helped Hugh rediscover the joy of friendly conversation—
something he'd had little chance to practice on Arundel. The four
airmen went on sipping as the hungry former castaway wolfed down
the first decent meal he'd had since before the loss of his ship. The al-
cohol and the meal worked their magic, and Hugh was just starting to
really relax when the shrill whistle of incoming artillery rounds sent
everyone sprinting for the slit trenches that lay just outside the tent.
Several of the Japanese shells hit in the ACORN 8 area, one of them
landing among a line of sailors waiting for chow, killing two men and
wounding nine others.[12]

When the shelling stopped, Hugh and his companions slowly
emerged from the shallow trenches. The sudden attack had cast a pall
on their impromptu gathering, and after a round of handshakes the
men parted company. The aviators walked back toward the airfield,
Turner for the return flight to Henderson Field on Guadalcanal and
the other three to check on the Duck. Fortunately, Luck's decision to
park the amphibian in a revetment meant that despite several nearby
explosions, the aircraft that had rescued Hugh had suffered only a few
small shrapnel holes in its wings.[13]

Hugh stayed at Munda until August 18, following Ward's orders
to eat as often as possible and sleep as much as he could. He also
spent several hours each day with Marine intelligence officers from
Mulcahy's staff and their counterparts from the Army's 43rd Infantry
Division. The former were particularly interested in Hugh's observations of Japanese barge traffic along Arundel's east coast—information that they deemed "most complete" and that was forwarded to

ComAirSols for use in planning aircraft and PT-boat attacks on the enemy vessels.[14] The Army intelligence officers, on the other hand, were more focused on Hugh's accounts of the numbers, locations, and armament of Japanese troops on the island. Though they did not reveal the reason for their interest, Hugh correctly assumed that they were assembling background data for an imminent invasion of Arundel—an attack that was ultimately launched by the 43rd's 172nd Infantry Regiment on August 27, took nearly a month, and resulted in the deaths of forty-four Americans and more than five hundred Japanese—and he urged them to undertake a search for Armbruster, Lawrence, and Mullane at the earliest opportunity.[15] Hugh was also able to officially report the deaths of Oberg, Deering, and the men who had died on the floater net.

Because there were no Japanese linguists at Munda, the intelligence officers could not decipher the information contained in the documents Hugh had recovered on Arundel. They therefore decided that he should share the contents of his two haversacks with representatives of the Combat Intelligence Center, the New Caledonia–based organization that had jurisdiction over captured enemy papers and whose teams of Japanese-speaking analysts were deployed throughout the Southwest Pacific. The closest detachment was at Henderson Field, and the intelligence officers' plan to send Hugh there coincided nicely with Ward's intention to evacuate him to Guadalcanal's newly opened USN Mobile Hospital No. 8, a facility much larger and far better equipped than the ACORN 8 dispensary. The physician duly signed Hugh's movement orders, and on the afternoon of August 18 the freshly shaven former castaway departed Munda as one of only two passengers aboard an R4D-1 twin-engine transport of Marine Utility Squadron 153 operating as part of the triservice South Pacific Combat Air Transport Command (universally known by the rather unfortunate acronym SCAT). The aircraft, a military cargo variant of the Douglas DC-3 airliner, landed at Henderson Field just after six in the evening.[16]

During the days he spent on Guadalcanal, Hugh split his time between medical examinations at "MOB 8" and conferences with the team from the Combat Intelligence Center. Their translations of the documents recovered from the Japanese bodies on Arundel—and of the names and other information inscribed on some of the garments and pieces of equipment—helped the analysts identify elements of several enemy units not previously known to be in the Solomon Islands.[17]

It was also on Guadalcanal that Hugh was first able to get solid information about what had happened to his shipmates following *Strong*'s loss. While he was obviously pleased to hear that Gus Wellings and the majority of the destroyer's crew had been rescued and that most had already been returned to the United States, he was devastated by the news that Fred Purdy, Del Downer, Bill Hedrick, and several other close friends had been reported dead.[18]

Hugh was also shocked to learn that, contrary to standard Navy practice, news of the sinking had been broadcast worldwide only one day after the event. Navy Department Communiqué No. 435 of July 6 stated that *Strong* "was torpedoed and sunk while engaged in the bombardment of Japanese positions on New Georgia Island," adding that "next of kin of the casualties . . . will be notified as soon as possible." The reality, of course, was that most of the relatives and friends of those aboard the vessel read or heard about the sinking days before they received any official notification from the Navy. And when those notifications finally were made, they actually contained *less* information than the premature news release. The telegram from Chief of Naval Personnel Rear Admiral Randall Jacobs delivered to Frances Miller in Tuscaloosa on July 9 was typical:

> *The Navy Department deeply regrets to inform you that your husband, Lieutenant H. B. Miller Jr., United States Naval Reserve, is missing following action in the performance of his duty and in the service of his country. The Department appreciates your great anxiety but details not now available and delay in receipt thereof must necessarily be expected. To prevent possible aid to our enemies please do not divulge the name of his ship or station.*[19]

The last injunction was, of course, an excellent example of the Navy figuratively trying to close the barn door after all the livestock had gone, given that the name of the vessel and the time and place of its destruction had already been widely publicized.[20]

While Hugh did not at that point know of the Navy Department telegram that had been sent to his wife, or that Al Grimes had already written to Frances to tell her that Hugh had been seen alive aboard a raft after the sinking, he obviously wanted to get word of his rescue to her as quickly as possible. He therefore secured permission for the Navy communications center on Guadalcanal to send a brief message to his wife stating that he was safe and in good health and asking her to also notify his parents. The message went first to the 12th Naval District in San Francisco, which passed it to Western Union for onward transmission. Surviving records do not indicate, however, whether Frances actually received the telegram.

Fortunately, Hugh had already met and befriended one of the few men in the entire South Pacific who could ensure that the story of the rescue of the castaway of Arundel Island would quickly reach not only Frances Miller, but also the world at large. The man had been the only other passenger on Hugh's August 18 flight from Munda to Henderson Field, and his name was Art Burgess.

TWENTY-NINE YEARS OLD AT THE TIME HE MET HUGH MILLER, Arthur E. Burgess Jr. had newsprint in his veins. He had written his first column at age ten for North Carolina's *Winston-Salem Journal*, where his father was the city editor, and was sports editor for the *Bluefield (WV) Sunset News and Daily Telegraph* after his parents moved there. Stints at several New York newspapers followed his graduation from Duke University, and in 1936 Burgess joined the Associated Press in Seattle. In 1941 he moved to Tacoma, from where he covered state politics and activities at the Army's Fort Lewis and the adjacent McChord Field.[21] Ineligible for military service for health reasons, in late 1942 Burgess volunteered for duty as one of the AP's military correspondents. He sailed for the South Pacific in early 1943 and after a few weeks in Nouméa moved forward to the Russell Islands.

Burgess soon proved himself a highly capable—and fiercely competitive—military correspondent. After covering the initial Allied

operations on New Georgia, he was the first war correspondent to
file a story from the newly captured Munda airfield, then witnessed
the overwhelming American victory in the August 6–7 Battle of Vella
Gulf as the only reporter aboard Commander Frederick Moosbrugger's flagship, the destroyer *Dunlap*. Returning to Munda, apparently
in search of transportation to Guadalcanal, Burgess heard about the
rescue of Hugh Miller. The two men were introduced at some point
by an enterprising Navy public information officer, who also arranged
Burgess's passage to Henderson Field aboard the same R4D-1 carrying
Hugh—undoubtedly on the condition that any resulting article would
contain no classified information. By the time the aircraft landed on
Guadalcanal, the AP reporter had what he later rightly called "one
helluva story," and he wasted little time filing it.

Slugged "Ex-Rose Bowl Star Saved After Being Missing 43 Days"
and datelined August 20, the piece opened with a name familiar to
many Americans: "Football coach Wallace Wade, in recommending
one of his players to the Navy, once wrote that the young man had
plenty of fortitude and could take care of himself in any circumstances.
Wade's judgment in that instance was sustained today with the return
from the list of the missing of little, red-bearded naval Lt. Hugh Barr
Miller Jr., 33, of Tuscaloosa, Ala."

Burgess went on to relate the story of *Strong*'s sinking, Hugh's sojourn on the island following the departure of the three young sailors,
the attack on the five-man Japanese patrol, and the rescue flight. While
the article got a few facts wrong—Vern Peterson was said to have piloted the Duck, for example—and intentionally omitted much detail
in the interests of both brevity and Navy-mandated secrecy, the story
was essentially correct. As the first published report of Hugh's time
on Arundel Island—one that was quickly picked up by newspapers
throughout the United States—Burgess's piece laid the foundation for
all subsequent reporting about the "castaway" and his exploits.

When the article appeared in the *Tuscaloosa News* on Monday, August 23, it amplified the official Navy notification of Hugh's changed
status delivered to Frances Miller that same day. In an early-morning
telephone call, a Captain Reynolds from Rear Admiral Jacobs's staff

had informed her that her husband was "officially reported to be a survivor." A follow-on telegram delivered to the family home that afternoon confirmed Reynolds's news and ended by saying, "The anxiety caused you by the previous message is deeply regretted."[22]

ALTHOUGH ART BURGESS'S ARTICLE WAS THE FIRST PUBLIC DIS-closure of Hugh's story, it was up to the former castaway himself to give the Navy an official account of his experiences during and after the sinking of *Strong*. Hugh had jotted down several pages of notes by the time he left for the New Hebrides on August 23 as one of eleven passengers aboard a SCAT R4D-5 transport.[23] Upon being admitted to Base Hospital No. 3 in Espíritu Santo for "further observation and treatment," Hugh managed to type the notes into final form, and the day after his arrival he submitted the completed *Report of Activities While Missing* to the "Senior Representative of Commander, Destroyers, Pacific Fleet, in South Pacific Area." The man bearing that somewhat unwieldy title was none other than Captain Francis X. McInerney, who had relinquished his command of Destroyer Squadron 21 only days earlier. Having himself been involved in the July 4–5 action during which *Strong* was lost, McInerney was particularly interested in Hugh's account of the ship's sinking. After reading the report through several times, the senior destroyer man in the South Pacific visited Hugh in the hospital and spoke with him at length, primarily about the later events on Arundel. McInerney was apparently impressed with Hugh's straightforward responses to questions about his time on the island, for the senior officer forwarded a copy of *Report of Activities While Missing* to the commander of all Allied air, sea, and land forces in the South Pacific Area, U.S. Navy Admiral William F. Halsey.

Hugh underwent additional intelligence debriefings during the thirteen days he spent at Base Hospital No. 3, but the primary reason for his stay, of course, was medical treatment. His physician, Lieutenant Commander J. H. Willard, noted that while Hugh's physical health continued to improve, he was not sleeping well, occasionally had trouble focusing his attention, was often anxious, and was smoking excessively. Although these are all symptoms of what we now refer to as post-traumatic stress disorder, the secondary diagnosis entered in Hugh's medical record on September 1, 1943, was "fatigue, combat, not due to own misconduct." After spending weeks alone on an enemy-infested island—constantly in danger, always looking over his shoulder, not knowing whether rescue would ever come, and having killed human beings for the first time in his life—it would have been strange had Hugh *not* been showing symptoms of combat fatigue. Nor was there any stigma attached to the diagnosis; the condition was as common in the South Pacific as malaria.

To help the former castaway deal with his psychic malaise, Willard suggested that Hugh write letters to family and friends. One of the resulting missives, written on September 2, was to Roy Luck's wife. After explaining who he was and how he had come to be rescued from Arundel Island, Hugh added: "The appreciation which I feel toward [Luck, Peterson, and Happer] for saving my life cannot be put into words, but more important than that is the purely impersonal courage and daring which they displayed and which, surely, is the reason why a fighting marine is superior to any other fighting man alive. Though one can never tell, I sincerely hope they will be decorated for their act of bravery. Your Major Luck . . . was in the best of health and spirits when I left Munda."[24] Hugh's hope that the three aviators would be decorated did not come to pass, though Luck, Peterson, and Happer ultimately received letters of commendation from Brigadier General Mulcahy for their rescue of the castaway of Arundel Island.[25]

The *Strong* survivors who were returned to the United States following the loss of their ship made the journey via Nouméa, and after almost two weeks in Espíritu Santo Hugh embarked on what he assumed would be the same route home. On the morning of September 4 Willard transferred Hugh to *Pinkney*, the same vessel that had carried him to New Caledonia following his hospital say in New Zealand. Escorted by the destroyer *Case*, the evacuation transport made good time and dropped anchor in Nouméa's Baie des Pêcheurs late on the afternoon of September 7. Hugh spent that night aboard ship as other more seriously injured men were offloaded and the following morning was one of several ambulatory patients transported by truck to USN Mobile Hospital No. 7.[26]

One of two similar Navy facilities in the Nouméa area, MOB 7 was a collection of prefabricated metal buildings and existing local structures east of the city along the edge of Magenta Bay. The hospital was designed to expand up to two thousand beds, if necessary, though at the time of Hugh's arrival it housed fewer than half that number of patients. Following an admission examination, the facility's chief of medicine, Lieutenant Commander R. N. Klemmer, noted that Hugh had gained ten pounds since his rescue from Arundel but was still vitamin deficient. His boils were improving, the scars from the bullet fragments were fading, and, other than continued sporadic intestinal issues, Hugh's physical health appeared to be steadily recovering. Klemmer noted that he also seemed to be doing better psychologically; while he still carried the secondary "combat fatigue" diagnosis, Hugh was less anxious and more willing to engage with others. Indeed, Klemmer wrote, "He goes to meals regularly and has requested 'liberty' nearly every day since [admission to MOB 7]."[27]

Hugh also spent a fair amount of time with the only other *Strong* crewman still in New Caledonia. Twenty-five-year-old Georgia-born Electrician's Mate 2nd Class Willard G. Langley was a "plank owner," meaning that, like Hugh, he had been assigned to the ship on the day of its commissioning and was the sole known survivor of the destroyer's forward engine room. The young sailor had suffered grievous wounds to an arm and leg when *Strong* was torpedoed and had been pulled into one of several rafts that had been tied together. After drifting for two days the rafts washed ashore on Kolombangara, where Langley and his companions stayed for more than a week before the chance discovery of a large rubber boat that had apparently been used during the landings at Rice Anchorage allowed them to paddle to New Georgia. Though Langley's uninjured companions were quickly repatriated to the States, the seriousness of his wounds resulted in the sailor's extended stay in MOB 7. Hugh's arrival at the hospital came as quite a surprise, for Langley had been told that the officer was missing and presumed dead. Despite the differences in

their ages and ranks, the two former castaways and fellow southern-
ers soon formed an easy friendship.[28]

Although Hugh assumed that he would spend a few weeks quietly convalescing in Nouméa before being evacuated to the States for
eventual reassignment, actions undertaken by two senior officers were
already ensuring that scenario would not play out.

A FEW DAYS AFTER SUBMITTING A COPY OF HUGH'S *REPORT OF
Activities While Missing* to Halsey, McInerney had dispatched to
the South Pacific Area commander a second message concerning
the former castaway. Dated September 11 and marked "Confiden-
tial," the document recommended "that Lieutenant Hugh B. Miller,
Jr., U.S.N.R., survivor of the ex–U.S.S. STRONG, be awarded the
Navy Cross for extraordinary heroism and meritorious conduct in
the performance of duty on the occasion of the sinking of the U.S.S.
STRONG on July 5, 1943 and his activities for 43 days thereafter."[29]

McInerney added that he was originating the recommendation
because Hugh's direct superior, Gus Wellings, had already "departed
from this area"—*Strong*'s former commander was en route to Bethesda
Naval Hospital in Maryland for further medical treatment—and included proposed wording for the citation. Halsey had already been
impressed both by the *Report of Activities While Missing* and by the
Combat Intelligence Center's determination that the information
and captured documents Hugh had provided following his rescue
were of significant value. Indeed, the South Pacific commander was
so intrigued by Hugh's report that he actually visited the former
castaway at MOB 7 to hear the story firsthand. The admiral and the
lieutenant spent nearly an hour together, and when Halsey returned
to his headquarters he approved McInerney's recommendation
and directed that the award ceremony be conducted at the earliest
opportunity.[30]

The Navy Cross is second only to the Medal of Honor in the service's order of precedence for valor awards, and Halsey preferred to
personally pin the medal on recipients within his command whenever possible. However, in Hugh's case he made an exception that was

both politically astute and a very public demonstration of his respect for a person who just weeks earlier the admiral had described as a meddlesome "do-gooder" whose impending visit to the South Pacific he "dreaded."[31] The woman was Eleanor Roosevelt, wife of President Franklin D. Roosevelt, and she was on what would eventually become a five-week, twenty-three-thousand-mile tour of the combat zone in her role as a representative of the American Red Cross.

That the then fifty-nine-year-old first lady initially elicited such grumpy sourness from Halsey is understandable. As one of the admiral's biographers later put it, Halsey believed the many VIP visitors to the South Pacific theater took up badly needed space in aircraft and lodgings and interfered with vital wartime duties of the admiral and his staff. Halsey believed that Mrs. Roosevelt's status as wife of the commander in chief would make her even more of a nuisance than most.[32] Halsey's opinion of Mrs. Roosevelt had changed rapidly following her August 25 arrival in New Caledonia, however. The admiral accompanied her on her first full day in Nouméa and later recorded that the president's wife visited three military hospitals, stopping at every bed and speaking to every patient. Halsey marveled at the first lady's endurance and patience and at the obvious effect she had on those she encountered.[33]

Indeed, Halsey was so impressed by Mrs. Roosevelt that he was "ashamed" of his "original surliness" and was determined to atone for it.[34] While he showed the first lady every kindness during the twenty-four hours she spent in Nouméa before departing for New Zealand and Australia for a series of visits to American and Allied installations, Halsey was determined to do more. He knew Mrs. Roosevelt was scheduled to return to New Caledonia on September 14 before flying on to Espíritu Santo and, she hoped, from there to Guadalcanal, and he realized that having her participate in the awarding of a Navy Cross would be a very visible sign both of his respect for her and of his acknowledgment that her tour was more than the mere VIP junket he had initially believed it to be. Halsey therefore directed that the ceremony be held on September 15 and informed his staff that the man the admiral referred to as his "one-man army" would be decorated by the first lady herself.[35]

While Halsey sincerely wanted to honor Hugh for his actions both during and after *Strong*'s sinking, he was also certainly aware that the young officer's unusual and intriguing tale would garner very positive publicity for the Navy. Mrs. Roosevelt's involvement in the presentation ceremony would guarantee the widest possible dissemination of the story—if, of course, the event was covered by as many reporters as possible. As the home of Halsey's headquarters and several other key American and Allied organizations, Nouméa was already well stocked with journalists both military and civilian, and the South Pacific commander's public relations (PR) staff ensured that every one of them was invited to the award ceremony. Among the higher-profile newsmen present on the early afternoon of September 15 were Burgess and his AP colleague Tom Lambert, Frank Tremaine of United Press, Archibald T. Steele of the *Chicago Daily News* and Clayton Gowran of the rival *Chicago Tribune*, and Jim Brown of the International News Service.

Conducted in front of Langley's hospital bed and with the wounded electrician's mate looking on, the ceremony began with Halsey himself reading the Navy Cross citation as Hugh and Mrs. Roosevelt listened:

> For extraordinary heroism and distinguished service while serving on board a destroyer which was sunk in Kula Gulf, British Solomon Islands, on the night of July 4–5, 1943, and during a period of forty-three days thereafter, Lieutenant Miller assisted in abandon ship operations, during which, with complete disregard for his own safety, he extricated two men who were entangled in a line on the ship's side. He remained with his ship until it sank, and although injured by exploding depth charges, supported two injured men in the water and placed them in a net. As senior officer of a group in two floater nets and two broken rafts, he directed attempts to reach friendly shores for four days and finally succeeded in landing on a small island close to enemy positions. Although weakened by his injuries, he continued to direct his party of one officer and four men in attempts to escape capture by the enemy. When Lieutenant Miller could no longer

proceed because of his injuries, he ordered the men to take all remaining equipment and to leave him behind. Thereafter he lived on cocoanuts [*sic*] and water, and after being strafed and injured by a Japanese plane, succeeded in obtaining two hand grenades from the bodies of dead Japanese with which he completely destroyed a five man enemy patrol which was pursuing him. On three different nights Lieutenant Miller attacked Japanese machine gun parties with grenades he obtained from the enemy's dead. After thirty-nine days on the island he was rescued by friendly aircraft and subsequently furnished our forces with valuable information concerning Japanese positions and units. His gallant and courageous conduct was in keeping with the highest traditions of the United States Naval Service.[36]

When Halsey finished reading, an aide handed the first lady the Navy Cross, which she pinned above the left breast pocket of Hugh's newly issued and somewhat oversize khaki uniform shirt. As she did so, Mrs. Roosevelt quietly commended Hugh for his heroism, at which the still somewhat gaunt former castaway blushed and stammered a polite "Thank you, ma'am." A Purple Heart medal bearing a small gold star affixed to its ribbon (given in lieu of a second decoration) soon joined the valor award on Hugh's chest, after which he, Halsey, and Mrs. Roosevelt posed for the several press photographers in attendance. The first lady then turned and spent a few moments speaking with Langley, after which she, Halsey, and Hugh made themselves available to answer questions from the gathered journalists.

As Halsey had hoped, articles and photos regarding the award of the Navy Cross to the "castaway of Arundel Island" appeared within days in newspapers throughout the United States, Australia, and New Zealand. However, one of the journalists who had attended the ceremony decided that the story deserved more than just a standard wire-service report. That decision helped ensure that the tale of Hugh's exploits would evolve from being just another account of individual wartime valor into an enduring and unique saga—one that ultimately would border on myth.

OF ALL THE REPORTERS PRESENT WHEN ELEANOR ROOSEVELT pinned the Navy Cross on Hugh Miller, only one had what might be called a longtime—albeit tenuous—acquaintance with the former castaway.

On January 1, 1931, then seventeen-year-old Pasadena High School student Frank Benjamin Tremaine had watched from the stands as Hugh and the Crimson Tide washed over Washington State in the Rose Bowl. After graduating from Stanford University in 1936 with a degree in journalism, Tremaine had joined United Press's Salt Lake City bureau and in June 1940 became the news organization's Honolulu-based Pacific bureau chief. On December 7, 1941, Tremaine filed the first news flash reporting the Japanese attack on Pearl Harbor, and his wife, Katherine, gave the first eyewitness accounts to mainland radio stations by telephone. The outbreak of war saw UP's Honolulu bureau quickly swell from two reporters to more than twenty, and in May 1943 Tremaine gave up his managerial position to embark on a yearlong stint as a war correspondent covering the South Pacific from Nouméa.

By the time he met Hugh the UP reporter had filed dispatches on a variety of actions, including the sinking of *Helena*, and he believed the tale of the Arundel Island castaway deserved to be told in far greater depth than could be accomplished in a newspaper article. After obtaining Halsey's permission, Tremaine therefore sat down with Hugh for several one-on-one interviews conducted over the course of three days, September 16–18. Using a partially censored copy of the *Report of Activities While Missing* as a starting point, the journalist asked Hugh to expand as much as he could on the events surrounding *Strong*'s sinking and his subsequent time on Arundel. Tremaine's resultant article ran to more than five thousand words, and almost as soon as he completed the manuscript he submitted it by mail to *Life* magazine.

By the time the article was finished, however, its subject was already on the move again. Though Dr. Klemmer noted that Hugh's general health was "improving," he determined that the patient's continuing vitamin deficiency and slow weight gain required "further attention" and directed that he be transferred to MOB 4 in Auckland for "treatment and disposition."[37] While Hugh was undoubtedly disappointed that he wouldn't be heading back to the States as soon as he had anticipated, we can assume he was not unhappy with the idea of continuing his recuperation in New Zealand. He boarded the USS *Cetus* on the evening of September 18, and the following morning the cargo ship pulled away from Nouméa's Grand Quay, passed through the open antisubmarine net at the harbor's mouth, and turned south.

The five-day voyage to "the Land of the Long White Cloud" was uneventful, and by four thirty on the afternoon of September 23 *Cetus* was safely moored alongside Auckland's Western Breakwater Wharf. Hugh disembarked with the cargo ship's few other passengers and was admitted to MOB 4 in time for dinner. On his second day back in New Zealand he underwent the by now customary physical, during which the examining medical officer found Hugh to be "mentally alert and cooperative" with normal vital signs, but still suffering the effects of "severe weight loss" and "vitamin deficiency." The doctor prescribed continued multivitamins, a full diet, and moderate exercise, and following a second exam a few days later he noted that Hugh had "no complaints" and was "sleeping and eating well." The patient himself described his delight with the food available in New Zealand in a September 26 letter to Colonel Eddie Fay: "These steaks and milk are really good," he wrote, "and I have put myself on a diet of at least one steak a day. Naturally, I get two."[38] His regimen worked, for on October 5 his physician recorded that in the almost two weeks since his admission Hugh had gained six pounds. By October 15 his health had improved to the point that he was granted five days' leave. While it is unclear how and where Hugh spent the time away from MOB 4, he used at least some of it to indulge in one of his favorite pastimes, hunting, for he would later write of bagging five red deer.

Hugh returned from leave on October 20 refreshed and in excellent spirits, though his buoyant emotions were dampened somewhat by a letter that arrived a few days later. Written more than two months earlier by Naomi Hedrick Minton, one of Bill Hedrick's two sisters, the letter had followed Hugh from hospital to hospital. Its purpose was straightforward: Mrs. Minton was seeking any information *Strong's* former machine-gun officer might be able to provide about her brother's fate. In his October 28 reply, Hugh wrote:

> *If I had any idea of what happened to Bill, I'd tell you because I know what you feel and what you have had to go through . . . but I do not know. The last time I saw him, he was going to do his duty and that was to destroy secret papers. . . . He was not at any time in my sight after the ship sank. I am genuinely sorry that I cannot be of more help. Bill was a grand boy and a real shipmate—he was conscientious and courageous—and I was very fond of him. . . . If he does not return, you may be* sure *that he was doing his duty bravely and cheerfully, and that he gave his life for his country and loved ones in a manner of which you may be justly proud.*[39]

Sadly, Bill Hedrick's family ultimately had nothing but their loving memories of the young officer to sustain them, for his body was never found.

ON NOVEMBER 1 HUGH HAD YET ANOTHER PHYSICAL, AFTER which he received the news he'd been waiting for. His health had improved to the point that his physician deemed him ready to return to the United States, and the following morning his status was changed to "discharged to duty." However, for reasons that are unclear—and undoubtedly to Hugh's immense frustration—he was not released from MOB 4 until November 10.

The orders he carried when he finally left the hospital directed him to report to the Naval Air Transport Service seaplane base on Auckland's Mechanics Bay for "onward movement," which was to be provided by Navy Transport Squadron 10 (VR-10). The Oahu-based unit operated a transpacific shuttle service for "high-value" passengers and cargo using Martin PBM-3R Mariner twin-engine flying boats. While surviving records do not indicate how Hugh qualified to make the long passage from New Zealand to North America by air rather than by troopship, his designation as "high-value" almost certainly resulted from his status as a Navy Cross recipient and from the Navy's desire to further publicize his story. The best way to do that would be to make the young officer available for interviews with mainland-based news organizations, and the sooner the better.

Hugh's transpacific journey initially took him back to several familiar locations. After departing Auckland the Mariner made stops of varying durations at Nouméa, Efate, and Espíritu Santo before striking out on the 940-mile leg to Funafuti Atoll. The flying boat then crossed another 700 miles of open ocean before reaching Canton Island in the Phoenix group, the jumping-off point for the 900-mile flight to Palmyra Atoll. From there it was another long haul, 960 miles to Honolulu, where Hugh was able to enjoy a daylong stopover. It wasn't much of a respite, however, for McInerney—who also happened to be on Oahu—took the "hero of Arundel Island" around to meet several senior officers. These included Admiral Mahlon S. Tisdale, commander of all destroyers in the Pacific Fleet, and Commander Gelzer Sims, who would himself soon be awarded the Navy Cross for his actions in command of USS *Maury* during the earlier Battle of Vella Gulf.[40]

With his whirlwind round of office calls completed, Hugh was rushed back to Ford Island to catch his plane for the final leg of the trip to the West Coast. He was one of some forty passengers aboard the aircraft, a Consolidated PB2Y-3R Coronado flying boat of California-based VR-2.[41] Unlike the shuttle from Auckland to Honolulu, the 2,400-mile flight to San Francisco Bay was made nonstop—one reason the four-engined Coronado was the aircraft of choice for the route instead of the smaller two-engined Mariner. Made at an altitude of about five thousand feet and an average cruising speed of just 170 mph, the trip took an undoubtedly exhausting fourteen hours but passed without incident. After landing the Coronado water-taxied to a pier at the former Pan American Airways flying-boat terminal on Treasure Island, in the middle of the Bay, where the weary passengers disembarked. Hugh was met by a Navy driver and barely had time to savor his return to the land of his birth before being whisked across the

Bay Bridge to 12th Naval District headquarters at the Federal Building in downtown San Francisco. He didn't know it yet, but his hopes of a speedy reunion with his wife were about to be dashed—again.

By THE TIME HUGH'S PLANE SPLASHED DOWN IN SAN FRANCISCO Bay, the story of his sojourn on Arundel Island had piqued the interest of the American people. Burgess's initial account had appeared in newspapers across the country and was quickly picked up by the major radio networks. On September 10, even before the Navy Cross award ceremony in Nouméa, Hugh had been saluted as the "Hero of the Week" on broadcaster Bob Hawk's nationally syndicated radio show, *Thanks to the Yanks*. The November 8 publication in *Life* of Frank Tremaine's article "The Battle of Arundel Island"—bearing the subhead "For 39 Days a Wounded, Shipwrecked Navy Lieutenant Was a One-Man Army Behind Jap Lines"—had further whetted the public's appetite for details. Knowing an excellent PR opportunity when they saw one, 12th Naval District public information officers had decided before Hugh's arrival that the "One-Man Army" should undertake a round of press events in San Francisco and Los Angeles. They therefore modified Hugh's travel orders to include a ten-day "delay en route" that would give them enough time to fully exploit the former castaway's considerable public relations value. Hugh was none too pleased with this development, later saying all he wanted to do "was get some new uniforms and go home," but having no choice in the matter he dutifully got on with the job.

Hugh's first event was a press conference on the morning of November 16. He began by giving an extended account of *Strong*'s sinking—though leaving out details that were still classified—and his subsequent time on the island, closely following the narrative in the *Life* article.[42] He then spent some time answering questions from the dozens of wire-service and newspaper reporters in attendance before being whisked off to lunch. The afternoon was taken up by another interview, though this one was decidedly different from the morning round.

Hugh sat down with an Ensign Preston of the 12th District's intelligence staff to record what in current military terminology is referred to as a "lessons-learned" report. After first describing *Strong*'s sinking in the sort of detail he could not reveal to the civilian journalists, the former castaway spoke at length about the ways in which he felt the survival equipment carried aboard Navy ships—including floater nets, life rafts, and life jackets—could be improved and offered several recommendations regarding the cans of fresh water and emergency rations that were supposed to sustain survivors until rescue. Hugh also mentioned how effective the Japanese insect repellent had been and urged that something equally good be developed for use by shipwrecked U.S. sailors. And, not surprisingly, he strongly suggested that Navy personnel operating in the South Pacific "be taught the ability to stalk, get around quietly in the woods and some of the elementary things about living in the woods on your own resources . . . how to build camps, how to build fires . . . and what food to look for. . . . The kid that doesn't know how to get around in the woods when he is in enemy territory is just a gone duck, he doesn't stand a chance."

The transcribed interview, titled "Recommendations After Being Rescued from Arundel Island," ran to six closely typed pages. Marked "SECRET," it was later widely circulated among those Navy technical agencies responsible for survival equipment and training.

After conducting several additional press interviews, Hugh left the City by the Bay at noon on November 19, bound for Los Angeles aboard the Southern Pacific Railroad's train number 98, the Coast Daylight. The 471-mile trip south highlighted some of the best scenery in California, all of which was new to Hugh. Although it was likely a relaxing journey, he knew things would be hectic in Los Angeles, for the 12th Naval District public information office had put together an ambitious schedule of interviews and meetings. What the PR men had *not* arranged was Hugh's lodging in Southern California—he'd done that himself. Before leaving San Francisco, Hugh had contacted Johnny Mack Brown, his old college friend now living in Los Angeles, and been offered a place to stay as long as he needed one. More important, however, was that Brown was about to introduce the

"Navy's One-Man Army" to some of the most important people in
one of the nation's most exclusive company towns—Hollywood.

Mack Brown had parlayed his Crimson Tide football fame, his
physique, and his good looks into a lucrative career in the movies,
primarily westerns. By the fall of 1943 Brown was a well-established
screen actor, and he was determined to introduce his Navy Cross–
wearing friend to the sorts of people who could put the amazing
story of wartime survival in the South Pacific onto the silver screen.
In between Hugh's public relations duties he was feted by some of
Hollywood's most influential movers and shakers. Among them
were actor (and future U.S. senator) George Murphy, singer Hoagy
Carmichael, and Louis B. Mayer, the immensely powerful vice president of Metro-Goldwyn-Mayer studios. Hugh later wrote that while
in Hollywood, he "had a hell of a lot of fun" and was the guest "at
about a dozen . . . sumptuous shindigs."[43]

Though Hugh obviously enjoyed himself at the various soirees, his
time in Hollywood was to have far-reaching consequences. As Mack
Brown had hoped, the story of the castaway of Arundel Island and
the desire to put the adventure-filled tale on film would continue to
attract some of the biggest names in the entertainment industry for
decades to come.

When Hugh left Southern California, he did so with orders granting him thirty days' leave before reporting to his next duty
station. He and Frances met in New Orleans for a joyous reunion
that was briefly interrupted by yet another press conference, at which
Hugh again recounted his time on Arundel. In answer to a question
about the state of the war in the Pacific at the time he left, the decorated officer replied, "Man, we are really mopping them up there now.
The Navy is all over the place—more doggone Navy than we ever
dreamed of having in the Pacific."[44]

From New Orleans the couple moved on to Tuscaloosa to visit with
Hugh's parents. The interlude in Alabama passed quickly, and during
the last few days of his time off Hugh traveled to Washington, D.C.,
to speak with friends in the Bureau of Personnel about his next assign-

ment. The orders issued to him when he left Los Angeles had directed that upon completion of his leave, he was to report to Norfolk, Virginia, to become a general gunnery instructor on the World War I–era battleship turned training vessel USS *Wyoming*. Hugh did not believe that he could best serve the Navy or the war effort by cruising around Chesapeake Bay in an obsolete warship, and while in Washington he was able to obtain new orders assigning him to the Anti-Aircraft Training and Test Center in Dam Neck, just south of Virginia Beach. He reported to his new duty station on January 3, 1944, and had just begun settling into the job when a new commanding officer arrived. The man soon showed himself to be a humorless and vindictive martinet, earning the dislike of his subordinates and prompting Hugh to describe him in a letter as a "little son of a bitch."[45]

After enduring the new commander's tirades and erratic behavior for several months, Hugh traveled back to Washington and pleaded with his friends in BuPers to find him a different assignment. As he later wrote, "being well acquainted with the aforesaid son of a bitch," they offered him several choices. Hugh selected the assignment he felt would make the best use of his skills—chief instructor at the Anti-Aircraft Training Center at Lido Beach on New York's Long Island. He and Frances found a small house about halfway between the base and New York City, and Hugh took up his new post during the first few days of July. He so excelled in his work that when the facility's commander was transferred on August 1, Hugh was named to replace him. He reveled in the assignment, writing to Colonel Eddie Fay in early January 1945 that it was "good duty" and that he had "a grand bunch of officers and men."

Nor was running the training center the only thing keeping him busy, he told Fay. He was still doing public appearances at the Navy's request, and he had started work on a book about his experiences on Arundel. While Hugh wrote that "it is very nice to be home again" and that he and Frances were expecting their first child around the end of the month, he added that he had little energy and was still dealing with some physical problems as a result of his injuries. Indeed, Hugh's health problems went even further than he admitted to Fay. The intestinal difficulties he had experienced as a result of his immersion-blast injuries had begun to manifest themselves again, and he had to be extremely careful about what and how much he ate in order to prevent severe cramping and diarrhea. Though Hugh sought to manage his condition and concentrate on the positive aspects of life—including the February 8 birth of his son Landon Cabell Garland Miller, the May 8 end of the war in Europe, and Japan's September 2 surrender—his condition worsened, and on September 10 he was admitted to St. Alban's U.S. Naval Hospital in nearby Queens.

By the time Hugh was released from the facility in January 1946, his condition—now officially labeled as a chronic irritable colon subsequent to severe immersion-blast injury—had improved considerably. Several other things in his life had changed as well. On October 2, 1945, he'd been promoted to lieutenant commander and simultaneously notified that he, along with thousands of other naval reservists, would be transferred to inactive status "at the earliest convenience of the government." Then, in November, the magazine *True* had published his bylined account of the events on Arundel Island under the title "Hide and Seek."[46]

At that time *True* was still an old-school "man's magazine" focused on outdoor sports, travel, and tales of globe-trotting adventure and had not yet deteriorated into the tacky rag that it would later become. Hugh's ten-thousand-word "book-length" article was plugged on the magazine's front cover as "The Most Suspense-Filled Story of the War" and on the table of contents as "Strange adventures of a Navy hero who was trapped on a Jap-infested Island." Though considerably longer than any previous account, it added little new factual information, relying instead on greatly expanded recitations of previously known incidents. The article nonetheless served to keep the tale of the "castaway of Arundel Island" alive and in the public eye, as did concurrent stories by authors writing for other publications, including "The Best Robinson Crusoe Story of the War" in the *Sunday Express* of London.

Hugh's time in St. Alban's had prompted some serious soul-searching on his part. Though he had initially seen the end of the war as the opportunity to return to a long-postponed civilian life and career, the knowledge that his health problems would likely plague him for the rest of his life caused him to reconsider his options. He could leave the service that he had come to love and seek work as a civilian attorney, but he would then be financially responsible for increasingly large medical bills. Or he could try to stay in the smaller postwar Navy, continuing to serve his country while at the same time gaining access to free health care for himself and his growing family. In the end, the decision was an easy one. Having been transferred to the inactive list a few weeks after his release from the hospital, Hugh—with Frances's agreement and support—used his now almost limitless free time to complete the paperwork necessary to return to active duty.

The "hero of Arundel Island" was about to begin a new chapter in his life—one in which the Navy, Admiral Bull Halsey, the U.S. Senate, and Hollywood would all ultimately make guest appearances.

11

CONGRESS, TELEVISION, AND THE SILVER SCREEN

THE SEPTEMBER 2, 1945, END OF WORLD WAR II IN THE PACIFIC MARKED the beginning of a period of radical change for all of America's military services, with millions of men—and hundreds of thousands of women—being released from the ranks almost as fast as their paperwork could be processed.

The postwar drawdown was particularly challenging for the Navy, which during the course of the conflict had amassed some twelve thousand vessels of all sizes and a personnel strength of nearly 3.4 million. Yet even as it set about mothballing or scrapping thousands of warships, transports, and auxiliary craft, the service needed to maintain a sufficient number of vessels to undertake a variety of vital tasks. While a major war at sea was considered highly unlikely—no prospective enemy had a fleet capable of threatening the United States in any meaningful way—the Navy still had to be ready to fight if called upon, while at the same time supporting the occupation of Japan, aiding in the repatriation of American troops from the former war zones, and conducting the usual sorts of peacetime deployments.

Because these disparate missions were to be accomplished by a force planned to consist of just 558,000 officers and enlisted sailors, the Bureau of Personnel was keenly interested in retaining capable and experienced individuals—particularly those with proven abilities in ship handling, logistics, administration, and the law. And since more than 80 percent of the wartime Navy had consisted of reservists, it was from that vast pool that the majority of the members of the new peacetime force would be drawn. Qualified officers and enlisted personnel were urged to consider remaining in the service; those who did apply to stay were evaluated on a variety of criteria, including length of service, overall capability, and recognized excellence. The latter category included awards for valor, with possession of either of the top two—the Medal of Honor and the Navy Cross—guaranteed to significantly boost an applicant's chances for retention.

And having received a valor award personally from Eleanor Roosevelt certainly wouldn't have hurt, either.

FOLLOWING HIS DECISION TO ATTEMPT TO STAY IN THE NAVY AND transfer into the Judge Advocate General's (JAG) Corps, Hugh Miller began methodically preparing himself for his hoped-for career change. As he was readying his application for a return to active duty, he embarked on a self-directed and rigorous crash course in the intricacies and peculiarities of military law. He renewed his membership in the Alabama Bar and began amassing the letters of recommendation that would support his request. When he submitted his application package during the last days of September 1946, it was accompanied by glowing letters of support from some true Alabama legal heavyweights—state supreme court justices T. S. Lawson and J. Edwin Livingston, Judge Robert B. Harwood of the court of appeals, Attorney General William N. McQueen, and Dr. William M. Hepburn, dean of the University of Alabama School of Law.[1]

On October 1 Hugh reported to the U.S. Naval Hospital in New Orleans for the physical that was required as part of his application. He was likely a little apprehensive, given that the examining physician would have leafed through his medical record and might possibly have already formed an opinion about Hugh's fitness—and any negative report would certainly have scuttled the former castaway's chances of remaining in uniform. Captain L. E. Bach found nothing disqualifying in Hugh's then current state of health, however, and officially declared him fit.

Within days Hugh received orders returning him to active duty and assigning him to not one but two jobs—as assistant district director of Naval Reserve in the New Orleans Office of the Commandant of the 8th Naval District and concurrently as commanding officer of the Surface Division (Reserve) in Montgomery, Alabama. Though neither position was in the legal field—his application for a transfer to the JAG Corps was still pending—Hugh threw himself into the work. For the next five months he shuttled between his two offices, splitting his time between largely administrative activities in the 8th District headquarters and the decidedly more "salty" Surface Division, which was responsible for preparing reservists for sea duty and operated several small training vessels.

On March 7, 1947, Hugh received orders transferring him to Washington, D.C., for assignment as the assistant chief of the General Law Division in the Office of the Navy's Judge Advocate General. Just over a month later, on April 11, Hugh was officially transferred from the Naval Reserve to the regular Navy, at which time he was also promoted to commander with a retroactive effective date of November 5, 1945. His regular commission was designated "For Special Duty Only, Law."[2]

The decade after Hugh's return to active duty was an eventful one. In his personal life the sadness caused by the death of his father in March 1948 was leavened by the joy surrounding the birth of his third son, Fitzhugh Lewis Miller, the following September 17. His professional life was marked by a series of increasingly important positions both Stateside and at Guantánamo Bay, Cuba, and by January 1958 he

was a captain and the highly regarded staff legal officer in the headquarters of the Chief of Naval Air Training in Pensacola, Florida.

Though Hugh had made a name for himself as one of the most
competent and respected members of the JAG Corps, he was also still
widely known as the "hero of Arundel Island." This was primarily
because the tale of his "adventure" had appeared as a chapter in several
"best stories of World War II" anthologies, and in the years following
the end of the conflict Hugh was often invited to speak at the meetings
of veteran groups and fraternal organizations. His renown had started
to wane somewhat by 1955, however, as books focused on events in
the Korean War became increasingly popular.

Then, in May 1956, no less a personage than William F. Halsey had
refocused the spotlight of fame on Hugh in a most dramatic way.

WHEN THE END OF WORLD WAR II SPARKED THE MASSIVE REDUC-
tion in the Navy's ships and personnel, Bull Halsey wanted to put
himself "on the beach" along with the millions of others who were
leaving the service. His retirement was not to be of the ordinary kind,
however, for in December 1945 he was promoted to fleet admiral—becoming only the fourth person to hold that five-star rank—and named
a special assistant to Secretary of the Navy James Forrestal. Over the
following year Halsey undertook several goodwill trips, notably to
Central and South Americas and in December 1946 at his own request
was removed from "active participation" in the Navy, though as a fleet
admiral he did not officially retire.[3]

Halsey's post-Navy life was a busy one. He joined the board of
directors of a Pennsylvania-based tire and rubber company, worked
to raise funds for the University of Virginia, and in late 1949 became chairman of the All-American Cable and Radio Corporation, a
subsidiary of International Telephone and Telegraph. He ultimately
became a director of ITT and president of another of its subsidiaries,
International Telecommunications Laboratories, based in New York
City. While these duties certainly required his attention, Halsey still
had more than enough free time to begin organizing his personal
papers in preparation for writing his memoirs—and it was during

this period that he decided to revisit the issue of Hugh Miller and the Navy Cross.

On May 4, 1956, Halsey dispatched a letter to Vice Admiral J. L. Holloway, the chief of the Bureau of Personnel, in which he recommended that Hugh's Navy Cross be upgraded to the Medal of Honor: "I know you will think it strange that I have taken so long to forward this recommendation. . . . It was only recently that I received the full details of Miller's exploits. . . . I had a general account [of Hugh's actions during *Strong*'s sinking and on Arundel] but never knew the full story until I read this narrative today. . . . In my opinion a Medal of Honor was never more richly deserved." If his recommendation came too late to meet the time restrictions then in place regarding awards of the decoration, Halsey said, "I believe the case is so deserving that a special bill should be presented by the Navy Department to Congress to grant him the Medal of Honor."[4]

While it is unclear to which "narrative" of Hugh's actions the fleet admiral was referring—the most likely candidates are the 1946 *True* article or the book manuscript Hugh had told Colonel Eddie Fay he had been working on—it is obvious that Halsey was determined that the former castaway receive the Medal of Honor. Just three days after writing to Holloway, Halsey sent a similar recommendation letter directly to Secretary of the Navy Charles S. Thomas. After laying out the basics of Hugh's story, the fleet admiral went into greater detail regarding the value of the information the castaway had acquired, pointing out that some of the intelligence data was very quickly used during the New Georgia campaign and resulted in the elimination of a "large number" of Japanese troops. Halsey also pointed out that small intelligence parties were sent behind enemy lines to verify Hugh's most important observations and that his information was confirmed in every case. The admiral ended his letter to Thomas by saying that he was of the firm belief that Hugh's information was so important to the success of the South Pacific campaign that he should receive "the highest recognition."[5]

Thomas passed Halsey's letter to Chief of Naval Operations Admiral Arleigh Burke and to the director of the Navy's Board of Decorations and Medals. Despite Halsey's ringing endorsement of the value of the intelligence information Hugh had provided, both Burke and the board advised that no change be made to the decoration already awarded, pointing out that by regulation any recommendation for the award of the Medal of Honor had to be made within five years of the events for which the decoration was sought.

BuPers chief Holloway communicated this information to Halsey in an August 7 letter, but suggested a possible way to circumvent the five-year rule. The "most feasible" solution, he said, was the introduction of a special bill in Congress that would waive the time limitation and allow the secretary of the Navy to authorize the award. The service would not oppose such a bill, Holloway wrote, in that it would be viewed (at least by him, apparently) as "appropriate recognition" for Hugh's "heroic action."[6] In a follow-on letter to Halsey a few weeks later, Holloway said that Democratic senator J. Lister Hill of Alabama had already drafted a proposed bill and would introduce the measure at the next regular session of Congress.[7]

True to his word, Hill introduced S. 394, "A Bill to Waive the Limitation on the Time Within Which a Medal of Honor May Be Awarded to Comdr. Hugh Barr Miller, Jr., United States Navy," at the opening of the Eighty-Fifth Congress on January 3, 1957. Given that the Senate had many pressing matters to address, the bill was not immediately considered, and in the interim the Navy's opposition to it grew. In a February 7 message to the service's chief of legislative liaison, the senior member of the Board of Decorations and Medals wrote that statutory limitations were imposed on the award of combat decorations because "time blurs the accuracy of the recollection of eye witnesses."[8]

Despite the Navy's expressed displeasure with S. 394, the Senate passed the bill on February 11. Exactly one month later a subcommittee of the House Armed Services Committee met to consider the two bills submitted as companions to the Senate's action. The first, H.R. 4724, was introduced by Alabama's Robert E. Jones and mirrored S. 394 in seeking to waive the five-year time limitation for award of the Medal of Honor, but only in Hugh's case. The second bill, H.R. 4323, was authored by Tennessee congressman Clifford Davis and sought to actually authorize the secretary of the Navy to award Hugh the medal. During its session the subcommittee heard testimony from a Lieutenant Commander Weller of the Bureau of Personnel, who explained the process by which the Navy awarded the nation's highest decoration for valor. The officer pointedly reminded his listeners that while the Medal of Honor is presented by the president in the name of Congress, it must be authorized by the secretary of the proposed recipient's service.[9] It was this last caveat that was to ultimately derail Hugh's case.

Thomas S. Gates Jr. became the fifty-fourth secretary of the Navy on April 1, 1957, barely four weeks before Congress passed the legislation pertaining to Hugh and the Medal of Honor. A World War II veteran who had served as a Navy intelligence and operations officer in both the Atlantic and the Pacific theaters, Gates had first heard of Halsey's campaign while serving as undersecretary of the Navy immediately before becoming secretary. When the fleet admiral resubmitted his recommendation on May 28, Gates quickly passed it to his friend and subordinate Arleigh Burke, asking for his recommendation.

On June 20 the chief of naval operations responded, stating that "a most careful review" indicated that the original award of the Navy Cross was "fully justified" and that Hugh "conducted himself in a manner to completely uphold the finest traditions of the Naval Service." Indeed, Burke said, "It is difficult to see how he could have done more."

However, Burke pointed out, award of the Medal of Honor required that the nominee must have distinguished himself "conspicuously by gallantry and intrepidity at the risk of his life above and beyond the call of duty." He then added that in wartime, there is often no opportunity for those qualities to be observed by others, saying that while Hugh did a "magnificent job" during and after *Strong*'s sinking and while marooned on Arundel Island, "the essential elements of [the requirements for the Medal of Honor] are not present." Burke ended his response by recommending that "no change be made in the award previously made."[10]

The chief of naval operations' opinions were echoed in a July 23 memorandum to Secretary Gates from the Board of Decorations and Medals.[11] In the end, Gates concurred with the opinions of both his chief of naval operations and the board. On November 26, 1957, the secretary officially declared that the Navy Cross Hugh had received in 1943 was "sufficient recognition" for his actions during and after the sinking of *Strong* and disapproved award of the Medal of Honor.

Although Gates's pronouncement permanently terminated Halsey's attempts to gain Hugh the nation's highest award for valor in combat, the retired fleet admiral's campaign had already succeeded in an entirely different way. The publicity surrounding his efforts had caught the interest of two men who, though separated by a continent, were both fascinated by Hugh's story and determined to bring it to a national audience. One was Navy public affairs officer Lieutenant Henry B. Norton Jr., and the other was movie producer William Hawks.

HANK NORTON MUST HAVE THOUGHT HE HAD HIT THE PUBLIC RE-lations mother lode when he first heard of the effort to award Hugh Miller the Medal of Honor. Here was a genuine Navy hero who had been shipwrecked on a Pacific island and, on the recommendation of one of America's most highly regarded World War II admirals, was apparently going to receive the nation's highest award for military valor — and through a special act of Congress, no less.

A Navy reservist on a two-year active-duty stint in the service's Washington, D.C.–based Office of Information, the thirty-two-year-old radio and television broadcaster was project officer for *Navy Log*, a dramatic anthology television series. Each episode was based on actual events and highlighted the heroism of a particular service member, though the civilian company that actually produced the series was allowed great latitude in embellishing the stories for dramatic effect. The show was a well-packaged blend of entertainment and pro-Navy publicity and had proved consistently popular since its September 1955 debut. Norton knew instinctively that Hugh's story would make an ideal addition to the show's lineup. And, as an alumnus of the University of Alabama himself, the public affairs officer also likely saw an opportunity to plug the alma mater that he and the former castaway shared.[12]

Norton contacted Hugh in June 1956 and, after securing the senior officer's permission to commit his story to film, passed the project on to Hollywood-based Gallu Productions. The company, which produced *Navy Log* under contract, hired veteran screenwriter Leonard Lee to pen the script. He apparently based his thirty-minute teleplay on information derived from Frank Tremaine's 1943 *Life* article, the 1945 story in *True*, and several long telephone conversations with Hugh. Lee completed the script in August, and the final revision—titled "Man Alone"—was reviewed and approved by Norton on September 5.

As might be expected of a man with Lee's credentials, the final script was tight, well written, and engaging. Although it altered some basic details—Armbruster, Lawrence, and Mullane became two men named Scott and Chadwick; Hugh's rescue took place under a hail of enemy gunfire; and Eleanor Roosevelt was not present at the awarding of the Navy Cross—it generally adhered to the facts. The challenges Hugh faced on Arundel and his responses to them were well portrayed, as were his various attacks on the Japanese. Given that the departure of "Scott and Chadwick" left the castaway alone, most of the dialogue in the short film was presented in a voice-over narration.[13]

Production began in late September at the General Services Studios in Hollywood, with thirty-year-old actor Don Hayden cast as Hugh.[14] Filming lasted just under three weeks, and when principal photography ended Sam Gallu traveled to Pensacola to record a brief interview with Hugh. The two-minute segment—during which a well-spoken Hugh displayed the short piece of broken knife blade that had been so important to him on Arundel—was inserted between the end of the episode and the credits. The show was broadcast on November 21 as the sixth episode of *Navy Log*'s second season and proved popular with both audiences and critics.

While the very positive response to "Man Alone" more than validated Hank Norton's belief that Hugh's story would resonate with American audiences, by the time of the show's telecast the young public affairs officer had already taken steps intended to present the "Navy's One-Man Army" to a much wider audience.

IN MID-OCTOBER NORTON HAD URGED HUGH TO OPTION HIS
story to one of the major Hollywood film producers and suggested
that William Hawks might be the perfect choice. Although it is unclear whether Norton knew Hawks or had had any previous dealings
with him, the public affairs officer apparently brought the producer
and the Navy hero together and helped broker the deal. By the end
of October Hugh had signed an exclusive three-year option that gave
Hawks sole rights to produce a major motion picture based on the
events on Arundel Island.

Though not as well known as his older brother, director and producer Howard Hawks, Bill Hawks was a Hollywood force to be reckoned with. He'd started as a theatrical agent, handling such luminaries
as William Faulkner, and had ultimately become a producer. In the
year before he met Hugh, Hawks had helped bring two big-budget
westerns to the screen—Raoul Walsh's *The Tall Men*, with Clark
Gable, Robert Ryan, and Jane Russell, and Delmer Daves's *The Last
Wagon*, starring Richard Widmark—and was riding high. He certainly
saw the potential in Hugh's story. Within weeks of gaining the option,
Hawks hired a screenwriter—possibly the same Leonard Lee who had
penned "Man Alone"—to produce a treatment for the film he was
already referring to as "Hide and Seek."[15]

Word of Hawks's new project circulated quickly among the motion picture elite, and on November 14—a week before the telecast of
"Man Alone"—Hollywood gossip columnist Hedda Hopper reported
that John Wayne wanted to star in "Hide and Seek." Knowing that the
actor had turned down many scripts, Hopper asked Hawks what was
so special about this particular one. After giving a brief outline of the
story, the producer concluded by saying that on Arundel Island, Hugh
Miller had led "a Robinson Crusoe existence before he was rescued"—
and thereby likely explained Wayne's desire to do the movie.[16] Just two
years earlier a relatively low-budget film version of Daniel Dafoe's
novel directed by famed Spanish auteur Luis Buñuel had done surprisingly well at the box office, in the process significantly boosting the
status of its star, Dan O'Herlihy. Wayne undoubtedly saw the inherent
benefits in doing a film that combined the adventures of a castaway

with the type of combat action that had been the hallmark of many of his previous films.

While "Duke" Wayne's interest in the project was an undeniably beneficial development in terms of attempting to secure studio support and financing, Hawks sought additional ways in which Hugh's name—and the movie project now connected to it—might remain in the public eye. And in that way his intentions coincided neatly with Norton's desire to build upon the positive public reaction to "Man Alone" in order to further enhance the Navy's reputation. At some point in early December the two men hit upon the ideal way to advance their convergent aims: they would arrange for Hugh to appear on the popular national television program *This Is Your Life.*

Produced and hosted by well-known radio personality Ralph Edwards, the weekly show—broadcast live from NBC's Burbank studios outside Los Angeles—was in many ways the first "reality" television program. An unsuspecting guest, usually a celebrity but occasionally someone who had made an important contribution to their community or the nation, was led through a thirty-minute on-camera review of their life and accomplishments before a studio audience. Edwards would bring on friends, coworkers, or family members of the guest for brief interactions, interspersed with photographs or short film clips that pertained to the person's life. Though the host's comments and questions were scripted, the guest's responses obviously were not, leading to frequent moments of real emotion and revelation. The show had been a major hit on national radio from the moment it debuted in 1948, and that popularity had only increased when it moved to television in 1952.

Documents in the archives of Edwards's production company indicate that he was first approached by Bill Hawks and was enthusiastic about the idea of having Hugh as a guest.[17] The fact that the Navy was willing to support his appearance by providing film footage, still photos, and background information—assistance facilitated by Norton—helped clinch the deal, and preparation for the episode ramped up during the last weeks of December and into early January 1957.

The most obvious requirement, of course, was Hugh's presence in California on the night of the broadcast, which had been set for

Wednesday, January 30. As it turned out, Hawks managed that one handily—he convinced Hugh to take ten days' leave from his duties in Pensacola and travel to Los Angeles for what Hawks said was a series of meetings with industry executives pertaining to "Hide and Seek." Edwards's staff was also quietly arranging for other key players in Hugh's life and the events on Arundel Island to be in Burbank for the broadcast.

Preparations for the show went smoothly—with one exception. The week before the broadcast Edwards discovered that he would have to undergo minor surgery, so to fill in as guest host for Hugh's episode he tapped a good friend and popular actor, forty-six-year-old Ronald Reagan.[18] Like Edwards, the future U.S. president—who during World War II had served Stateside as an officer in an Army Air Forces motion picture unit—had an easygoing style, a rich voice, and a knack for on-camera improvisation. All were attributes that would later serve him as well in politics as they had in Hollywood.

On the afternoon of the broadcast Hawks took Hugh—who was wearing his dark service dress uniform—to watch a rehearsal at the NBC Burbank studios, telling him that they would then go to a film screening at the nearby Warner Brothers lot. The two men were sitting in a hallway outside the soundstage where *This Is Your Life* had just gone live when Reagan came through a nearby door, followed by a huge TV camera on a dolly and two grips carrying lights. After announcing to Hugh that he was that night's guest of honor, the host escorted the somewhat startled Navy officer onto the set to the applause of the audience. Reagan seated Hugh on a fake log surrounded by equally artificial palm trees and underbrush and launched into the evening's entertainment.[19]

Over the course of the next thirty minutes the suave host, reading from the "red book" that was Edwards's signature prop, asked his increasingly relaxed subject a series of leading questions about his time on Arundel Island. Interspersed with Hugh's straightforward and well-delivered responses were the surprise appearances of a series of guests, with the first being Gus Wellings. He was followed in turn by Milt Hackett; Wallace Wade; Hugh's older brother, Robert; and the three Marines who had rescued the man Reagan referred to as "the wartime Robinson Crusoe," Roy Luck, Vern Peterson, and Jack Happer.[20] Hugh reacted with delight when each man appeared, and there was much handshaking and backslapping. Each of the guests stayed only a few moments, just long enough to share a memory or brief anecdote, and was then hustled offstage so that Reagan could continue. After neatly summing up the story and mentioning the role Eleanor Roosevelt played in the Navy Cross award ceremony, the host brought out Hugh's wife, Frances, and his three sons. The program concluded with the family receiving a variety of sponsor-provided gifts, and when the show went off the air the man of honor, his family, all the guests, and Reagan repaired to the swank Hollywood Roosevelt Hotel for a postbroadcast reception that lasted well into the night.

Hugh's appearance on *This Is Your Life* more than fulfilled the expectations of Hank Norton and Bill Hawks. It was one of the program's most highly rated episodes, further burnishing the Navy's image while at the same time adding to the media buzz surrounding both the ongoing effort to award Hugh the Medal of Honor and the "Hide and Seek" movie project.

Unfortunately, that buzz and Bill Hawks's fervent belief that "Hide and Seek" would be a blockbuster were not enough to actually get it made.

DESPITE JOHN WAYNE'S EARLIER AND WIDELY REPORTED ENTHUSIasm about starring in the movie version of Hugh's time on Arundel Island, by mid-1957 the iconic star had committed to several other projects that would keep him busy for the following three years.[21] And though Bill Hawks continued to shop the project around Hollywood, enthusiasm for "Hide and Seek" began to wane. One likely reason for the decline in both Wayne's and the industry's interest was—as is often the case in Hollywood—the success of a somewhat similar film.

On March 15 the 20th Century Fox studios had released John Huston's *Heaven Knows, Mr. Allison*. Set late in World War II, the fictional drama tells the story of a Marine (Robert Mitchum) shipwrecked on a Pacific island whose only other inhabitant is a novice Catholic nun

(Deborah Kerr) stranded when the priest with whom she had traveled to the island dies. The rough-edged Sergeant Allison and the deeply religious Sister Angela gradually form a cautious friendship that is strengthened by their isolation and the need to elude capture by the Japanese. Though the two have clearly fallen in love, they ultimately part following the invasion of the island by American forces, he respecting her vows and she dedicating her life to God. While the film obviously differed in many ways from Hugh's story, the mere fact that it was a "castaways on a Pacific island in wartime" tale, featured two major stars, and did very well at the box office was apparently enough to persuade Wayne and other major players in Hollywood that to do "Hide and Seek" at that point in time would look like a crass attempt to cash in on the success of *Heaven Knows, Mr. Allison*.

There is, of course, another credible reason for Hollywood's declining interest in "Hide and Seek"— Secretary of the Navy Gates's decision in late November 1957 not to authorize the Medal of Honor for Hugh. The expectation that the former castaway would receive the nation's highest award for valor in combat had certainly been a key point in Hawks's pitch to prospective investors and studio heads. Then, as now, successfully moving a motion picture project from the purgatory of "development" into actual production depended on the convergence of many disparate factors, and success often required having a unique "hook." The medal was just that hook for "Hide and Seek," and while Gates's decision did not necessarily sink the project, it certainly took the wind out of its sails.

Hollywood's memory is notoriously short, however, and barely three years later another industry icon was touting his interest in bringing the story of the "Navy's One-Man Army" to the silver screen. On November 14, 1960, Dorothy Manners—a protégé of Louella Parsons—wrote that Robert Stack had bought the rights to "Hide and Seek." The actor had served as a Navy gunnery instructor in World War II and was currently the lead in television's then highest-rated program, the Roaring Twenties crime drama *The Untouchables*. Stack was looking for a vehicle with which to return to movie work and intended to produce the film through his Langford Productions and star as Hugh. He was ultimately unable to do either, though, primarily because his series' success left him no time for other projects. The show ran for four seasons, finally going off the air in 1963. That same year Stack sold his interest in Langford to Desilu, the company founded by Lucille Ball and Desi Arnaz that had produced *The Untouchables* and many other popular television programs. The "Hide and Seek" project was part of the sale, though Desilu never moved forward with it. The production company was sold in 1967, becoming part of Paramount Television, which itself ultimately became CBS Television Studios. "Hide and Seek" presumably conveyed to CBS, though a recent check of the company's archives failed to locate any mention of it. It, too, has apparently become a castaway.

THE FILM INDUSTRY'S GRADUAL LOSS OF INTEREST IN HUGH'S SAGA did not prevent its appearance in printed media, however. The tale was occasionally mentioned in newspaper articles commemorating such events as Veterans Day, the Fourth of July, and Armed Forces Day. But the exploits of the "hero of Arundel Island" got the widest exposure in "the sweats"—the lurid "men's adventure" periodicals that had evolved in the 1950s from the earlier and far less crass likes of the original *True*.

In December 1958 the magazine *Male* was the first to run the story, when it published "I Swear You'll Never Hunt Me Down." Penned by Mark Sufrin, himself a World War II veteran and the writer of the acclaimed 1957 documentary film *On the Bowery*, the article followed the basic facts of Hugh's story but presented them in the chest-thumping, testosterone-fueled prose common to the men's pulp genre. The author seems to have written the article using information gleaned from the earlier *Life* and *True* pieces, without actually communicating with Hugh. Sufrin would go on to write more than a dozen books on topics ranging from political biography to science fiction, but he either had a special affection for Hugh's story or found it particularly lucrative, for he later twice sold slightly modified and more strident versions of it—to *Men* in December 1961 as "Like Hell I'll Surrender" and to *Adventure for Men* in January 1971 as "Lt. Hugh Miller: The Rose Bowl Quarterback Who Killed Two-Dozen

Japs." He was not the only writer to sell a sensationalized (and usually wildly inaccurate) version of Hugh's story to the pulps, of course; among the better known of the others was Stan Smith, whose "Castaway Lt. Miller's 43-Day War on Jap-Held Arundel Island" ran in the May 1963 issue of *Bluebook for Men*.

In more recent years the story of Hugh's time on Arundel has appeared in several books dealing with various aspects of World War II in the Pacific, in biographies of Wallace Wade, in histories of the University of Alabama football program and its players, and in Landon C. G. Miller's 2009 slim self-published account of his father's wartime experiences, *Lt. "Rose Bowl" Miller: The Navy's One Man Army*. And it is safe to assume that the story of the red-bearded castaway's sojourn on that enemy-held island more than seventy years ago will continue to intrigue writers, and readers, for many years to come.[22]

EPILOGUE

A S HOLLYWOOD PONDERED HOW TO TURN HUGH'S WARTIME EXPERIENCES
into a blockbuster film and writers sought new ways to tell the
tale in print, the man himself got on with the truly important
things in his life—his family and his career.

Although the death of his mother in April 1958 was a hard blow
for Hugh, he took comfort in the strength of his marriage to Frances and his pride in his growing sons. His eldest boy, Hugh Barr III,
had been raised mainly by his mother, Anne, but Hugh and Frances
were able to see him with some regularity. The younger boys, Landon
and Fitzhugh, grew up as "Navy brats" whose early lives were shaped
by the frequent moves necessitated by their father's changing assignments. These included time in Seattle as the 13th Naval District legal
officer (and armed services coordinator for the 1960 World's Fair); a
return to the Office of the Chief of Naval Air Training in Pensacola;
a stint as the staff legal officer for the commander of the Naval Air

Force, Atlantic Fleet, in Norfolk; and, finally, as a military judge for general and special courts-martial back in Pensacola.

Sadly, the greatest tragedy in Hugh's life occurred even as his naval career advanced. On September 19, 1965, Hugh Barr III—who had joined Pan American Airways several years earlier as a navigator—was killed in the crash of the airline's *Clipper Constitution* in the British West Indies. The Boeing 707—which in 1957 had been the first of its type accepted by Pan Am—was on a scheduled flight from Fort de France, Martinique, to New York with several intermediate stops. While on approach to Antigua's Coolidge International Airport in bad weather, the aircraft hit the upper slope of thirty-two-hundred-foot Chances Peak volcano on the island of Montserrat; all twenty-one passengers and nine crew members died instantly.[1]

Hugh was understandably shattered by his son's death, and the emotional impact of his loss almost certainly exacerbated the increasingly burdensome physical issues with which he had been dealing since the 1943 sinking of *Strong*. While these included the chronically painful "football" knee that he had reinjured on Arundel and various other orthopedic complaints, the most serious were those caused by his immersion-blast injuries. From the time of his initial hospitalization at Munda onward, he had been plagued by stomach cramps and severe spastic colitis. Through diet and exercise Hugh had been able to control his symptoms well enough to perform his duties, though as he aged these remedies proved increasingly less effective.

By the spring of 1971 Hugh had determined that his physical limitations would no longer allow him to carry out his assigned tasks, and he submitted his retirement papers. At a June 30 ceremony in Pensacola, with Frances looking on, Hugh was awarded the Legion of Merit in recognition of his "sustained superlative performance" throughout the course of his naval career. With a final salute to his commanding officer, Captain Hugh Barr Miller Jr. retired from the Navy after twenty-nine years, nine months, and four days of service.

He didn't stay retired long, however, for within weeks of leaving the Navy, Hugh went to work as the director of administration for the Pensacola law firm Levin, Warfield, Graff, Mabie, and Rosenblum. It was a position that made excellent use of his legal and organizational skills, while also allowing him to spend time with his family—which by now included four grandchildren. The law firm's flexible work hours also gave Hugh the time he needed for his increasingly frequent six-hundred-mile round-trip journeys to Gainesville, Florida.

His destination on these trips was the city's sprawling Veterans Administration hospital complex, where he initially received treatment for issues related to his colitis. He also received regular physicals, and it was during one of these routine examinations in the spring of 1978 that doctors discovered Hugh had developed an abdominal aortic aneurysm. The condition—an abnormal bulge in the wall of the lower section of the aorta, the main artery carrying blood from the heart to the rest of the body—is extremely serious, in that the rupture of the bulge can cause life-threatening internal bleeding.

Hugh's physicians immediately scheduled him for surgery intended to repair the aneurysm. However, during the procedure the surgeon discovered that Hugh was riddled with what was later dispassionately listed as "widely spread metastatic carcinoma"—cancer that had likely resulted either from the internal trauma the patient had suffered during the sinking of his ship so many years before or from his lifelong smoking habit, or a combination of both. Realizing that Hugh was already terminal, the physicians aborted the surgery, closed the incision, and sent him to the recovery room. He was later transferred to a ward and made as comfortable as possible.

On June 21, 1978, the aneurysm did what the Japanese had been unable to do. The bulge burst, causing a sudden bleed that killed the "castaway of Arundel Island." Hugh Barr Miller Jr., holder of the nation's second-highest award for valor in combat and the man whom Bull Halsey had called "the bravest man I ever met," was sixty-eight years old.[2]

ACKNOWLEDGMENTS

M Y MULTIYEAR QUEST TO PRODUCE THE MOST ACCURATE, COMPLETE, AND engaging account possible of Hugh Miller's sojourn on Arundel Island—and of the events that precipitated and followed it—was not a journey I made alone. Many people have offered their time, memories, documents, expertise, advice, and support, and I sincerely appreciate the kindness shown to me by each and every one of them. I am, of course, solely responsible for any errors or omissions in this volume.

Every author needs a muse, and I am stupendously lucky in that mine is also my dearest friend, my companion in adventures large and small, and, best of all, my wife, Margaret Spragins Harding. Her love, intelligence, compassion, and limitless optimism suffuse my life, and this book—and those that preceded it—could never have been written without her insight and support. As I never tire of proclaiming, she is simply the best thing that has ever happened to me.

I am also tremendously indebted to Tambrie "Tammi" Hedrick Johnson, niece of *Strong*'s assistant communications officer, Ensign William Hedrick. Over the course of her years-long personal search for information about her uncle's life and death, Tammi has become the acknowledged expert on all things USS *Strong*. I was incredibly fortunate to stumble upon her truly wonderful website (projectuss-strongdd467 .com) very early in the research phase of this book. Tammi provided absolutely crucial information unavailable elsewhere, introduced me to the families of *Strong* crew members—and to a few of the crew members themselves—and over time has become a great and valued friend. This book has benefited immeasurably from her help and guidance, and I am truly indebted to her.

Special thanks must also go to Fitzhugh Miller, for providing documents, artifacts, and photographs pertaining to his father's life and career, as well as for being willing to allow an outsider to tell Hugh Barr Miller's amazing story. I am also sincerely grateful to Mrs. Gayden C. Metcalfe, daughter of Hugh Miller's first wife, Anne, for insights on her mother's life.

The members of the USS *Strong* DD467/758 Association—particularly Jim Kelley and Reuel Kaighn (and the latter's delightful wife, Barbara)—allowed me to attend their reunions and pick their brains. They are a wonderful group of people, and I am proud to be an associate member of their fine organization. I was especially fortunate—and honored—to have had the opportunity to meet and speak with Milton O. Hackett, colleague of Hugh Miller, fellow survivor of *Strong*'s sinking, and an association member. Though his ability to move and speak clearly had declined by the time we met, his memories of *Strong* and Miller remained clear. Sadly, he passed away in October 2013, just weeks after our meeting.

I would also like to thank:

Andy Hoder, son of *Strong* gun crew captain Stanley Hoder, for providing documents that illuminated his father's time aboard ship.

Willis Naphan, son of Alfred Naphan, for sharing with me his father's reminiscences about life aboard *Strong* and the events surrounding its sinking.

Thomas Culbert, my ace researcher, for his willingness to spend countless hours in dusty archives doggedly seeking out the long-forgotten documents that have proved essential to the accuracy of this book.

Tetsuya Yamada for his research in Japanese-language sources and expert translations.

My staff (and friends) at World History Group's *Military History*: David Lauterborn, managing editor; Brian Walker, art director; Sarah Cokeley, senior editor; and Jennifer Berry, photo editor. They are a delight to work with.

Delbert Reed, a true gentleman who shared with me his extensive knowledge of University of Alabama football and of Hugh Miller's time with the Crimson Tide.

Gretchen Wayne, daughter-in-law of John Wayne and current president of Batjac Productions, for providing essential information on the legendary actor and "Hide and Seek."

Kevin Ray of the University of Alabama's W. S. Hoole Special Collections Library for providing copies of pages from the 1929–1931 editions of the *Corolla*, the school's yearbook, pertaining to Hugh Miller's activities on and off the football field.

Bronwyn Foott, Barbara Wojtkowski, and Amy Han of the Hargrave-Andrew Library at Australia's Monash University for their help in locating and obtaining copies of maps and terrain studies of Arundel, Kolombangara, and New Georgia islands produced during World War II by the Allied Geographical Section.

Dr. Evelyn Cherpak, former head of the Naval Historical Collection at the U.S. Naval War College, for her help in locating letters and other documents pertaining to Joseph H. Wellings's naval career.

Shirley Soenksen of the University of Northern Colorado's James A. Michener Library for help in locating copies of correspondence between Edward Fay and Hugh Barr Miller.

Kirsten Strigel Carter of the Franklin D. Roosevelt Presidential Library and Museum for her help in obtaining documents and photographs pertaining to Eleanor Roosevelt's South Pacific tour and her encounter with Hugh Miller.

Francesca Pitaro of the Associated Press Corporate Archive for her help in obtaining background information on Art Burgess.

Nikki McIntyre of the Mississippi Bar for her help in researching Hugh Barr Miller's time with the firm of Percy & Farish after his graduation from the University of Alabama.

James Zobel of the MacArthur Memorial Library for his help in obtaining a copy of Colonel Frederick P. Munson's oral history regarding the World War II Combat Intelligence Center and its review of the Japanese documents Hugh Miller recovered on Arundel Island. Additional information on Munson's wartime activities was provided by Carol A. Leadenham of the Hoover Institution Archives.

Paul W. Grasmehr of the Pritzker Military Museum and Library in Chicago for his help in obtaining a copy of the book *Sea Raiders* by Freeman Westel.

The staff of the Maine Maritime Museum Research Library for their help in obtaining information and photos pertaining to the building of USS *Strong* and the history of Bath Iron Works.

And, finally, the research and archives staffs of the National Museum of the Royal New Zealand Navy, the New Zealand National Maritime Museum, and the Auckland War Memorial Museum for their hospitality and cheerful assistance during my visit to research Hugh Miller's time in Aotearoa.

BIBLIOGRAPHY

PRIMARY SOURCES

Official Documents

Documents were obtained from the National Archives and Records Administration's Modern Military Records Center in College Park, MD, or from NARA's National Personnel Records Center in St. Louis.

Activities of Task Forces Under the Command of Rear Admiral Walden L. Ainsworth, U.S. Navy, Solomon Islands Campaign, 10 December 1942 to 4 June 1944.

Air Command New Georgia. *Daily Intelligence Summary, 16 August 1943.*

Amphibious Force ACORN 8. *War Diary, 19 May–2 September 1943.*

Bombardments of Munda-Vila Stanmore, January–May 1943. Combat Narratives: Solomon Islands Campaign, vol. 9. Washington, DC: Office of Naval Intelligence, 1943.

Chronological Summation of Japanese Submarine Losses, no. 9. Pt. 9 in the volume *The Imperial Japanese Navy in World War II* (Japanese Monograph 116), Military History Section, General Headquarters, Far East Command, Tokyo, February 1952.

Combat Tour of Marine Fighting Squadron 123 from 11 August 1943 to 27 August 1943.

Commander, Destroyer Division 20. *War Diary, 1–30 November 1942.*

Commander, Destroyer Squadron 21. *Operations Order No. 10–43, July 1, 1943* (including annexes).

_____. *War Diary, 1–30 June 1943.*

_____. *War Diary, 1–31 July 1943.*

Commander, Task Force 18. *War Diary, 1–31 March 1943.*

_____. *War Diary, 1–30 April 1943.*

_____. *War Diary, 1–30 June 1943.*

_____. *War Diary, 1–31 July 1943.*

Commander, Task Force 19. *War Diary, 1–31 January 1943.*

Commander, Task Force 31. *War Diary, 1–31 August 1943.*

Commander, Task Group 18.6. *Bombardment of Vila-Stanmore Area, Kolombangara Island, 15–16 March 1943.*

Commander, Task Group 36.1. *Action Report, Night Bombardment of Vi-la-Stanmore and Bairoko Harbor, Kula Gulf, 4–5 July 1943.*

_____. *Action Report, Night Engagement Off Kula Gulf During the Night of 5–6 July 1943.*

Commander, Task Group 66.19. *War Diary, 27–31 January 1943.*

Commander, Task Unit 36.1.4. *Action Report, Shore Bombardment Kula Gulf Area, Night of July 4–5, 1943.*

Commander in Chief, U.S. Fleet. *Battle Experience, Solomon Islands and Alaskan Areas, March 1943.* Chap. 42, "Bombardment of Vila-Stanmore Area by Task Group 18.6, March 15–16, 1943." Washington, DC: Naval History and Heritage Command.

Commander in Chief, U.S. Pacific Fleet. *Command Summary, 1 July 1943 to 31 December 1943.* Washington, DC: Naval History and Heritage Command.

Commanding Officer, Ex–USS *Strong. Action Report of Bombardment of Kula Gulf Area and Circumstances of Sinking of USS* Strong, *5 July 1943, Amplifying Report.*

Commanding Officer, USS *Honolulu* (CL-48). *Action Report, Bombardment Kula Gulf Area—Night of 4–5 July 1943.*

Commanding Officer, USS *Nicholas* (DD-449). *Action Report, Vila Plan-tation-Bairoko Harbor Bombardment, July 5, 1943.*

Commanding Officer, USS *St. Louis* (CL-49). *Night Bombardment of Vi-la-Stanmore and Bairoko Harbor, Kula Gulf, 4–5 July 1943.*

Commanding Officer, USS *Strong* Contingent. *Report of Material Dam-age Sustained by USS* Strong *(DD-467) by Torpedo Hit During Action Against the Enemy on the Morning of July 5, 1943.*

Daily War Diary, Commander, Destroyer Squadron Twenty-One, July 4 and 5,
    1943.
Executive Officer, USS *Chevalier* (DD-451). *Statement in Regard to Action*
    of This Vessel During Shore Bombardment of Enemy Installations on
    Kolombangara and New Georgia Islands Morning of July 5, 1943, and
    Rescue of Survivors from USS Strong *Subsequent Thereto.*
German and Japanese Submarines and Their Equipment. Office of Naval
    Intelligence Publication 220, 1943.
Gulf Sea Frontier Force. *War Diary, Month of April 1942.*
Headquarters, Marine Aircraft Group 11. *War Diary, 1 August–31 August*
    1943.
Headquarters, New Georgia Air Force (Forward Echelon, 2nd Marine Air-
    craft Wing). *War Diary, 14 August–20 October 1943.*
History of the USS Strong *(DD 467).* Washington, DC: Ships' Histories Sec-
    tion, Division of Naval History, Navy Department, 1951.
Lieut. Donald A. Regan, USNR: Miscellaneous Lessons Learned from Torpe-
    doing and Sinking of the USS Strong, *4–5 July 1943.*
Lieut. Hugh Barr Miller Jr., Correct Status of Missing USS Strong *Crew*
    Members. Submitted February 10, 1944, in response to a query from
    Commander A. C. Jacobs, USNR, Casualties and Allotments Section,
    Bureau of Naval Personnel.
Lieut. Hugh Barr Miller Jr., Recommendations After Being Rescued from
    Arundel Island. Pt. 2, *Narrative by Lt. Hugh Barr Miller Jr.* Office of
    the Commandant, 12th Naval District, 16 November 1943.
Lieut. Hugh Barr Miller Jr., USNR, Report of Activities While Missing, Au-
    gust 24, 1943.
Marine Torpedo Bombing Squadron 143. *War Diary, 1 August–31 August*
    1943.
Marine Utility Squadron 153. *War Diary, 1–31 August 1943.*
Medical Officer, Ex–USS Strong: *Battle Casualties—Killed, Missing,*
    Wounded and Survivors, July 17, 1943.
Miller, Commander Hugh B., Jr. *Narrative of Events in Connection with the*
    Recommendation for the Award of the Medal of Honor.
"The Old Black Cats" [Patrol Squadron 12/VP-12]. Intelligence Division,
    South Pacific Force, U.S. Pacific Fleet, June 29, 1943.
Operation Order No. 10–43, Commander Task Group Thirty-Six Point One
    (CTF-18), July 1, 1943.

Operations in the New Georgia Area, 21 June–5 August 1943. Combat Narratives: Solomon Islands Campaign, no. 10. Washington, DC: Office of Naval Intelligence, 1944.

Personal Narrative, Rear Admiral Walden L. Ainsworth, USN, Cruiser-Destroyer Task Forces, Solomons Campaign. Recorded January 17, 1946.

Second Marine Aircraft Wing, FMF, Special Action Report, 14 August 1943 to 20 October 1943.

Strike Command Air, Solomons, War Diary, 26 July–19 November 1943. Terrain Study No. 40: New Georgia. Allied Geographical Section, Southwest Pacific Area, 17 December 1942. Australian War Memorial, Canberra.

Terrain Study No. 54: Area Study of New Georgia Group. Allied Geographical Section, Military Intelligence Section, General Headquarters, Southwest Pacific Area, 28 March 1943. Australian War Memorial, Canberra.

Torpedo and Mine Damage and Loss in Action, 17 October 1941 to 7 December 1944. Preliminary Design Section, Bureau of Ships, Navy Department, 1 May 1945.

U.S. Atlantic Fleet. *War Diary, 1–30 November 1942.*

U.S. Naval Activities, Wellington, New Zealand. *War Diary, April 1–30, 1943.*

U.S. Naval Operating Base, Auckland, New Zealand. *War Diary, January–October 1943.*

U.S. Navy Base Hospital No. 4. *History, March 17, 1943 to December 31, 1945.*

USS *Chevalier* (DD-451). *Ship's Damage Report—Shore Bombardment Kula Gulf Area, Night of July 4–5, 1943.*

————. *War Diary, 1 November–30 November 1942.*

————. *War Diary, 1 July–31 July 1943.*

USS *Gwin* (DD-433). *Action Report, Landing at Rice Anchorage, Kula Gulf, 5 July 1943.*

USS *Honolulu*, (CL-48). *War Diary, 1 July–31 July 1943.*

USS *Pinkney* (APH-2). *War Diary, 1 June–30 June 1943.*

————. *War Diary, 1 July–31 July 1943.*

USS *Ralph Talbot* (DD-390). *War Diary, 1 July–31 July 1943.*

USS *Rixey* (APH-3). *War Diary, 1 April–30 April 1943.*

USS *Strong* (DD-467). *Action Report, Air Raid on Guadalcanal, 16 June 1943.*

————. *Action Report, Bombardment of Vila-Stanmore, 15/16 March 1943.*

————. *Action Report, Bombardment of Vila-Stanmore, 12/13 May 1943.*

————. *Action Report, Submarine Attack by USS* Strong, *7 April 1943.*

_____. *Battle Casualties—Killed, Missing, Wounded and Survivors, July 17, 1943.*

_____. *Muster Rolls, 7 August 1942–30 June 1943.*

_____. *War Diary, 7 August–31 August 1942.*

_____. *War Diary, 1 September–30 September 1942.*

_____. *War Diary, 1 November–11 December 1942.*

_____. *War Diary, 12 December 1942–2 January 1943.*

_____. *War Diary, 2 January–31 January 1943.*

_____. *War Diary, 1 February–28 February 1943.*

_____. *War Diary, 1 March–31 March 1943.*

_____. *War Diary, 1 April–30 April 1943.*

_____. *War Diary, 1 May–31 May 1943.*

War Damage Report No. 43: USS Helena *(CL50) Loss in Action.* Preliminary Design Section, Bureau of Ships, Navy Department, September 15, 1944.

Interviews

Fawcett, Donald W. Audio-recorded September 20, 2014.

Hackett, Milton O. Audio-recorded August 7, 2013.

Merriman, James. Audio-recorded September 20, 2014.

Miller, Fitzhugh. Audio-recorded September 12, 2013, by Tambrie Johnson.

Munson, Brigadier General Frederick P. Audio-recorded July 3, 1971, by D. Clayton James.

Memoirs

Grimes, Alton B. "USS *Strong* (DD-467) World War II Operations." March 1989 (unpublished). Author's collection.

Hackett, Milton O. "The USS *Strong* Is Sunk: Recollections." February 1987 (unpublished). Author's collection.

SECONDARY SOURCES

Books

Borden, Charles A. *South Sea Islands.* London: Robert Hale, 1961.

Bowling, Lewis. *Wallace Wade: Championship Years at Alabama and Duke.* Durham, NC: Carolina Academic Press, 2010.

Coakley, Robert W., and Richard M. Leighton. *The War Department: Global Logistics and Strategy, 1943–1945.* United States Army in World War II. Washington, DC: U.S. Army Center of Military History, 1968.

Coates, Colonel John Boyd, Jr. *Neurosurgery.* Surgery in World War II, vol. 1. Washington, DC: Department of the Army, 1958.

Craven, Frank W., and James L. Cate, eds. *The Pacific: Guadalcanal to Saipan, August 1942 to July 1944.* The Army Air Forces in World War II, vol. 4. Chicago: University of Chicago Press, 1950.

Crenshaw, Russell Sydnor. *South Pacific Destroyer: The Battle for the Solomons from Savo Island to Vella Gulf.* Annapolis, MD: Naval Institute Press, 2009.

Domagalski, John J. *Sunk in Kula Gulf: The Final Voyage of the USS* Helena *and the Incredible Stories of Her Survivors in World War II.* Washington, DC: Potomac Books, 2012.

Drea, Edward J. *MacArthur's ULTRA: Codebreaking and the War Against Japan, 1942–1945.* Lawrence: University Press of Kansas, 1992.

Feldt, Eric A. *The Coastwatchers: Operation Ferdinand and the Fight for the South Pacific.* New York: Oxford University Press, 1946.

Freedman, Russell. *Eleanor Roosevelt: A Life of Discovery.* New York: Houghton Mifflin, 1993.

Halsey, William F., and J. Bryan III. *Admiral Halsey's Story.* New York: Whittlesey House, 1947.

Hara, Capt. Tameichi (IJN), with Fred Saito and Roger Pineau. *Japanese Destroyer Captain.* New York: Ballantine Books, 1961.

Hinton, Jack, and June Hinton. *The Friendly Invasion of New Zealand by American Armed Forces, June 1942–October 1944.* Auckland: J&J Hinton, 1993.

Horan, James D. *Action Tonight: The Story of the American Destroyer* O'Bannon *in the Pacific.* New York: G. P. Putnam's Sons, 1945.

Marine Air Reserve. *Marine Wings: Stories of War and Peace as Written by the Pilots.* Rogers, MN: DeForest Press, 2007.

Matloff, Maurice, and Edwin M. Snell. *Strategic Planning for Coalition Warfare, 1941–1942.* United States Army in World War II: The War Department. Washington, DC: U.S. Government Printing Office, 1980.

May, Stephen J. *Michener's South Pacific.* Miami: University Press of Florida, 2011.

McComb, Dave. *U.S. Destroyers, 1942–45, Wartime Classes.* Oxford: Osprey, 2010.

Mead, Senator James M. *Tell the Folks Back Home.* New York: D. Appleton–Century, 1944.

Miller, Edward S. *War Plan Orange: The U.S. Strategy to Defeat Japan, 1897–1945*. Annapolis, MD: Naval Institute Press, 1991.

Miller, John, Jr. *CARTWHEEL: The Reduction of Rabaul*. United States Army in World War II: The War in the Pacific. Washington, DC: Office of the Chief of Military History, 1959.

Miller, Landon C. G. Lt. *"Rose Bowl" Miller: The U.S. Navy's One Man Army*. Self-published, 2009.

Morison, Samuel Eliot. *Breaking the Bismarcks Barrier, 22 July 1942–1 May 1944*. History of United States Naval Operations in World War II, vol. 6. Boston: Little, Brown, 1959.

_____. *Operations in North African Waters, October 1942–June 1943*. History of United States Naval Operations in World War II, vol. 2. Boston: Little, Brown, 1947.

_____. *The Rising Sun in the Pacific, 1931 to April 1942*. History of United States Naval Operations in World War II, vol. 3. Annapolis, MD: Naval Institute Press, 2010.

Munholland, Kim J. *Rock of Contention: Free French and Americans at War in New Caledonia, 1940–1945*. New York: Berghahn Books, 2007.

National Institute for Defense Studies. *Senshi Sosho*. War History Series, vol. 19, IJN series. Tokyo, 1997.

Norton-Taylor, Duncan. *I Went to See for Myself*. London: William Heinemann, 1945.

_____. *With My Heart in My Mouth*. New York: Coward-McCann, 1944.

Phillips, Jock, and Ellen Ellis. *Brief Encounter: American Forces and the New Zealand People, 1942–1945*. Wellington, New Zealand: Historical Branch, Department of Internal Affairs, 1992.

Potter, E. B. *Bull Halsey: A Biography*. Annapolis, MD: Naval Institute Press, 1985.

Prados, John. *Islands of Destiny: The Solomons Campaign and the Eclipse of the Rising Sun*. New York: NAL Caliber, 2012.

Raven, Alan. Fletcher-*Class Destroyers*. Annapolis, MD: Naval Institute Press, 1986.

Reilly, John C., Jr. *United States Navy Destroyers of World War II*. Poole, Dorset: Blandford Press, 1985.

Rentz, Major John N., USMCR. *Marines in the Central Solomons*. Washington, DC: Historical Branch, Headquarters, USMC, 1952.

Roscoe, Theodore. *U.S. Destroyer Operations in World War II*. Annapolis, MD: Naval Institute Press, 1953.

Rottman, Gordon L. *World War II Pacific Island Guide: A Geo-military Study*. Westport, CT: Greenwood Press, 2002.

Scutts, Jerry. Fletcher *DDs in Action*. Carrollton, TX: Squadron/Signal, 1995.

Snow, Ralph Linwood. *Bath Iron Works: The First Hundred Years*. Portland, ME: Anthoensen Press, 1987.

Stack, Robert, with Mark Evans. *Straight Shooting*. New York: Berkley Books, 1981.

Stille, Mark. *Imperial Japanese Navy Destroyers, 1919–1945*. Vol. 1, *Minekaze to Shiratsuyu Classes*. Oxford: Osprey, 2013.

_____. *Imperial Japanese Navy Destroyers, 1919–1945*. Vol. 2, *Asashio to Tachibana Classes*. Oxford: Osprey, 2013.

_____. *Imperial Japanese Navy Submarines, 1941–1945*. Oxford: Osprey, 2007.

U.S. Navy. *Administration of the Navy Department in World War II*. Washington, DC: U.S. Government Printing Office, 1959.

_____. *Building the Navy's Bases in World War II: History of the Bureau of Yards and Docks and the Civil Engineer Corps, 1940–1946*. Vol. 2. Washington, DC: U.S. Government Printing Office, 1947.

_____. *The Logistics of Advanced Bases*. United States Naval Administrative Histories of World War II, vol. 21. Washington, DC: U.S. Government Printing Office, 1948.

Watson, Mark Skinner. *Chief of Staff: Prewar Plans and Preparations*. United States Army in World War II: The War Department. Washington, DC: U.S. Government Printing Office, 1950.

Newspaper Articles

AMSTERDAM (NY) EVENING REPORTER
"Writer Survives Crash, Falls Victim to Malaria." October 2, 1943.

BATH (ME) DAILY TIMES
"Sunday Launching Sets New Record for Iron Works." May 18, 1942.

BINGHAMTON (NY) PRESS
"Terry Film Teener, Matron in Real Life." February 12, 1957.

BIRMINGHAM (AL) NEWS
"Cmdr. Hugh B. Miller on Way to Top Medal." February 9, 1957.

BIRMINGHAM (AL) POST HERALD
"Hugh Miller Boosted for Medal of Honor." February 12, 1957.

CHARLESTON (SC) NEWS AND COURIER
"Berkeley County Boy Tells Thrilling Adventure Tale." November 1, 1943.

FLORENCE (AL) TIMES
"Terry Moore Drops Divorce Proceedings." August 13, 1957.

LOS ANGELES TIMES
"Alabamans Victorious: Cougars Bow by 24–0 Score." January 2, 1931.
"Cougars Can't Navigate Crimson Tide." January 2, 1931.
"Hedda Hopper: Wayne Seeks Role of Naval Hero." November 14, 1956.
"2 Castaway Sailors, Flyer Rescued from Raft at Sea." July 27, 1943.

MILWAUKEE (WI) SENTINEL
"Dorothy Manners: Stack Ponders Retires." November 14, 1960.

MINNEAPOLIS (MN) STAR TRIBUNE
"Goodwin Luck Was Good, Lucky and Courageous." May 20, 2010.

NEW YORK TIMES
"First Lady Presents Navy Cross to Hero." September 22, 1943.
"'Hide and Seek' to Court." March 16, 1957.
"House Clears Medal Award." May 8, 1957.
"Top Medal for Navy Hero." February 12, 1957.

SANTA CRUZ (CA) SENTINEL
"War Writer's Wife in Santa Cruz." October 3, 1943.

SNOHOMISH COUNTY FORUM (GRANITE FALLS, WA)
"Red Beard Saves Life of Wrecked Warship Survivor." July 6, 1944.

TUSCALOOSA (AL) NEWS
"Hugh Barr Miller Dropkicks for Goal!" September 28, 1930.
"Hugh Barr Miller Rescued After Killing Five Japs." August 23, 1943.
"Hugh Miller Is on Leave in New Orleans." December 3, 1943.
"Illness Fatal to Mrs. Miller." April 3, 1958.
"Lt. Hugh Miller Listed Missing." July 11, 1943.
"Mrs. Miller Tells of Saving President's Home in 1865." October 27, 1955.
"Mrs. Roosevelt Decorates Tuscaloosa's Hugh Miller." September 21, 1943.

Monographs

Military History Section. *Southeast Area Naval Operations, Part I, May 1942–February 1943*. Japanese Monographs, no. 98. HQs., U.S. Army Forces Far East, 1947.

———. *Southeast Area Naval Operations, Part II, February 1943–October 1943*. Japanese Monographs, no. 99. HQs., U.S. Army Forces Far East, 1947.

The Story of Ward-Belmont. Produced by the school, 1951.

Wellings, Joseph H. *On His Majesty's Service: Observations of the British Home Fleet from the Diary, Reports, and Letters of Joseph H. Wellings, Assistant U.S. Naval Attaché, London, 1940–41*. Naval War College Press, Newport, RI, 1981.

Film/TV Scripts

"Man Alone." *Navy Log*, episode 5703. Written by Leonard Lee.

Magazine/Journal Articles

Gage, Lieutenant Commander E. Lyle, MC, USNR. "Immersion Blast Injury — Clinical Experiences." *U.S. Naval Medical Bulletin* (February 1945).

Miller, Hugh Barr, Jr. "Hide and Seek." *True*, November 1945.

Roupe, R. H. "Fireworks in Kula Gulf." *Our Navy* (June 1, 1946).

Smith, Stanley Edson. "Castaway Lt. Miller's 43-Day War on Jap-Held Arundel Island." *Bluebook for Men*, May 1963.

Sufrin, Mark. "I Swear You'll Never Hunt Me Down." *Male*, December 1958.

———. "Lieut. Hugh Miller: The Rose Bowl Quarterback Who Killed Two-Dozen Japs." *Adventure for Men*, January 1971.

———. "Like Hell I'll Surrender!" *Men*, December 1961.

Tremaine, Frank. "The Battle of Arundel Island." *Life*, November 1943.

Wellings, Rear Admiral Joseph H., USN. "The Night *Strong* Was Sunk." *Shipmate* (July–August 1977).

Williams, Surgeon-Commander E. P. P., RN. "Problems and Treatment of Immersion Blast in the Royal Navy." *South African Medical Journal* (May 26, 1945).

Miscellaneous

Ralph Edwards Productions Collection. Film & Television Archive, University of California, Los Angeles.

NOTES

PRELUDE

1. Commander, Task Group 36.1, *Action Report, Night Bombardment of Vila-Stanmore and Bairoko Harbor, Kula Gulf, 4–5 July 1943.*

2. The highest regularly occupied position was the Mark 37 fire-control director that loomed directly above where Miller stood. While the crewmen within the turret-shaped Mark 37 were protected from the elements, the men on the unenclosed flying bridge—which in addition to Miller and his talker included the three-man crew for the 20mm mount on that level and at least two lookouts—were fully exposed to the weather.

CHAPTER 1. ROLL TIDE

1. Details of Hugh Miller's family history and early life are drawn from a variety of sources, including the *Dictionary of Alabama Biography*, data provided by family members, and Miller's official Navy biography.

2. Miller's memories of Uncle Jim are drawn from an eight-page personal biography he prepared before his appearance on the *This Is Your Life* television show in 1957. Hereafter cited as Miller personal biography.

3. Ibid., 3.

4. Details of Wade's life are drawn largely from Lewis Bowling's excellent biography *Wallace Wade: Championship Years at Alabama and Duke.*

5. Miller personal biography, 4.

6. Ibid.

7. In later years, several reporters would erroneously credit Hugh with quarterbacking the 1931 Rose Bowl team. That task was actually undertaken by John "Monk" Campbell.

8. Anne's presence at the Rose Bowl game was verified to the author by Mrs. Gayden Metcalfe, Anne's daughter by her second marriage.

9. *Greenville (MS) Delta-Democrat Times*, July 15, 1943.

10. Copies of Anne Gayden Miller's original Bill for Divorce, Hugh Barr Miller's Waiver of Process, and the Washington County Chancery Court's Final Decree are all in the author's possession. Following her divorce from Hugh, Anne attended the Chicago Teacher's College (now Northeastern Illinois University) and eventually married Joseph E. Call of Greenville. Anne lived a long, full life and passed away on May 22, 2007, at the age of ninety-four.

11. Miller personal biography, 5.

12. *Administration of the Navy Department in World War II*, 270.

13. Ibid., 273.

14. H. B. Miller to Commandant, Seventh Naval District, June 23, 1941.

15. Though his commissioning ceremony was held on September 29, Hugh's commission was dated nine days earlier and his official date of rank was September 18. Copies of the pertinent documents are in the author's possession.

16. Details drawn from *Gulf Sea Frontier Force, War Diary, Month of April 1942*, 4–5.

17. Details of Wellings's early career are drawn from his compiled reports and reminiscences of his time in London, published by the Naval War College in 1981 under the title *On His Majesty's Service: Observations of the British Home Fleet from the Diary, Reports, and Letters of Joseph H. Wellings, Assistant U.S. Naval Attaché, London, 1940–41*.

18. Miller personal biography, 5.

CHAPTER 2. TAKING SHIP

1. The exact value was $40,879,200.00, or $6,813,200.00 per vessel. These numbers are drawn from both the Navy Department's January 27, 1941, public announcement of the contract award and from Ralph Linwood Snow's exhaustive and fascinating history of BIW, *Bath Iron Works: The First Hundred Years*, 335, 638.

2. The three largest private companies were Bethlehem, New York, and

Newport News shipbuilding, with Federal Shipbuilding and Electric Boat joining BIW in the smaller category.

3. Ibid., 327.

4. Known, as it happens, as the Harding Plant—though not through any connection to the author's family. The plant was erected on the site of the former Harding Station of the Maine Central Railroad.

5. Between 1940 and 1942, BIW's expansion cost $2.8 million in company funds and $2.4 million provided by the federal government.

6. The keel for the future USS *Fletcher* (DD-445) wasn't laid until October 2, 1941.

7. The rank is hereafter rendered Lieutenant (jg).

8. *Muster Roll of the Crew, USS* Strong, August 7, 1942.

9. "Sunday Launching Sets New Record for Iron Works," *Bath (ME) Daily Times*, May 18, 1942.

10. Cochrane was promoted to rear admiral upon taking command of BuShips in November 1942. He led the organization until the end of the war and ultimately retired from the Navy as a vice admiral.

11. Data on the number of personnel, the locations from which they were drawn, and their time in service are taken from the ship's muster rolls for August and September 1942.

12. Snow, *Bath Iron Works*, 333.

13. Ibid., 334.

14. Like several other BIW-produced *Fletcher*s, *Strong* was apparently also fitted with a second sonar system, the QCJ-6. This was removed from the other vessels during the Boston yard period, and we may assume—though no records survive—that the QCJ-6 was also removed from *Strong*.

15. The elevation and position of the second tub led sailors to refer to it as the sky top.

16. A copy of this document, sent to the Navy Yard's commander by C. L. Dean of Kiernan's Supervisor of Shipbuilding office at BIW and dated August 6, was found in the BuShips files (Record Group 19) at NARA and is in the author's possession.

17. Miller personal biography, 6.

18. Ibid.

19. Details of *Strong*'s movements and activities for September 1942 are drawn from the ship's *War Diary* for that month.

20. Three early *Fletcher*s were constructed without the aftmost launcher in order to provide space for an aircraft catapult. Somewhat confusingly, the

launchers themselves were designated Mark 14 (amidships) and Mark 15 (aft of the second funnel). The launchers varied only in that the rearmost one was fitted with a round covered shield over the operators' position atop the tubes to protect the two men from the blast and noise of Mount 53's gun. Both sets of tubes fired the Mark 15 torpedo.

21. Details of *Strong*'s movements and activities for October 1942 are drawn from the ship's *War Diary* for that month.

22. Zigzagging was a tactic developed during World War I to make it more difficult for an enemy submarine commander to determine the true course and speed of potential target vessels. The surface ships would steer the same predetermined course for a set period of time, then change direction in unison. The tactic was intended to both spoil the submarine's aim at individual ships and make it more difficult for the attacker to infiltrate convoys of multiple vessels.

23. In earlier joint talks held in Washington from January through March 1941, the two nations had adopted a strategy that designated the Atlantic Ocean and Europe as the "decisive theater" in any conflict that might pit America and Great Britain against an Axis coalition. The secret, high-level January–March 1941 staff conferences in Washington were referred to as the American-British Conversations, and the comprehensive report the talks produced was known as ABC-1.

24. Details of *Strong*'s movements and activities for November 1942 are drawn from the ship's *War Diary* for that month, from which Wellings's statement is also drawn. Details of the makeup of UGS-2 are from Robert W. Coakley and Richard M. Leighton, *The War Department: Global Logistics and Strategy, 1940–1943*, 485–486.

25. Alton B. Grimes, "Atlantic Prelude," chapter in "USS *Strong* (DD-467) World War II Operations," the latter hereafter cited as Grimes memoir.

26. Gus Wellings was a prolific letter writer throughout his naval career, and dozens of the missives he wrote to his wife during the war are archived in the Naval Historical Collection at the U.S. Naval War College in Newport, RI.

27. It was actually the physician's second such operation aboard *Strong*—he had also performed an at-sea appendectomy while the destroyer was part of convoy UGS-2 bound for North Africa.

28. Several former *Charles Carroll* crew members have asserted that the ship was actually hit by a torpedo, but no records have yet been discovered that support that theory.

29. Details of *Strong*'s movements and activities for January 1943 are drawn from the ship's *War Diary* for that month.

CHAPTER 3. WAR AMONG THE ISLANDS

1. Details of *Strong*'s movements and activities for January 1943 are drawn from the ship's *War Diary* for that month.

2. A detailed account of the establishment of BOBCAT—and the unusual degree of Navy-Army cooperation in both its development and its operation—can be found in Chapter 4 of U.S. Navy, *The Logistics of Advanced Bases*, 36–65.

3. Grimes memoir, in the section "The Broad Pacific."

4. Letter dated January 25, 1943.

5. At the time of the Pearl Harbor attack, Michener was working as a textbook editor at Macmillan Publishing in New York. Though raised as a Quaker, he ultimately decided that it was his duty to serve his country and spent many months vainly attempting to gain an officer's commission in the Army. In early 1943 he was instead commissioned as a Navy officer and after various Stateside jobs was dispatched to the Pacific. In April 1944 he arrived at Espíritu Santo in the New Hebrides, where he met Lieutenant Colonel Eddie Fay; the two soon became fast friends. For a comprehensive and very well-written account of Michener's time in the Pacific and the effect it had on his career as a writer, see Stephen J. May's *Michener's South Pacific*.

6. Rosenberg survived the war and stayed in the Navy, ultimately achieving the rank of commander. He died in Las Vegas in 2007 at the age of ninety-five.

7. This period is based on the conflict having begun with the December 7, 1941, Japanese attack on Pearl Harbor rather than with Congress's official declaration of war the following day. Britain, Australia, and New Zealand had, of course, been engaging German and Italian submarines and surface raiders in the Pacific since September 1939.

8. The talks and their conclusions are exhaustively detailed in Mark Skinner Watson, *Chief of Staff: Prewar Plans and Preparations*, 337–378.

9. In 1904 an Army-Navy committee known as the Joint Board was tasked with developing a series of operational plans that could quickly be put into action in the event of war. Each of the board's subsequent plans focused on a potential conflict with a specific nation, and each was assigned a color as a code name: Black for Germany, Purple for Russia, Red for Great Britain, Orange for Japan, and so on. While most of the plans were essentially

intellectual exercises, Japan's defeat of Russia in 1905 and post–World War I acquisition of League of Nations mandates over several former German colonies and possessions in the Pacific ensured that the Orange Plans were constantly updated through the years. Two basic assumption about Japan's goals remained unchanged: its desire to become a world power would lead it to attack its Asian neighbors to acquire land and natural resources, and because such actions would directly threaten American economic and political interests in Asia and the western Pacific, Japan would first attempt to neutralize American military and naval power in the Pacific. The last Orange Plan revision was made in 1938, after which its tenets were incorporated into the series of broader plans that culminated in Rainbow 5.

10. Maurice Matloff and Edwin M. Snell, *Strategic Planning for Coalition Warfare, 1941–1942*, 149.

11. TF 17's support force, Task Group 17.3, included the Australian heavy cruiser HMAS *Australia* and light cruiser HMAS *Hobart* and was commanded by Australian-born Royal Navy rear admiral John Grace.

12. In 1863 the screw sloop USS *Wyoming* engaged and defeated several vessels belonging to a regional Japanese warlord in retaliation for the enemy vessel's earlier, unsuccessful, attack on an American merchant ship. The battle took place off the southwestern tip of Honshu, near Shimonoseki.

13. These engagements included the August 24–25 Battle of the Eastern Solomons, the October 11–12 Battle of Cape Esperance, and the decisive November 12–15 naval Battle of Guadalcanal.

14. While all of America's military services have long used abbreviations and acronyms, the Navy traditionally likes its to be pronounceable. This can be helpful, of course, but can also be taken to extremes. Consider, for example, the likes of COLanForASCU (Commanding Officer, Landing Force Air Support Control Unit) and ComNavEastLantMed (Commander U.S. Naval Forces Eastern Atlantic and Mediterranean). The author of this volume once worked as a civilian writer-producer for the delightfully loopy-sounding San Diego–based NetSeaPac—the Naval Education and Training Center, Pacific.

15. The Type 93 is often referred to as the Long Lance, though this name was given to the weapon after the war by noted U.S. naval historian Samuel Eliot Morison and was not known by the IJN.

16. XIV Corps, consisting primarily of the Army's 23rd ("Americal") and 25th Infantry Divisions and the 2nd Marine Division, had assumed responsibility for operations on the island from the 1st Marine Division in December 1942.

17. This was Admiral Ainsworth's own description of his orders from Halsey, as he recalled in a classified personal narrative recorded on January 17, 1946, *Personal Narrative, Rear Admiral Walden L. Ainsworth, USN, Cruiser-Destroyer Task Forces, Solomons Campaign*. That document is hereafter cited as *Personal Narrative, Ainsworth*.

18. The submarine USS *Grayback* had been stationed off Munda to act as a navigational aid to the bombardment group, and PBY patrol aircraft had been used for both reconnaissance and to adjust naval gunfire. Details of the Munda raid are drawn from *Activities of Task Forces Under the Command of Rear Admiral Walden L. Ainsworth, U.S. Navy, Solomon Islands Campaign, 10 December 1942 to 4 June 1944*, hereafter cited as *Ainsworth Task Forces*.

19. The figure of two thousand is a postwar estimate based on captured documents and interrogations of former Japanese military leaders. At the time of *Strong*'s first bombardment of Vila-Stanmore, Allied intelligence analysts estimated the number of Japanese military personnel based in and around Vila-Stanmore to be as high as nine thousand. See *Bombardments of Munda-Vila Stanmore, January–May 1943*, 48n.

20. Ibid., 48–49.

21. This information and subsequent operational details of the Vila-Stanmore bombardment are drawn from *Action Report, Bombardment of Vila-Stanmore, 15/16 March 1943* and from Chapter 42 of *Battle Experience, Solomon Islands and Alaskan Areas, March 1943*.

22. Beginning in 1942 PBY-equipped patrol squadrons based at Espíritu Santo began flying night bombing raids against Japanese positions on Guadalcanal and ships in the surrounding waters. The aircraft were painted black, and the exhaust stacks on their engines were fitted with dampers to reduce their light signature. VP-12 was the first unit tasked with night operations, which were expanded to include spotting for naval gunfire missions in darkness.

23. Details of *Rixey*'s movements and patient numbers are drawn from USS *Rixey* (APH-3), *War Diary, 1 April–30 April 1943*. Details of the establishment and operation of Mobile Hospital No. 4 are drawn from *U.S. Naval Operating Base, Auckland, New Zealand, War Diary, January–October 1943* and *U.S. Navy Base Hospital No. 4, History, March 17, 1943 to December 31, 1945*.

24. *Aotearoa* is usually translated as "Land of the Long White Cloud." In this very well-traveled and admittedly jaded author's opinion, taken as a whole New Zealand is simply the most beautiful country on earth.

CHAPTER 4. ON A COLLISION COURSE

1. Details of *Pinkney*'s movements and activities for June 1943 are drawn from the ship's *War Diary* for that month.

2. Built in the late 1930s as a commercial fruit carrier, *Cap des Palmes* was converted into an armed merchant cruiser and served the Vichy French until captured by Free French forces during the November 1940 Battle of Gabon off the coast of West Africa. After further modification in the United States, the vessel undertook escort duties in the Pacific for the remainder of the war and is often referred to as a frigate in official French and American sources.

3. Details of *Strong*'s and TG 18.6's activities and movements for the months of April and May 1943 are drawn from the *War Diaries* for those months for *Strong*, *Honolulu*, and Commander, Task Force 18.

4. Details of *O'Bannon*'s attack on the submarine are drawn from the destroyer's *War Diary* for April 1943, from *Strong*'s *War Diary* for the same period, and from Grimes memoir, in the section "We Hunted for the Vila Express."

5. Among the many monographs on Japan's World War II military and naval operations produced after the war—at the behest of the Allied occupation forces and written by former Japanese military and diplomatic personnel using surviving official records—was *The Imperial Japanese Navy in World War II*. Part 9 of that massive volume, *Chronological Summation of Japanese Submarine Losses*, lists all such losses by date and location, and has only one vessel, *RO-34*, as having been sunk in the Solomons during the month of April 1943 (see 242). See also the *RO-34* entry on the excellent website www.combinedfleet.com. Additional details on *RO-34* are taken from *Imperial Japanese Submarines, 1941–1945*, 41–42.

6. San Cristóbal is now Makira.

7. Purdy had attended a radar short course before the ship deployed.

8. Details of *Strong*'s attack on *RO-34* are taken from *Action Report of Submarine Attack by USS Strong, 7 April 1943*. In that after-action report Gus Wellings wrote, "When the submarine was illuminated it was broadside to the *Strong*. . . . It was fully surfaced and very long. As one signalman said, 'What a big son of a bitch.' The size and shape of the conning tower and hull when compared to the O.N.I. [Office of Naval Intelligence] silhouettes indicated that the submarine was of the I-121–123 class. A net cutter was observed on the bow. No deck gun was observed and no number was seen on the hull or

conning tower." There are a few things to consider regarding Wellings's identification. First, the ONI document he refers to (Publication 220, *German
and Japanese Submarines and Their Equipment*) depicts the four units of the
I-121–123 class of large minelaying subs as having both bow net cutters and
forward deck guns. Second, none of the subs, more accurately referred to as
Type KRS, was lost in the Solomons in 1943. Third, the 248-foot long *RO-34*,
though shorter than the 279-foot-long *I-121–123* boats, had a very similar
silhouette, with both forward mounted deck gun and bow net cutter. And
finally, as mentioned earlier, *RO-34* was the only Japanese submarine sunk
anywhere near the Solomon Islands in April 1943. The obvious conclusion—
as reached by the Navy itself after the war—was that *O'Bannon* had damaged
RO-34, but the sub was finally sunk by *Strong*. The actual identity of the sub
was not known, of course, until it was revealed by postwar examinations of
IJN records. Those records showed that an April 16 radio message ordering
RO-34 to return to Rabaul had not been acknowledged and that on May 2 the
IJN listed the submarine and the sixty-six men aboard it as "presumed lost."
That designation was officially changed to "lost" as of July 14.

9. Given that most of *Strong*'s daily deck logs for the month of June 1943
were lost with it, details of its activities and movements for most of the period
are drawn from the CTF 18 and ComDesRon 21 *War Diaries*. Gus Wellings's
Action Report—Air Raid on Guadalcanal, 16 June 1943 did survive, however,
and details of the destroyer's actions during the engagement are drawn from
that document.

10. Letter dated June 21, 1943.

11. Although the name of this vessel is unknown, it likely was actually an
ambulance transport (casualty evacuation) vessel—the only true hospital ship
in the region at the time was USS *Solace*, which during the month of June
1943 was anchored in Nouméa, New Caledonia.

12. Letter dated June 23, 1943.

13. Details on Operation TOENAILS are drawn from "TOENAILS:
The Landings in New Georgia," which is Chapter 6 in John Miller Jr.,
CARTWHEEL: The Reduction of Rabaul, and from *Operations in the New
Georgia Area, 21 June–5 August 1943*.

14. Ainsworth's TG 36.1 was essentially TF 18 minus *Leander, Radford,
Jenkins*, and *Taylor*, which would be engaged elsewhere. The *Gridley*-class
destroyer USS *McCall* was temporarily attached to TG 36.1 but left the formation on June 29 to join TG 36.3, built around the aircraft carrier *Sara-
toga*. Details on TG 36.1's composition and initial actions are drawn from

Ainsworth's Task Forces; Personal Narrative, Ainsworth; and Commander, Task Force 18, *War Diary, 1–31 July 1943*.

15. As its name implies, a high-line is a line passed between underway ships in order to transfer matériel and, on occasion, people strapped into bosuns' chairs.

16. On June 1 VP-54 had formally relieved VP-12, which then returned to the United States for refit.

17. *Operation Order No. 10–43, Commander Task Group Thirty-Six Point One (CTF-18)*, July 1, 1943.

18. These instructions are contained in Annex B to the operation order cited above.

19. This is the organization outlined in the originally classified 1944 publication *Operations in the New Georgia Area*, 19. Some postwar accounts identify the mine and screening groups as one operational entity. The *Gleaves*-class destroyer *McCalla* should not be confused with the *Gridley*-class *McCall*, which sortied from Espíritu Santo with, but then detached from, TG 36.1.

20. This comment was included in Commander, Task Group 36.1, *Action Report, Night Bombardment*, which Ainsworth submitted to CinCPacFlt on July 30.

CHAPTER 5. DEATH BY LONG LANCE

1. This comment is included in Military History Section, *Southeast Area Naval Operations, Part II, February–October 1943*, 26, in the series of monographs prepared just after the war by former Japanese officers at the direction of the American occupation authorities.

2. Originally the commander of the IJN's Southeast detachment, in May 1943 Sasaki (whose first name is sometimes also given as Minoru) was given overall responsibility for the defense of the New Georgia group of islands. At that time the IJN passed operational control of the 8th Combined Special Naval Landing Force and 6th Kure SNLF (Munda), Yokosuka 7th SNLF (Kolombangara), and Kure 7 SNLF (Rekata) to him. These dispositions are drawn from ibid.

3. Miller, *CARTWHEEL*, 97–98.

4. Some American sources identify him as commander of DesDiv 21, but contemporary Japanese sources agree on DesDiv 22.

5. The 3,700-ton figure is at full displacement. The full wartime Japanese designation for *Niizuki*'s radar—Type 2, Model 1, Modification 2—was ab-

breviated as No. 21 Mod 2 or simply No. 21(2). See Mark Stille's excellent *Imperial Japanese Navy Destroyers,* vol. 2, *Asashio to Tachibana Classes,* 30–38, for details on ships of the *Akizuki* class.

6. Mark Stille, *Imperial Japanese Navy Destroyers,* vol. 1, *Minekaze to Shiratsuyu Classes,* 8–16.

7. Details of Japanese planning for the July 4–5 reinforcement run to Vila-Stanmore are found in Chapter 4 of *Navy,* 19:226–230, of the *Senshi Sosho,* the massive War History Series compiled after World War II and currently held by the National Institute for Defense Studies in Tokyo.

8. It is unclear why *Satsuki* did not launch torpedoes.

9. Operational details of the night's action were gleaned from several sources, including Commander, Task Force 18, *War Diary, 1–31 July 1943;* the *War Diaries* of *Nicholas, Honolulu, St. Louis, O'Bannon, Chevalier,* and *Gwin; Operations in the New Georgia Area;* and the action reports prepared by Commander Destroyer Squadron 21, Commander Task Group 36.1, and Commanding Officer, Ex–USS *Strong.* Personal accounts of the sinking and its aftermath will be cited individually.

10. Hugh Miller's account of the torpedoing of *Strong* and his actions before arriving on Arundel Island are drawn from his August 23, 1943, *Report of Activities While Missing;* his November 16, 1943, *Recommendations After Being Rescued from Arundel Island;* his article "Hide and Seek" in the November 1945 issue of *True;* and his postwar *Narrative of Events in Connection with the Recommendation for the Award of the Medal of Honor.*

11. Grimes memoir.

12. Details of the damage inflicted on *Strong* are drawn from Commanding Officer, USS *Strong* Contingent, *Report of Material Damage Sustained by USS* Strong *(DD-467) by Torpedo Hit During Action Against the Enemy on the Morning of July 5, 1943;* and *Torpedo and Mine Damage and Loss in Action, 17 October 1941 to 7 December 1944,* 24–26.

13. Additional details on the actions of *Strong*'s officers following the torpedoing are drawn from Grimes memoir; Milton Hackett's unpublished 1987 memoir, "The USS *Strong* Is Sunk: Recollections" (hereafter cited as Hackett memoir), and the author's 2013 interview with him; and Rear Admiral Joseph H. Wellings, USN, "The Night *Strong* Was Sunk" and his July 13, 1943, letter to Commander W. N. Freseman, a longtime friend and at that time aide to Admiral William D. Leahy, President Franklin Roosevelt's military chief of staff (hereafter Freseman letter).

14. Regan's heroic actions are detailed in Grimes memoir.

15. The radio traffic among the various ships of the task group was recorded, and a complete transcription was titled "Communications Log" and appended to Commander, Task Group 36.1, *Action Report, Night Bombardment*.

16. Essentially a cargo net with cork flotation devices attached to each strand of rope, a floater net would keep men from sinking but would keep only their chest and shoulders above the water.

17. Wellings, "Night *Strong* Was Sunk," 25.

18. Ibid.

19. The quotes and details are drawn from ibid.

CHAPTER 6. ADRIFT IN KULA GULF

1. As its designation implies, the Mark 27 was an electro-optical fire-control device that determined the course a torpedo launched from the destroyer should follow toward an intended target. The information generated by the director—which included relative bearing to the target and projected point of intercept—was automatically transmitted to the torpedo course indicator mounted atop each set of quadruple tubes.

2. Details on depth-charge safety and launching procedures aboard *Strong*, and of the actions taken to ensure the weapons were on "safe" immediately before and just after the ship's sinking, are taken from Commanding Officer, USS *Strong* Contingent, *Report of Material Damage*; and Commanding Officer, Ex–USS *Strong*, *Action Report of Bombardment of Kula Gulf Area and Circumstances of Sinking of USS* Strong, *5 July 1943, Amplifying Report* (hereafter cited as *Amplifying Report*), p. 3, para. f.

3. The author is indebted to Willis Naphan for details of his father's recollections of the events surrounding *Strong*'s sinking. It is interesting to note that Naphan was of Arab Christian descent; both his parents had immigrated to California from Lebanon. The family name was originally Nabhan.

4. Surgeon-Commander E. P. P. Williams, RN, "Problems and Treatment of Immersion Blast in the Royal Navy." This journal article and Lieutenant Commander E. Lyle Gage, MC, USNR, "Immersion Blast Injury—Clinical Experiences," provided the bulk of the information on this topic.

5. Colonel John Boyd Coates Jr., *Neurosurgery*, 242.

6. It is entirely possible that the three later explosions resulted not from the weapons having been jarred off "safe," but because of what is known as

"sympathetic detonation." This is when the shock wave created by the explosion of one device causes other nearby devices to go off.

7. As noted earlier, details of Hugh's experiences before, during, and after *Strong*'s sinking and of his time on Arundel Island are drawn from several sources: the official documents include his *Report of Activities While Missing*, *Recommendations After Being Rescued*, and *Narrative of Events*. The unofficial sources include the article "The Battle of Arundel Island" by Associated Press reporter Frank Tremaine in the November 8, 1943, issue of *Life*; "Hide and Seek" in the November 1945 issue of *True* (which was quite possibly ghostwritten by Tremaine); Hackett memoir; Grimes memoir; and numerous contemporary newspaper articles. For full details on these sources, please see the bibliography.

8. The floater nets were stowed in open-top baskets attached to the sides of the ship's funnel and other elevated places and simply floated free as the vessel sank. The ship's several forty-man canvas-covered balsa life rafts worked on the same "self-launching" principle.

9. Morphine syrettes looked like a cross between a syringe and small tube of toothpaste and were intended for emergency pain relief in battle or, as in this case, following a disaster at sea. After use the empty syrette was pinned to the injured person's clothing to indicate the dosage of morphine administered.

10. Hackett memoir.

11. Grimes memoir. Regan provides greater detail in his postrescue report, *Miscellaneous Lessons Learned from Torpedoing and Sinking of the USS Strong, 4–5 July 1943.*

12. Wellings, "Night *Strong* Was Sunk." Wellings also lauds Rodrigos in his *Amplifying Report*.

13. *Communications Log*, part of Commander, Task Group 36.1, *Action Report, Night Bombardment*.

14. The problem in *Chevalier*'s Mount 53 had developed while the ship was trying to suppress the enemy artillery fire from Kolombangara and Enogai Inlet that was straddling the crippled *Strong*. The gun crew had evacuated the turret, and no one was injured when the round detonated.

15. Details of damage to *Chevalier* are drawn from *Ship's Damage Report—Shore Bombardment Kula Gulf Area, Night of July 4–5, 1943.*

16. Details on TG 36.1's actions following *Strong*'s sinking are drawn from Commander, Task Group 36.1, *Action Report, Night Bombardment*, and from the July 4–6 entries in *Honolulu's War Diary*.

17. Freseman letter. Sadly, it later turned out that Rodrigos had been far more gravely injured than it had initially seemed. The explosion of the sinking destroyer's depth charges caused severe trauma to his brain, though the extent of his injuries did not become apparent until after his return to the United States. Blinding headaches, vision and hearing problems, and significant personality changes led to his admission to the Navy hospital in Oakland, California, where he died on October 27, 1943. The cause of death was a number of blood clots in his brain that had gone undiagnosed.

18. Ibid.

19. USS *Ralph Talbot* (DD-390), *War Diary, 1–31 July 1943*.

20. Hackett memoir.

21. Ibid.

22. Like all but a few of those lost in the sinking of *Strong*, Summers's status as determined by the Defense Prisoner of War/Missing Personnel Office (DPMO) was initially "MIA/BNR"—Missing in Action/Body Not Recovered. He and all World War II MIAs are now referred to as Service Personnel Not Recovered Following World War II. In January 2015 DPMO and the Joint POW/MIA Accounting Command were combined to form the Defense POW/MIA Accounting Agency (DPAA).

23. Details of the Japanese perception of, and actions before and during, the July 6–7 Battle of Kula Gulf are drawn from National Institute for Defense Studies, *Senshi Sosho*.

24. The general details on TG 36.1's battle with Akiyama's Reinforcement Group are drawn from Ainsworth's *Action Report—Night Engagement Off Kula Gulf During the Night of 5–6 July 1943* and from the chapter "The Battles of Kula Gulf and Kolombangara" in Samuel Eliot Morison's rousing *Breaking the Bismarcks Barrier, 22 July 1942–1 May 1944*. Details on the damage inflicted on *Helena* are drawn from *War Damage Report No. 43: USS* Helena *(CL50) Loss in Action*. For an excellent in-depth account of *Helena*'s final voyage and the ordeals suffered by some of its survivors, see John J. Domagalski's *Sunk in Kula Gulf: The Final Voyage of the USS* Helena *and the Incredible Stories of Her Survivors in World War II*.

25. Different sources give a different total complement number. The one cited here is from *War Damage Report No. 43*. While the majority of *Helena*'s survivors were picked up within hours of its sinking, many—like the men aboard *Strong*—ended up adrift or were cast away on nearby islands. Their stories are well told in the aforementioned Domagalski, *Sunk in Kula Gulf*.

26. This account is drawn from Wolter's *Survivor's Firsthand Account in August, 1943*, part of the Wellings Collection at the Naval War College in Newport, RI. There is some confusion surrounding the discovery of Purdy's body, in that a November 1, 1943, interview with Robert Gregory in his hometown, Charleston, South Carolina, newspaper gives a substantially different account than that found in Wolter's official statement. In the article Gregory said that he was one of eleven *Strong* survivors who made it onto rafts that ultimately washed ashore on Japanese-occupied Kolombangara, and it was on that island that Purdy's body was found. Gregory's account says that he and his companions were stranded on Kolombangara for ten days before finding a rubber raft that had washed ashore. The young sailor—Gregory was just seventeen at the time of *Strong*'s sinking—then said that he and his companions paddled the rubber raft twenty-two miles across Kula Gulf in one night, landed on New Georgia, and contacted American forces.

27. Letter dated July 27, 1943, from Whitman to Wellings, graciously provided to the author by Willis Naphan.

28. Ibid.

29. Oddly, the May 1944 citation for Butler's Navy and Marine Corps Medal—a decoration that is six orders of precedence below the Navy Cross—cites the actions for which Butler was recognized to have occurred on Arundel Island rather than New Georgia. This is despite the fact that both Whitman and McGee clearly stated that everything happened on New Georgia.

30. This assumption was half right. As mentioned earlier, Hackett and his group made it ashore, contacted American forces, and were ultimately evacuated to Guadalcanal. McElduff and his companions, however, were never seen again and were listed as missing in action until August 10, 1945, when their status was changed to "Lost at Sea, Body Not Recovered."

CHAPTER 7. CAST UPON A HOSTILE SHORE

1. Primary sources for this chapter are as specified in Chapter 6, note 25.

2. Arundel Island is now called Kohinggo.

3. While all of these geographical features still exist, I will refer to them throughout as they appeared in 1943. I have also chosen to refer to them in the past tense so as not to cause confusion for the reader.

4. This information is drawn from "Terrain Study No. 54, Area Study of New Georgia Group," produced in March 1943 by the Allied Geographical Section, Military Intelligence Section, General Headquarters, Southwest Pacific Area.

5. The island was named after John Thomas Arundel, a commercial director in the Pacific Islands Company, which sought to form plantations and other businesses on islands nominally under the political control of the British Solomon Islands Protectorate.

6. These sailors of the Imperial Japanese Navy are often inaccurately referred to as the equivalent of American and British marines; the SNLFs did not have the autonomy of the Allied organizations, nor did their numbers compare.

7. Ibid.

8. Coconut water and meat are both highly nourishing, providing natural sugars, protein, vitamins, minerals, and antioxidants. However, as many people who have had to survive on a coconut-only diet for more than a few days have quickly discovered, coconut is also a highly effective natural laxative.

9. Oberg is one of 517 Navy personnel whom the DPAA still officially lists as "Personnel Not Recovered After World War II," despite the fact that the approximate location of Oberg's burial was reported by Hugh Miller soon after his own rescue.

10. Like Oberg, Deering is listed by DPAA as among the "Personnel Not Recovered After World War II," despite the fact that the approximate location of his grave was also reported by Hugh Miller after his rescue.

11. Miller was partially correct in his assumption. Nautical charts from 1943 indicate that Diamond Narrows, the body of water separating Arundel from New Georgia, was only 224 feet wide at its narrowest point. However, while there were some shallow spots along the shoreline at low tide, water depths in the very center of even the narrowest part of the channel ranged from 7 to 14 feet, which would have required anyone attempting to cross to either swim or use some sort of flotation device for at least part of the way.

12. Armbruster, Lawrence, and Mullane are all officially listed as "Service Personnel Not Recovered Following World War II."

CHAPTER 8. ALONE AMONG ENEMIES

1. A carrier-based torpedo plane, by mid-1943 Grumman's single-engine TBF (and the license-built General Motors TBM) was used primarily as a horizontal bomber.

2. This aircraft was likely the TBF flown by 1st Lieutenant J. L. Labatt of Marine Torpedo Bombing Squadron 143 (VMTB-143), which was shot down that day while completing a scouting flight of the Hathorn Sound and Munda areas.

3. Eric A. Feldt, *The Coastwatchers: Operation Ferdinand and the Fight for the South Pacific*, 103–105. Feldt's 1946 history is an excellent examination of the important work done by the members of his organization.

4. The sailors aided by Evans on Kolombangara and his colleagues on Vella Lavella were the lucky ones. Following the destruction of *Strong* and *Helena*, the Japanese captured scores of American seamen who had managed to reach shore. Though a few prisoners who were thought to possess potentially valuable information were transported to Rabaul for interrogation, the majority of those unfortunate enough to fall into Japanese hands were either killed immediately upon discovery or executed within days—often by beheading. Their corpses were then either burned or buried in unmarked graves.

5. In 1943 the Japanese were using motorized landing craft of three basic sizes. Smaller vessels without bow ramps were generally referred to as *Sho-hatsu*; those craft with bow ramps were the fourteen-meter *Daihatsu* class and the seventeen-meter *Toku-Daihatsu* class. Though Hugh Miller could not have known it at the time, both types of vessels were operated by the Vila-based 8th CSNLF Landing Craft Company and the Shipping Company of the IJN's New Georgia Sector. For additional details, see Major John N. Rentz, USMCR, *Marines in the Central Solomons*, 177. In most official American records of the period, the landing craft are generally referred to as "barges."

6. In his accounts of the following action Hugh Miller stated variously that it took place on either August 1 or 2, but the August 1–31, 1943, *War Diary* of Commander, Task Force 31—who had operational control of the Lever Harbor–based PTs—clearly states that the events transpired on the night of August 3–4, the first occasion on which the unit's boats engaged Japanese watercraft in Hathorn Sound and the southern end of Kula Gulf.

7. While the exact identity of this particular Elco-built eighty-footer is unclear, it was one of the six PTs (*115, 116, 126, 155, 156,* and *160*) assigned to the initial Grasse Lagoon flotilla. This group, led by legendary PT boat skipper Lieutenant Commander Robert Kelly, was also referred to as the Lever Harbor squadron.

CHAPTER 9. BACK IN THE WAR

1. Once again, for reasons now lost to history, no report of a Caucasian man on Arundel Island was made that day to any Allied organization in the Solomon Islands. A thorough search of the surviving records for Marine Air Wing 1; ComAirSols; Commander, Motor Torpedo Boats Pacific; and ComSoPac's Nouméa-based Combat Intelligence Center revealed no mention of

the Miller sighting on August 4. There were considerable numbers of Allied aircraft active that day—primarily bombing Japanese positions at Bairoko Harbor, Vila, and around Munda—and the units involved included VMTB-143, but no aircraft losses were recorded.

2. Known as *hinomaru yosegaki* and carried by the majority of Japanese military personnel in World War II, these flags were symbols of good luck given to men before they deployed. Inscribed with patriotic slogans, religious sayings, and good wishes for health and success in battle, the flags were often worn wrapped around the body. They were highly prized as souvenirs by Allied service members.

3. Ground troops of both the army and the special naval landing forces were active on Arundel during this time, but the men killed by Hugh Miller in this first incident were, as their insignia proved, army infantrymen. The NCO was a junior corporal (sometimes rendered as lance corporal) and the other man a private first class.

4. The Japanese destroyers were *Shigure* (damaged) and *Arashi*, *Hagikaze*, and *Kawakaze* (sunk). Moosbrugger's force consisted of *Craven*, *Dunlap*, *Lang*, *Maury*, *Stack*, and *Sterett*. None of the American vessels was damaged, and there were no U.S. casualties.

5. One of the documents Hugh recovered indicated that the men were members of the 8th Combined Special Naval Landing Force. How their bodies came to be on Arundel remains unclear.

CHAPTER 10. BACK TO THE WORLD

1. Unfortunately, surviving records do not provide the names of the two enlisted crewmen.

2. Details on Turner's flight are drawn from VMTB-143's *War Diary* for the period August 1–31, 1943; from the *War Diary* for the same period generated by HQs., Marine Air Group 11; and from the accounts cited in the previous chapter for Hugh Barr Miller's time on Arundel. Interestingly, Miller's various accounts, as well as some of the newspaper stories about his rescue, state that Turner was returning from a bombing raid on Vila-Stanmore when he spotted the red-bearded castaway. However, the official documents make it clear that VMTB-143 did not undertake any combat missions on August 16. Turner's was one of twelve test hops flown by squadron aircraft that day, with several of the planes making flights equal in distance and duration to Turner's.

3. Waiting to raise the TBF's flaps until the aircraft had climbed to five hundred feet was a standard procedure, in that when flying with its gear up

and flaps down the Avenger had a well-documented tendency to quickly lose two to three hundred feet of altitude—depending on the machine's gross weight—when the flaps were retracted.

4. Exactly who the first Allied pilot was to land at Munda is unclear. While Navy and Marine Corps aviators have claimed that distinction, film footage shot during the repair of the strip indicates that a P-40 Warhawk of the Royal New Zealand Air Force was likely the first Allied aircraft to use the strip. However, war correspondent Art Burgess of the Associated Press, one of the first reporters to land at Munda, wrote in a story datelined August 14 that the first to land was a USAAF P-40 flown by Lieutenant Coteworth B. Head of San Francisco.

Details on Munda's capture, repair, and use by American aircraft are drawn from Rentz, *Marines in the Central Solomons*, 142–148; Frank W. Craven and James L. Cate, eds., *The Pacific: Guadalcanal to Saipan, August 1942 to July 1944*, 238; and *Combat Tour of Marine Fighting Squadron 123 from 11 August 1943 to 27 August 1943*.

5. Upon his return to Guadalcanal, Turner was interviewed by a pool reporter, to whom he described that initial landing on Munda: "Well, I must admit I was rather proud of my landing. . . . Setting a plane down on a strange field is none too easy. But I can be thankful to the 'god of pilots' that nothing happened to mar the flight." The story of the rescue, and the Texas-born pilot's role in it, was subsequently picked up by the *McKinney (TX) Courier-Gazette*, which ran the piece on October 22, 1943.

6. Details on Peterson and Luck and their role in the recovery of Hugh Miller from Arundel Island are drawn primarily from Luck's postwar account, "South Pacific Duck Rescue," which was published as a chapter in Marine Air Reserve, *Marine Wings: Stories of War and Peace as Written by the Pilots*, 25–32. Additional details are drawn from Air Command New Georgia's *Daily Intelligence Summary, 16 August 1943* and from *Second Marine Aircraft Wing, FMF, Special Action Report, 14 August 1943 to 20 October 1943*.

7. Turner later repeated his colorful description of Hugh to the pool reporter on Guadalcanal, and it appeared in the *McKinney (TX) Courier-Gazette* article mentioned above.

8. After taking off from Munda Luck had put the J2F-5's propeller into low pitch, knowing that doing so would make the Duck sound like a Mitsubishi F1M "Pete" biplane floatplane, several of which were based at Rekata Bay on the northeast coast of Santa Isabel Island. Luck hoped the sound

would cause any enemy troops that might see or hear the Duck to assume it was one of their own. Marine Air Reserve, *Marine Wings*, 28.

9. Built by General Motors and officially designated the CCKW, the six-wheeled cargo truck weighed two and a half tons, hence the nickname. It was among the most common vehicles used by U.S. military forces in World War II.

10. ACORN stood for "Airfield Construction, Operation, Repair Navy," and ACORN 8 was one of many that operated in the Pacific theater during World War II. Details on ACORN 8 are drawn from the unit's *War Diary* for the period May 12 through September 2, 1943.

11. Details of Hugh Miller's medical condition following his rescue and in the years thereafter are contained in the many individual "Medical History" cards and other documents contained within his official—and voluminous—Navy medical file, a copy of which was provided to the author by Fitzhugh Miller.

12. Ibid. In his *Marine Wings* chapter, Roy Luck wrote that the shells had been fired by two Japanese artillery pieces emplaced on the southwest tip of Arundel Island and that both were subsequently knocked out by bombs dropped by Guadalcanal-based Dauntless SBDs.

13. Turner remained in the Marine Reserve after World War II and was called back to active duty during the Korean War, flying F7F-3N Tigercat twin-engine fighters with Marine Night Fighter Squadron 513. On December 6, 1952, he was returning to Kunsan Airfield after a mission when mechanical problems forced him to ditch in the Yellow Sea. He survived the crash and was ultimately rescued but, sadly, died of the effects of exposure. He was thirty-one years old.

14. Air Command New Georgia, *Daily Intelligence Summary*.

15. No search for the three *Strong* sailors was conducted, and all remain listed as "Service Personnel Not Recovered After World War II."

16. Marine Utility Squadron 153, *War Diary, 1–31 August 1943*. The aircraft that bore Hugh Miller to Guadalcanal was Bureau Number 37671, flown by Captain Donald G. Donahoe and 1st Lieutenant James H. Clouse.

17. The linguists also translated the inscriptions on the *hinomaru yosegaki* flag Hugh had taken from one of the bodies. In addition to such slogans as "Good luck and long life for a warrior," "Crushing evil and spreading truth," and "Strength!" the flag bore the names of sixteen people, most of them probably friends and relatives of the individual to whom the flag had belonged. The names on the flag, as translated at the author's request in

2014, are Atsushi Tanaka, Eiji Aman, Tetsuo Aman, Eizo Sonoda, Hideharu (or Hideji) Takayama, Hirozo Kawano, Katsumi Onizuka, Katsuo Sueyoshi, Takao Sueyoshi, Masato Mukae, Yukimasa Mukae, Noburo Kusunoki, Nubuo Kajisa, Ryozo Kumamoto, Tsutomu Ohno, and Yoshio Mizuno.

18. It is likely that Hugh was shown an updated list of the dead, missing, and rescued. The first such accounting had been compiled by Al Horne, *Strong's* medical officer, in a July 17 report to Pacific Fleet headquarters titled *Battle Casualties—Killed, Missing, Wounded and Survivors of the Ex-USS* STRONG *(DD467)*.

19. A copy of the telegram, marked "Pers-2224b-CEM," was included in Hugh Miller's Navy personnel file, a copy of which was provided to the author by Fitzhugh Miller.

20. Several *Strong* survivors later advanced theories about how news of the sinking got out prematurely. Among them was the one put forth by Clarence Gustavson. In his unpublished postwar memoir, "South Pacific Blues," the former signalman 3rd class surmised that the leak had originated from HMNZS *Leander*, which sent a signal regarding the sinking "in the clear," meaning the message was not encrypted and was thus somehow heard, and reported on, by news organizations in Australia. Gustavson apparently believed that U.S. Navy public relations personnel based in Sydney had then released the communiqué as a damage-control effort.

21. Burgess was actually born in North Carolina, on December 9, 1914, but grew up in Bluefield, West Virginia, and always referred to himself as a native of that state.

22. A copy of the telegram, marked "Pers-2224b-JMK," was included in Hugh Miller's Navy personnel file.

23. Like the aircraft that transported Hugh from Munda to Henderson Field, this second R4D (BuNo 37671) also belonged to VMJ-153. It was flown by 1st Lieutenant Robert J. Thompson and Master Technical Sergeant Glennon A. Johnston. Marine Utility Squadron 153, *War Diary*.

24. Marine Air Reserve, *Marine Wings*, 32.

25. *Second Marine Aircraft Wing*, 6.

26. USS Pinkney *(APH-2)*, *War Diary, 1 July–31 July 1943*.

27. "Liberty" is officially sanctioned time off, usually for a period of eight to twelve hours.

28. Langley's story is included in the newspaper article "Berkeley County Boy Tells Thrilling Adventure Tale," published November 1, 1943, in the *Charleston (SC) News and Courier*.

29. Letter, marked "Pl5 Serial 0198," McInerney to Halsey, September 11, 1943.

30. Halsey mentions the meeting in *Admiral Halsey's Story* (written with J. Bryan III), 164. The volume is based on the diary Halsey maintained throughout the war.

31. These characterizations are quoted by author Russell Freedman in *Eleanor Roosevelt: A Life of Discovery*, 135. The admiral's initial dislike of, and subsequent admiration for, the first lady are also mentioned prominently in E. B. Potter's *Bull Halsey: A Biography* and in *Admiral Halsey's Story*.

32. Potter, *Bull Halsey: A Biography*, 236.

33. *Admiral Halsey's Story*, 166. It is unclear whether Mrs. Roosevelt met either Hugh Miller or Willard Langley during her initial visit to Nouméa.

34. Freedman, *Eleanor Roosevelt*, 136.

35. *Admiral Halsey's Story*, 167.

36. This is the actual text read by Halsey. Typewritten on a sheet of paper with the heading "South Pacific Force of the United States Pacific Fleet, Headquarters of the Commander," it was marked "Temporary Citation." A permanent version of the citation prepared for the secretary of the Navy's signature in November 1943 is shorter and worded somewhat differently— for example, it includes the name of Hugh's ship, which the original omitted for security reasons—but is essentially identical in content. This permanent version of the citation was published in *Bureau of Naval Personnel Information Bulletin*, no. 323, in February 1944.

37. These determinations were noted on a "Medical History" card dated September 18, 1943, and signed by Klemmer. The card is included in Hugh's medical record.

38. Letter to Lieutenant Colonel Edward Fay, dated September 26, 1943. A copy is in the author's collection.

39. Letter to Naomi Hedrick Minton, dated October 28, 1943. A copy is in the author's collection.

40. Details of Hugh's return trip to the United States and his meetings in Honolulu are drawn from his January 2, 1945, letter to Lieutenant Colonel Edward Fay. Sims's Navy Cross was awarded for his "skillful maneuvering" and "bold and aggressive attacks" against Japanese warships during the battle on August 6–7, 1943.

41. Unlike amphibians, flying boats have no landing gear and must operate solely from the water.

42. The *Life* article was one of Frank Tremaine's most widely read pieces, and it helped cement his reputation as a journalist equally adept at both straight news and long-form narrative. He went on to cover the rest of World War II in the Pacific and was aboard USS *Missouri* in Tokyo Bay for the September 2, 1945, Japanese surrender. After the war he was UP's first Tokyo bureau chief and went on to assignments in Central America and California and then covered the Korean War. Tremaine ultimately became the renamed United Press International's senior vice president. He retired in 1980 after a forty-four-year career and died at the age of ninety-two on December 7, 2006—sixty-five years to the day after breaking the news of the Pearl Harbor attack.

43. Miller to Fay letter, Jan. 2, 1945.

44. Quoted in the *Tuscaloosa News*, December 3, 1943.

45. Miller to Fay letter, Jan. 2, 1945.

46. Though obviously based to a great extent on the book manuscript Hugh had mentioned to Colonel Eddie Fay in January 1945, the finished article shows all the hallmarks of having been heavily edited. It is likely the piece was cowritten—possibly with Frank Tremaine—though no evidence exists to support that possibility.

CHAPTER 11. CONGRESS, TELEVISION, AND THE SILVER SCREEN

1. Copies of the letters are in the author's collection.

2. Details here and following regarding Hugh Miller's assignments and dates of rank are drawn from his official personnel file, a copy of which was provided to the author by Fitzhugh Miller.

3. See Potter, *Bull Halsey: A Biography*, 366–371. The five-star rank had been authorized by the U.S. Senate in December 1944, and four Army and four Navy officers were elevated to that rank. In April 1946 Congress authorized all eight officers to remain on active duty for life, with pay and benefits, even after they no longer filled an official billet.

4. A copy of the letter and other documents pertaining to Halsey's effort to have Miller awarded the Medal of Honor were provided to the author by the Secretary of the Navy Council of Review Boards.

5. Ibid.

6. Ibid.

7. Ibid.

8. Ibid.

9. The subcommittee's proceedings are recorded in House Report No. 26. Contrary to popular belief, the decoration is not the "Congressional Medal of Honor," though it is awarded in the name of Congress.

10. Ibid.

11. Ibid.

12. Information on Norton and the role he played in *Navy Log* generally and in the "Man Alone" episode specifically—and later in Hugh Miller's appearance on *This Is Your Life*—is drawn from letters, scripts, and other documents contained in Box 62 of the files of Ralph Edwards Productions. The files are currently held by the Film & Television Archive of the University of California, Los Angeles.

13. Oddly, although the title page of the "as telecast" script for "Man Alone" (*Navy Log* #5703) lists Leonard Lee as the writer, the credits at the end of the film read "Written by Sam Gallu." The script is included in the Edwards Collection at UCLA, and a copy is in the author's possession.

14. Founded in 1919, the independent lot on North Las Palmas Avenue is now known as Hollywood Center Studios and remains a popular venue for TV and film production.

15. While we do not know the name of the screenwriter, Lee would have been a logical candidate. He had already written "Man Alone" and was thoroughly familiar with the story, he had a proven track record as a writer for both feature films and TV, and he likely would have come with the endorsement of Hank Norton, the man who by all accounts put Hugh Miller and William Hawks together. Hawks's choice of the title "Hide and Seek" was obviously taken from the 1945 *True* article.

A treatment is essentially a multipage proposal for a film written in prose form and in the present tense. It is used to elicit financial and artistic interest in a story before the actual script is written.

16. Hopper's article containing this quote was syndicated to hundreds of newspapers around the country and ran on November 14, 1956, under the headline "Wayne Seeks Role of Naval Hero."

17. Ralph Edwards Productions, Box 62.

18. The future California governor and president of the United States also hosted the following week's program, which featured actress Constance Hope.

19. Ibid. The author is in possession of both the episode's script—designated YLN231—and a DVD of the broadcast.

20. Peterson eventually retired from Eastern Airlines as a senior captain

and died in 2001. Luck worked as a power-plant engineer for Northwest Airlines from 1946 to 1982 and passed away in 2002. Happer remained in the Marine Corps for a few years after the war before going into business in Southern California and died in 1970.

21. In an early 2015 e-mail exchange with the author, Gretchen Wayne—the star's daughter-in-law and the current president of his Batjac Productions—said that the company had no records of Wayne's interest in "Hide and Seek."

22. The only previous attempt to tell Hugh Miller's story in book-length form—other than Hugh's—was made by Donald H. Kumferman. In 1979 the civilian general engineer working at the China Lake Naval Weapons Station in California began detailed research intended to produce a book about the events on Arundel Island. Over the next thirteen years he contacted former members of *Strong*'s crew—including Gus Wellings and Don Regan—and members of Hugh's family and requested hundreds of pages of relevant documents from the Navy and the National Archives. In 1992 Mr. Kumferman copyrighted his resulting manuscript, titled "The Navy's One-Man Army: The True Story of One Man's Extraordinary Exploits in World War II." While the basic facts of the story are relatively accurate, the writer's many years of research did not serve him well. The work—a copy of which is in this author's possession—contains many significant errors and quite a few exaggerations that border on fabrication. It was never published, and Mr. Kumferman died on May 29, 1994.

EPILOGUE

1. The complete accident report for Pan Am Flight 292 can be found on the Flight Safety Foundation's website, www.flightsafety.org.

2. A copy of Hugh Miller's death certificate is in the author's possession. Hugh's wife, Frances, survived him by twenty-one years, passing away on August 14, 1999. The two are buried next to one another in Hazlehurst Cemetery.

INDEX

275